Theatre and Phenom

Univers

**WITHDRAW ITEM IN NEXT
ROUND – NO. OF CHECKOUTS
BELOW RETENTION LEVEL**

Daniel Johnston

Theatre and Phenomenology

Manual Philosophy

© Daniel Johnston 2017

All rights reserved. No reproduction, copy or transmission of this publication may be made without written permission.

No portion of this publication may be reproduced, copied or transmitted save with written permission or in accordance with the provisions of the Copyright, Designs and Patents Act 1988, or under the terms of any licence permitting limited copying issued by the Copyright Licensing Agency, Saffron House, 6–10 Kirby Street, London EC1N 8TS.

Any person who does any unauthorized act in relation to this publication may be liable to criminal prosecution and civil claims for damages.

The author has asserted his right to be identified as the author of this work in accordance with the Copyright, Designs and Patents Act 1988.

First published 2017 by
PALGRAVE

Palgrave in the UK is an imprint of Macmillan Publishers Limited, registered in England, company number 785998, of 4 Crinan Street, London, N1 9XW.

Palgrave® and Macmillan® are registered trademarks in the United States, the United Kingdom, Europe and other countries.

ISBN 978–1–137–53051–6 hardback
ISBN 978–1–137–53050–9 paperback

This book is printed on paper suitable for recycling and made from fully managed and sustained forest sources. Logging, pulping and manufacturing processes are expected to conform to the environmental regulations of the country of origin.

A catalogue record for this book is available from the British Library.

A catalog record for this book is available from the Library of Congress.

For Antonette Collins

Table of Contents

Acknowledgements   xi

Part I   1

1 Introduction: Before the Curtain   3
To Be or Not to Be: The Wonder of Being   3
How to Use this Book   4
Apply Philosophy (Consult a Doctor if Symptoms Persist)   5
A View from the Bridge: Outline of the Text   8
Notes   10

2 Preparing the Part: Theatre and Philosophy   11
Frivolous Entertainment or Genuine Self-Knowledge?   11
Sworn Enmity or Suppressed Love?   13
I Can See Clearly Now: Truth or Fiction   21
Exercises and Topics for Discussion   24
Notes   24

3 Setting the Stage: Phenomenology in Context   27
Tying the Knot: Knowledge in your Fingertips   27
Husserl: Return to the Things Themselves   32
Sartre, Merleau-Ponty, Levinas: Existence, Embodiment, Ethics   34
Heidegger: The Question of Being   38
Being and Time: Another Starting Point   41
The Turn: From the Being of Beings to Being Itself   47
It's All in Your Head: Criticisms of Phenomenology   48
Exercises and Topics for Discussion   50
Notes   51

4 Revealing the Scene: Doing Phenomenology in the Theatre — 53
Back to the Old Drawing Board: A Philosophy of Beginnings — 53
Thinking Outside the Box: Phenomenology in the Humanities and Social Sciences — 57
Thinking Through Your Body: Phenomenology and Theatre Studies to Now — 65
Demolishing Tradition (While Fossicking for Truth) — 72
One Size Doesn't Fit All: Theatre Phenomenology — 76
Exercises and Topics for Discussion — 77
Notes — 78

Part II — 81

5 Stanislavski's Phenomenology of Being-in-the-world: Action and Involvement — 83
Theatre for Disclosing a World — 83
An Actor's Work — 86
Action and Inauthenticity — 89
Being-in-the-world and Dasein — 92
Spatiality and Involvement — 93
Action and Involvement — 95
State of Mind — 97
Communion and Being-with-others — 99
Stanislavski the Phenomenologist — 101
Exercises and Topics for Discussion — 103
Notes — 104

6 Artaud's Phenomenology of Anxiety: Language and Being-towards-death — 107
Theatre for Metaphysical Transformation — 107
La Peste as Destruktion — 111
Falling Understanding and the Everyday Falling Self — 115
Being-with-others and the They — 118
Moods, Anxiety, and Being-towards-death — 121
Being Oneself: A Theatre of Homecoming — 126

Exercises and Topics for Discussion	129
Notes	130

7 Brecht's Phenomenology of Being-with-others: Authenticity and History — 131

Philosophical Theatre for Political Change	131
Authenticity and Rehearsal as Uncovering Truth	133
Epic Theatre and Resoluteness	143
Der Verfremdungseffekt and Showing the Things Themselves	149
Gestus and Being-with-others	153
Historicality, Temporality, and Selfhood	158
A Theatre of P-Effects	169
Exercises and Topics for Discussion	172
Notes	173

8 Conclusion: Lights Up on Manual Philosophy — 175

The World Disclosed: Your Fingerprints Were All Over It	175
Basic Problems in Theatre Phenomenology	177
A Theatre of Truth: *Aletheia*	180
Binocular Vision or Seeing Double: Semiotics and Phenomenology	183
What's Your Next Gig? From Phenomenology to Creativity	186
Notes	187

Bibliography	189
Index	201

Acknowledgements

I owe special thanks to Ian Maxwell, my PhD supervisor, whose encouragement, insight, and friendship made this work possible from the initial seed of an idea. I am also indebted to the special community that is the Department of Theatre and Performance Studies at the University of Sydney. In particular, I send my sincere gratitude to Paul Dwyer and Tim Fitzpatrick for taking me on as a research assistant to learn the ropes. This work also owes much to feedback and comments from Gay McAuley, Amanda Card, Laura Ginters, Glen McGillivray, J. Lowell Lewis, and Kate Rossmanith.

While completing this book, I have also been part of the wonderful team at Sheffield Hallam University who have given support and a caring environment for research.

The University Postgraduate Award Scholarship co-funded by the University of Sydney and the Commonwealth Department of Education, Science and Training generously financed three-and-a-half years of research towards my thesis upon which this book is based. IFTR/FIRT (the International Federation for Theatre Research) also generously provided support allowing me to attend their conferences. Many of the ideas in this work have also been developed through conference papers at PSI (performance studies International).

A previous version of Chapter Four has appeared elsewhere as Johnston, D. (2011) 'Stanislavskian Acting as Phenomenology in Practice', *Journal of Dramatic Theory and Criticism*, Fall (1), 65–84. Some sections from Chapter Six were also taken from Johnston, D. (2010) 'Phenomenology, Time and Performance', conference proceedings from *time.transcendence.performance* (Melbourne: Monash University).

Finally, thank you to my generous parents-in-law Barry and Rosemary Collins together with Dad and Babette for their continued support to our family throughout this academic escapade.

Part I

1

Introduction: Before the Curtain

To Be or Not to Be: The Wonder of Being

How often do you stop to think about the fact that there is *something* in the universe rather than *nothing*? When do we, as human beings, pause to marvel at the wonder of Being? It is even more amazing that we have conscious awareness of life at all. Take a mental step back and consider how the world presents itself to you. Are we just complex computers processing a set of facts about the world or is there something else going on? What is the role of perception in processing the 'outside' world? How do we experience 'internal' thoughts and emotions? Are we simply 'thinking' machines sifting through this material? How do we move from thought to action in our everyday activities? More broadly, we might consider how life is meaningful in the first place. What does it mean 'to be'?

Many of these questions are important to actors in formal training, preparing for a role, and even in the moment of performance. They are questions that go to the heart of drama – most famously in Hamlet's well-known monologue (alluded to in the section title above) in which the Danish prince contemplates the relationship between existence and action. The theatre is a place to wonder at Being. But in order to 'use' conscious action for the sake of theatrical representation, we need to understand it and find out how it works in the creative process. For this reason,

I argue that actors are 'manual philosophers' in that they put theory into action. In fact, we might even ask whether consciousness is a 'thing' that can be 'used' in the first place. Maybe consciousness isn't even the right word for what we are asking about in the questions above. But where can we look for help in forming an answer?

The problem with traditional philosophy (if that is where we turn) is that often it doesn't match up with our lived experience of the world. Reading through impenetrable philosophical tracts containing copious jargon and complex arguments can be difficult. In some cases, we might even begin to suspect that it is just a sophisticated word game or obscure puzzle meant only for insiders. The same may well be true of many critical studies in theatre that invoke the key topic of this book: phenomenology. It's a mouthful to say let alone understand.

In the classic 1980s cult film *The Princess Bride* (based on William Goldman's novel), the Sicilian would-be philosopher-villain Vizzini repeatedly exclaims the word 'inconceivable', surprised by the feats of the hero, Wesley (disguised as the Dread Pirate Roberts), who is in hot pursuit. Vizzini's henchman Inigo Montoya eventually challenges his master for this semantic choice: 'You keep using that word. I do not think it means what you think it means.' Just as we might laugh at Vizzini's inappropriate use of 'inconceivable' ('improbable' might be what he really means), so too might we direct Montoya's challenge at the academic use of the key term in this book: 'phenomenology'. The word gets bandied about to talk about embodied experience, subjective feeling, and perhaps even gestures towards a mysterious metaphysical force behind reality. The challenge here is to dispel the mystery surrounding phenomenology (while perhaps channelling Vizzini's sense of amazement) and sustain a willingness to be disproved by the world as it is (and preferably not get poisoned in the process as he does).

How to Use this Book

This book is intended to provide an introduction to theatre and phenomenology. It doesn't claim to be a comprehensive guide to either on its own or even cover every angle in the relationship between the two. You might want to dip in and out of the chapters below depending upon your familiarity with the subject matter. The philosophers covered here are largely what could be called 'first- and second-wave' phenomenologists. That being the case, you could supplement your reading with some of the contemporary debates in the movement.

At the end of each chapter I have included some exercises to try out and topics for discussion. You can select, adapt, or ignore them as you wish. You might even want to create a writing portfolio containing your responses to each task in order to map your development in thinking and description. Take each section as a challenge for further reading and look for the limits in the arguments and apparent contradictions that arise from the perspectives issued.

The text is divided into two parts. The first introduces the theoretical framework and the second examines three theatre practitioners as case studies in phenomenological interpretation. You could use Chapter 2 as a survey of the big-picture of the relationship between theatre and philosophy. As a general introduction to phenomenology Chapter 3 might be handy as a stand-alone reading. If you are looking for a broad brushstroke overview of phenomenology in theatre studies, Chapter 4 might fit the bill. The chapters in Part II might be of interest as counterpoint interpretations to other material you may have read concerning the history and philosophy of acting. Even if you are looking at practitioners other than those discussed here, the idea is to consider how you might take a phenomenological approach to them too.

Think about the boundaries of phenomenological reading and the way in which it seeks to unsettle the bases of traditional academic thought. Your task is to continue the radical questioning of presuppositions and foundations of your discipline and practice.

Apply Philosophy (Consult a Doctor if Symptoms Persist)

If we are going to look to philosophy for help, how might we go about it? Performance philosopher Laura Cull (Cull, 2012; Cull and Lagaay, 2014, p.15) takes issue with the idea that we can simply 'apply' philosophy to performance rather than engage with performance as a philosophical practice in and of itself. The risk of applying philosophy is that you could simply include examples of performance that confirm a philosophical theory or approach. Through such selectivity, the examples would match neatly with the philosophical view that has already been assumed true:

> Here, and with respect to the idea of performance as philosophy, the difficulty lies in the question of to what extent we are starting our investigations with a fixed definition of 'philosophy' (or 'research' or 'thinking') already in mind, or – correlatively – to what extent we are willing to allow our very definitions of these terms to be altered by the nature of the new activities seeking to be included within their categories. (Cull and Lagaay, 2014, p. 26)

David Krasner and David Saltz (2006, pp. 7, 8) also note the difference between 'doing' and 'using' philosophy too. Many scholars analyse performance by invoking theories developed in literary theory and cultural studies, for example 'using' Judith Butler, Jean Baudrillard and Pierre Bourdieu to analyse a particular production or practice. The validity of such arguments may well stand or fall depending on each 'theory' rather than in the scholar's own argument. Yet performance philosophy can also be studied in its own right despite drawing on previous theorists. The analyses of performance philosophy are therefore distinct from critical studies and prescriptive manifestos in that they see theatre as a philosophical practice (Krasner and Saltz, 2006, p. 2).

On the surface, the content below seems vulnerable to Cull's criticism, although I have deliberately left the door open for dialogue, debate, and dispute. I examine concepts from Martin Heidegger's phenomenology in order to interrogate theatre theory and practice. But as I will go on to explain in Chapter 3, phenomenology is a suitable approach here precisely because it doesn't provide a rigid definition of philosophy from the outset or even necessarily constitute a singular methodology of inquiry. I make no claim that the theatre makers considered here were directly and explicitly influenced by phenomenology. Nor do I suggest that they understood themselves as philosophers or their work to be philosophical in the same way.

What's more, this book is not a defence of phenomenology *per se*. But instead of simply cherry-picking coincidental or superficial parallels between philosophical phenomenology and examples from theatre history, I ponder how each approach asks the question of Being in its own way. Heidegger's might not be the definitive philosophy in this regard, but he provides a very useful starting point for the investigation. His philosophy provides a launch pad for asking how theatre interrogates the meaning of Being. Rather than simply 'apply' philosophy to each case, we might consider how theatre can answer back and bring something new to the inquiry. The exercises at the end of each chapter are intended to stimulate such dialogue and perhaps event change the way that you think about your own practice.

The key proposition here, following from Bruce Wilshire (1982), Bert States (1985), and Stanton Garner (1994), is that theatre-making can be understood as practical phenomenology in at least some forms. Wilshire goes on to suggest that we think of theatre as 'contemplation through acting'.[1] A philosophical reflection on the topic will advance new arguments and alternative approaches to thinking about theatre and performance. Theatre itself is capable of engaging in the dialogue:

> Like philosophy, theater often sheds light on a reality obfuscated by appearances. Moreover, theater like philosophy, exposes that reality by representing and analysing human action and demonstrating causal relationships […] Theater and philosophy shed light on thought, behavior action and existence while simultaneously enhancing our comprehension of the world and ourselves. (Krasner and Saltz, 2006, pp. 2, 3)

The chapters that follow here attempt to flesh out Martin Heidegger's thought and pry open the space between theatre and philosophy. Of course, it may be possible to relate many other philosophers to theatrical practice in such a way. I am not prescribing how theatre should be made or simply analysing theatrical forms of the past. I will consider how theatre-making as philosophy reflects on the meaning of existence, what sorts of things there are in the world, and how those things relate to each other, and how we ought to live. Interpreting various approaches to theatre through phenomenology is not straightforward and it would be a grave mistake to ignore the social and historical contexts in which they were born.

The examples of theatre covered in this book are largely from the Western tradition. This is not to say that important and valuable investigations might not be made in non-Western cultural performance forms.[2] Indeed, the complex relationship between theatre and philosophy is revealing of how we understand what it means to be in so far as those practices enact a set of beliefs about what a self is in Western culture. As an antidote, you might apply some of the exercises and questions at the end of each chapter to non-Western traditions, too.

A View from the Bridge: Outline of the Text

The initial trajectory of this book follows a progression from the general to the specific. First I contemplate philosophy in the widest sense. I then introduce the specific philosophical approach of phenomenology in Chapter 2 and sketch some of its major connections with the humanities, social sciences, and theatre studies. Chapter 3 introduces the broad movement of phenomenology, presents a brief overview of Heidegger's phenomenology, and provides some background to his major work *Being and Time (BT)* within the context of the movement. Chapter 4 considers how phenomenology has been adapted in the humanities and social sciences, and particularly in theatre studies. At the end of Part I, I attempt to articulate different phenomenological methodologies for understanding theatre practice.

Part II examines three artists – Constantin Stanislavski, Bertolt Brecht, and Antonin Artaud – and thinks about how features of Heidegger's phenomenology can help us to understand their theatre theories and practices. Chapter 5 explores Stanislavski and Heidegger's concept of Being-in-the-world. Chapter 6 interrogates Artaud in relation to selfhood and language through Heidegger's term 'Destruktion'. Chapter 7 interprets Brecht with reference to Historicality, Temporality, and Authenticity. Finally, I draw some conclusions about theatre as manual philosophy while questioning the future of phenomenological theatre theory.

Standing on the bridge between philosophy and theatre can be perilous.³ Many theatre-makers might see this work as overly theoretical. On the other side, philosophers might see it as not rigorous enough. Another perspective is to 'mind the gap' between the two and carefully attend to their differences rather than bring them together (Puchner, 2013). In their introduction to phenomenology, Stewart and Mickunas suggest 'what is needed is a bridge between phenomenology and the various methodologies of the human sciences – such as anthropology, sociology, psychology, history of religions, and so forth' (1990, p. 145). This is one attempt to lay foundations at the traversal point, however dangerous. My intention is to explore the tensions and borders between theatre and phenomenology and map some of the terrain between.

The three conceptions of theatre that I have chosen to focus on in the second part of this book – Stanislavski's method of physical actions, Artaud's Theatre of Cruelty, and Brecht's epic theatre – obviously differ in their respective definitions of performance and approaches to acting. Each practitioner played a different role in the theatre process: Stanislavski was a director and actor, Artaud was an actor, poet, and manifesto-writer, and Brecht was a playwright and director. Their views and ideas also changed and developed considerably throughout their careers in both theory and practice. It is possible to take some key ideas from their writings that have been widely influential in theatre theory, however, and consider the distinctively phenomenological trajectories of the practices they entail. As we will explore, each theorist engages with Being in different ways and provides a different entry point into the process of 'unconcealing' Being. Stanislavski develops a phenomenology of the world in order for the actor to prepare for a role. Artaud resists the concept of world in order to achieve a transcendent performance mode that would be a direct experience of Being itself. Brecht hopes for an acting style that will present different perspectives on social problems and challenge contemporary, complacent attitudes towards human existence that are always historically and temporally located. Or as Peter Brook puts it more succinctly, 'for Artaud, theatre is fire; for Brecht, theatre is clear vision; for Stanislavsky, theatre is humanity' (Brook, 1988, p. 43).

A final word of warning, however: it would be a mistake to see these different perspectives on performance as always mutually exclusive or that drawing upon one rules out the others. Late in his career, Brecht realised that his approach was not entirely incommensurate with Stanislavski's.[4] Artaud's insistence upon the body as the site of performance, Brecht's *gestus*, and Stanislavski's emphasis on the physical elements of acting all highlight the performing body. Emotion also seems to have a complex role in each of these practitioners' work and it would be wrong to say that epic theatre always abolishes feelings, or that Stanislavski's system works solely from an emotional centre. The point is that each of these practitioners theorise the theatre in a specific cultural context and emphasised various elements of performance while not necessarily ruling out other approaches. Again, my intention here is not simply to compare and contrast elements of these different theories of performing but to consider what sort of phenomenology each presents and how they engage in asking the question of Being. Each arrives at a potentially conflicting and contradictory phenomenology of the world partly because of the unique cultural and historical moment from which it sprang forth and partly because each seeks to uncover different aspects of Being and existence. Part of the challenge is to make these contradictions useful and productive in the search for creative inspiration.

Notes

1 Parry and Wrathall make a similar argument about art in *Art and Phenomenology* (focussing mainly on the fine arts) in general and invite other studies to look more closely (including theatre) (Parry, 2011, p. 8).
2 Zarrilli et al. (2006) note the eurocentric tendency of many past approaches to theatre history. Also see Meyer-Dinkgräfe (1996), for instance, which looks at Indian theories of acting as a frame for rethinking consciousness and the actor. It should be noted, however, that Dinkgräfe calls upon 'Vedic science', a twentieth-century movement associated with transcendental meditation, to discuss consciousness. Indian philosophy and psychology are considerably more complex and varied than even this perspective on phenomenology.
3 See Meyrick (2003) for a discussion of the tension between theory and practice in the academy and industry.
4 See Eric Bentley's 'Are Stanislavsky and Brecht Commensurable?' in Martin and Bial (2000).

2

Preparing the Part: Theatre and Philosophy

Frivolous Entertainment or Genuine Self-Knowledge?

In the second century, Lucian of Samosata made the intriguing assertion (quoting the 'enlightened Lesbonax of Mytilene') in his text *On Pantomime* that actors are 'manual philosophers' (1905, p. 259).[1] The text consists of a dialogue between Crato, who is suspicious of the representational arts and Lycinus, lover of the theatre. Lycinus argues that these amazing player-artists are possessors of wondrous self-knowledge. In his estimation, the performer's task is

> to identify himself with his subject, and make himself part and parcel of the scene that he enacts. It is his profession to show forth human character and passion in all their variety; to depict love and anger, frenzy and grief, each in its due measure, Wondrous art! – on the same day, he is mad Athamas and shrinking Ino; he is Atreus, and again he is Thyestes, and next Aegisthus or Acrope; all one man's work. (1905, p. 259)

In other words, the audience is presented with many varied worlds through the actor's art of self-transformation. Born on the periphery of the Roman Empire around 125 CE, Lucian was a Syrian *rhetor* (public orator) famous for his convincing presentation skills and for offering pleas to various courts on behalf of clients – a skill which funded his long journey to the epicentre of the Greek world to Athens, then through Italy. Eventually he lived out his life as a public official in Egypt. He became a writer of satire and later returned to perform his works in public for profit. He parodied ancient literary forms and philosophical movements having been 'converted' to the study of philosophy at the age of 40. Of course, the performance genre he had in mind in *On Pantomime* – a kind of dance-drama – is different from what we think of as theatre today, but the arguments nonetheless apply to dramatic representation more broadly.

In response to Lycinus, Crato says he would rather contemplate the sages of old through the philosophy of Plato and Aristotle than 'watch the antics of an effeminate creature got up in soft raiment to sing lascivious songs and mimic the passions of prehistoric strumpets' (1905, p. 239). For him, logic and abstract reasoning are placed above sentimental affectation. But Lycinus continues to argue that such performers are 'soothsayers of the soul of man' and appeals to Homer's opinion that spectators of the theatre leave 'gladder and wiser' than when they had entered (1905, p. 240). Furthermore, the spectacle of theatre is 'no less than a fulfilment of the oracular injunction KNOW THYSELF; men depart from it with increased knowledge; they have something that is to be sought after, something that should be eschewed' (1905, p. 261). Unlike philosophy, however, performance must be experienced rather than discussed and debated: Lycinus explains that if he would only accompany him to the theatre he would fall under its spell through 'the golden wand of Hermes' (1905, p. 263). The power of the theatre is not something to be contemplated in the abstract, but to be apprehended directly by the senses and through feeling. In the end, Crato concedes the argument (in a rather abrupt about-face) and announces himself to be converted.

We can't be entirely sure whether Lucian argues earnestly in this dialogue, or whether he is merely poking fun at the philosophical importance of performance. Indeed, the speakers in the text enact rhetorical flourishes and parade their skills of argument and persuasion much in the same way that Lucian himself did. On the one hand, the central question of the dialogue is whether actors are doing something philosophical in their art or whether they simply exhibit superficial form and style without any real substance. The query goes to the heart of what this book is about: in what sense can we think of theatre-making as manual philosophy? On the other hand, we could read Lucian as unmasking the theatrical nature of philosophy in its capacity to elicit an emotional response, its use of dramatic form, and its engaging narrative involvement. Such charge leads to what we might call 'sophistry' – using rhetorical smoke and mirrors rather than valid argumentation. The insinuation is that philosophy in some cases might be masquerading as transparent truth when employing the techniques of frivolous entertainment. Perhaps Lucian has chosen 'pantomime' as his topic for this dialogue precisely because considering pantomimes as philosophers seems so ludicrous. But successful parody captures the essence of the object it lampoons: Lucian might be onto something in his claim about at least some actors. Perhaps we might even question any fundamental opposition between truth in theatre and philosophy as a false contrast.

Nevertheless, the call for acting to *become* philosophical has persisted throughout the ages. The perplexing twentieth century avant-garde theatre maker Antonin Artaud used the phrase 'active metaphysics' in his call for theatrical reform in the 1930s. Far from simply being a theoretical reflection of the world, on his view, theatre was meant to be an alchemical force acting on life. And of course, Bertolt Brecht was fond of quoting Karl Marx when he proclaimed that the point of philosophy – and by extension theatre – is to change the world, not merely to represent it as philosophers have done in the past. The thought of theatre as applied philosophy is an enduring one. But before exploring further, there are several issues to navigate in our journey in search of philosophical theatre.

Sworn Enmity or Suppressed Love?

Since time immemorial, theatre and philosophy have maintained a complex and troubled relationship (Stern, 2013; Puchner, 2002, 2013). Yet the philosophical features of theatre can't be boiled down to just one thing. The types of theatrical questions that the ancient Greeks asked were quite different in many respects from the Elizabethans; and both are different from contemporary intersections between theatre and philosophy. Just as theatrical forms have changed so too have the practices of philosophy in parallel with advances in technology and changes in social organisation.

In *The Republic*, Plato reluctantly rejects the representative arts as having any place in an ideal civilisation (Plato, 1992, p. 74). He simultaneously deploys the dramatic form of dialogue to communicate his own philosophy (famously using his teacher, Socrates, as the primary speaker in the majority of his works). Elsewhere in *Ion*, he forces the protagonist Ion (who is a reciter of poetry) to admit that he has no real knowledge of what he is doing but merely 'a knack' (Plato, 1987). Stern (2013, p. xi) notes that often philosophers and theatre-makers are one and the same people: Seneca, Machiavelli, Voltaire, Diderot, Rousseau, and Sartre. And many of these attack theatre while simultaneously participating in its practice. Theatre scholars Krasner and Saltz argue that value of philosophy is not necessarily in reaching agreement on truths but in stimulating further dialogue (2006, pp. 3, 4). They suggest that philosophical works often have a dramatic structure. A philosophical text often poses a question (the initial disturbing event), present arguments and counterarguments (plot development leading to a climax) and finally offers a philosophical conclusion (dramatic resolution). Philosophical statements are also performative in that they *do* something in the world, even if it is only within an exclusive clique of philosophical readers.[2]

It is beyond the scope of this book to introduce philosophy as a whole. Nevertheless (at risk of oversimplifying), we might say that philosophers tend to ask questions such as:

- What sorts of things are there? (metaphysics)
- What type of being do things have and how can we sort them into categories? (ontology)
- How do we know the world and what is knowledge? (epistemology)
- How can we make valid arguments about things? (logic)
- How ought we to behave in life? (ethics)
- What is art? What is beauty? What is the nature of artistic representation? (aesthetics)

Various forms of theatre have asked similar questions, albeit in a different and perhaps less direct way. One might well look at classical Greek tragedy, for instance, as pondering the meaning of existence, facing the most horrific circumstances that life can throw at us, and asking how we can know the right way to act in the world.³ The theatre doesn't necessarily provide straightforward answers to these questions. And this is precisely the point. If theatre is philosophical, it is in a different way from traditional practices of philosophy because audience members participate in making sense of what they see. For example, some scholars argue that Shakespeare's ambiguity (in terms of textual meaning and political stance) is key to his widespread appeal and lasting literary fascination (Rossiter, 1961). Shakespeare's type of philosophy is not one of propositional reasoning, but of thought and feeling, requiring the audience to reach its own conclusion.

There is no consensus about how to present a philosophical argument either. Substantial differences in this respect can be found in the so-called analytic/continental divide. Broadly, analytic philosophy deals with the meaning of certain concepts such as 'knowledge', 'belief', 'truth', and 'justification' and judging a thesis by assessing the propositions and valid reasoning that make up an argument. Continental philosophy, by contrast, grew from the ideas of Hegel and Nietzsche and continued in the traditions of phenomenology, hermeneutics, existentialism, the Frankfurt school, and post-structuralism. Philosophers in this tradition often aim to challenge and unsettle the claims of science, knowledge, truth, language, morality, self and value (Krasner and Saltz, 2006, p. 5). Scholars in the disciplines of cultural studies, theatre studies, and performance studies tend to invoke philosophers from European tradition (most often French and German), whereas philosophy departments draw predominantly upon Anglo-American philosophers (Krasner and Saltz, 2006, pp. 4–7). Partly, it is an unwritten rule to reference particular authors in the field – flying the flag signifying the camp that you support. Some might allege that much continental philosophical writing is dense, inaccessible, and obscure. Others might quip that analytic philosophical writing is stale, not engaging, not reflective of lived experience, and overly technical. Part of the breach here is ideological (occupying a position in relation to political systems of power and discourse). The divide between analytic and continental philosophy is often tribal, too – contingent upon the historical evolution of disciplines within the humanities and social sciences that tend to reference their respective key works and ideas, perhaps like the feuding Montagues and Capulets. Nevertheless, as philosopher Bernard Williams puts it (also quoted by Krasner and Saltz), the distinction between these two philosophical traditions may well be meaningless, 'rather as though one divided cars into front-wheeled drive and Japanese' (Williams, 1996, p. 25).

The relationship between performance and philosophy has also attracted interest recently with the emergence of an interdisciplinary field called 'performance philosophy'. This newly minted area of study aims to sharpen and unsettle both 'performance' and 'philosophy' while also questioning its own boundaries and methodologies. In other words, the inquiry seeks to search out the limits of what performance and philosophy are, and ask how it is best to conduct research into these terms in the first place. At a time when performance practice is attempting to be accepted as research by performance studies scholars ('performance-as-research') and what counts as philosophy is interrogated by philosophers, Laura Cull rightly suggests that this development is particularly salient (Cull and Lagaay, 2014, p. ix). Cull argues convincingly for a field of research that accepts philosophy can be understood as performance and performance as philosophy, without reducing them to the same thing:

> Following Film Philosophy's lead then, might the idea of performance as philosophy be thought beyond the notion of 'influence' – beyond, for instance, cases where scholars have been able to evidence that a performance practitioner has engaged with a particular philosopher's work (Ibsen with Kierkegaard or Wagner with Schopenhauer, and so forth)? […] Might we, in other words, say that performance itself thinks, that performance itself philosophizes – not in a way that reduces it to being the 'same as' philosophy (as if philosophy was always the self-same thing anyway) but in a way that enriches our very concept of philosophy? (Cull and Lagaay, 2014, p. 25)

So rather than simply examine philosophical influences as points of origin for theatrical works, we can consider how those works destabilise the foundations and definitions of philosophy itself.[4] Part of the argument below in Chapter 5 is that superficial modes of performance lacking reflexive awareness and merely seeking outward representation do not qualify as philosophy. This type of acting and theatre-making is analogous to thought that blindly accepts past world-views and takes a surface approach to meaning and existence. Furthermore, there might be a difference between saying that types of theatre are philosophical and that they are a form of philosophy themselves. The former might simply imply that a particular play raises some philosophical questions; the later suggests that performance actively seeks to investigate those questions and provide or provoke some answers.

I would argue that Anton Chekhov, for example, does both.[5] Both form and content (if we naively assume a separation between the two) in *The Cherry Orchard* point towards philosophical questions about the existential meaning of work and labour in a society transitioning from being ruled by hereditary aristocracy to mercantile capitalism and the rising middle class (Chekhov, 2009). The overarching story of the Ranevsky family as the paradigm of aristocratic decline in Russia demonstrates this point. But more explicitly in Act 2, Trofimov, the eternal student, muses upon the relationship between past and present in their shared life-world:

> All Russia is our orchard. The world is big and beautiful, and there are many wonderful places in it. (*Pause.*) Just think, Anya, your grandfather and great-grandfather, and all your ancestors were serf-owners, owners of living souls. So isn't it possible that behind each trunk there are human beings looking out at you? Isn't it possible that you could hear their voices? To own living souls – surely that has transformed all of you, those who lived before and those who live now, so that your mother, you, your uncle don't even notice that you are living in debt, at someone else's expense, at the expense of those people who weren't allowed to go further than your threshold … We lag behind by at least two hundred years, we have exactly nothing, no definite relationship to the past, we only philosophize, complain about boredom and drink vodka. Isn't it clear that to start to live in the present, we must begin to atone for our past, to finish with it? And only suffering can atone for it, only extraordinary, ceaseless labor. Remember that, Anya. (Chekhov, 2009, p. 274)

Chekhov investigates the ethical responsibility of characters towards the 'Other' – in this case the serfs previously subjugated by rich landowners. Not all philosophical ponderings in the theatre might be so explicit, though.

Another approach might interrogate the implicit philosophy behind the performance practices of every age. Theatre historian Joseph Roach writes in *The Player's Passion: Studies in the Science of Acting*, that the 'history of theater is the history of ideas' (1987, p. 11). Roach offers a conceptual archaeology of different ways in which humans have historically understood the relationship between individuals and the world they inhabit. Specifically, he investigates how scientific theories of emotion throughout the past have informed performance practices in the past. More broadly, we could think about the philosophy of self: historical concepts of selfhood are also implicit in approaches to acting of each era. Such a rethinking (and de-universalisation) of acting also makes the relationship between philosophy and theatrical practice historically (and culturally) contingent. If every instance of performance contains an 'implicit theory of acting' as director and theatre scholar Phillip Zarrilli suggests (1995, p. 4), each instance also contains an implicit theory of self, ontology, and other philosophical concepts. The idea runs parallel to Arjun Appadurai's (1990) examination of 'topographies of the self' based on his cross-cultural observation of displays of emotion. The specific 'map' of selfhood through which we understand the construction and interpretation of emotion is relative to the society in which we live. In a Western context, we tend to think about emotion as 'inside' our body and mind whereas in an Indian context, emotion is in the 'in-between'. Many post-structural theories also emphasise the contingent (rather than *a priori*) the nature of subjectivity in relation to meaning, identity, and social practice. For instance, philosopher and historian Michel Foucault draws attention to the historical contingency of embodied subjectivity in his genealogies of sexuality, psychiatry, discipline, government, and systems of power.[6] In this sense, all human practices are based upon a specific worldview and an embodied understanding of the relationship between self and world. If such a line of thinking is correct, performance making is not epiphenomenal but a key point of access for interpreting culture and epistemology. The history of acting is deeply intertwined with the history of philosophy.

Could we say that all human activities are philosophical, then? What is it that makes theatre uniquely philosophical compared to other everyday pursuits? Might it not be that any activity engenders an implicit understanding of the world? Riding a bicycle, for instance, may contain within it a practical understanding of gravity and physics, an ethics of environmental sustainability, hopefully the rules of riding on the road, and as such a 'theory of riding'. For the most part, however, bike-riding is not reflexive or deliberately aiming to investigate its own nature. The epistemological distinction between (1) practical or procedural knowledge (including 'know-how') and (2) propositional knowledge ('knowing that') is relevant here. Knowing how to do something does not necessarily entail being able to articulate that knowledge. At least some types of acting training and preparation for a role analyse knowledge in everyday life in such a way that it becomes explicit and reflexive: a 'knowing that' which is developed in rehearsal is transformed back into a 'knowing how' in performance. Theatrical presentation contains an articulation of that knowledge – communication beyond statements and propositions about the world while at the same time engaging with the entire expressive apparatus of the actor. Of course, there may be other human activities that are philosophical by virtue of their reflexive awareness (and the point here is not to dismiss them in this respect).

The task of understanding theatrical practices of the past poses the further question of how each historical worldview is also shaped by technological and material conditions that in turn alter the way that we understand our very consciousness. Jade McCutcheon and Barbara Sellers-Young (2013) consider the way in which technology has changed the way that we experience the world and create performance in *Embodied Consciousness: Performance Technologies*. Throughout history, we have understood consciousness as a central processing unit, a machine, a theatre, a wax tablet, and shadows flickering on the wall of a cave. In trying to grapple with that which is 'closest' to us (consciousness itself), we reach outside for analogies. Neuroscience won't solve the matter. Performance constitutes a way of engaging with consciousness through contemporary technology. In this sense, it is as much an investigation of the present as it is of the past.

For Martin Heidegger, philosophy asks 'what is Being and what does it mean to be?'[7] Even if Lucian's comments above are tongue-in-cheek, understanding the processes of theatre throughout history can offer deep insight into the nature of the human self (as conceptualised at different points in the past). This book pushes the debate even further: not only does the study of theatre history reveal something about the philosophical world view of the past, it can also carry out an investigation of our own historical understanding of Being and the individual in relation to the world. Philosopher Bruce Wilshire suggests that

> theatre as phenomenology is a fictive variation of human relationships and of human acts *in act*. Theatre should not be regarded as contemplation set over against action and creation, but as contemplation through action and creation. (Wilshire, 1982, p. 357)

The process of performing shines a spotlight on the performer's own existence – as an entity engaged in meaningful dealings with the world, and even contemplating Being. Sometimes this philosophical investigation is undertaken in exploring a fictional world, sometimes in rehearsing a role, and other times in understanding the creative organism of the performer during actor training. But rather than contemplate abstract eternal truths, theatre deals with in the concrete, the physical, and the local – specific problems of the here and now. Theatre is always of its time in the sense that it necessarily draws upon contemporary conventions, materials, and performance traditions; it is also about its time, and revels in reflexivity – what performance theorist and director Richard Schechner calls 'twice behaved behavior' – a showing of a doing (and the doer) – as 'restored behavior' (Schechner and Turner, 1985, pp. 35–115). In this sense, performance is a collective reflection upon existence. One might even be tempted to call it 'symphilosophy', a term coined by Friedrich Schlegel (Pinkard, 2002, p. 147). In the field of performance studies, the relationship between performance and society (both in terms of making sense of the social world and bringing about social change) has been theorised by Schechner and anthropologist Victor Turner (Schechner and Turner, 1985; Turner, 1990). In technologically complex societies, theatre contains vestiges of the 'liminal' (in-between) phase of 'redressive processes' (ways of restoring order to a communal crisis). Such a process overturns everyday time and space through 'ludic deconstruction' (a playful experimentation with forms) (Turner, 1990, p. 10). Alongside legal and political processes, ritual is a way of repairing the social fabric of a society. Turner suggests that theatre is 'liminoid' (a ritual-like 'in-between-ness').[8] For Schechner (2003), the future of theatre lies in returning to this ritual efficacy over and above mere entertainment. On his view, theatre can once again be both a symbolic and practical means of making sense of and transforming society. The idea builds upon Turner's interpretation of the relationship between stage drama and social drama, whereby theatre can provide an implicit rhetorical structure for dealing with crises affecting society as a whole (1985, p. 17).

Over the last century, the terms 'drama', 'theatre', and 'performance' have taken on different meanings within the academy.[9] Drama tends to be understood as the study of dramatic texts and as a subset of literary studies. The discipline of theatre studies widens its object of analysis to include processes of production and the historical context of social practice. Performance studies looks towards links with performance in everyday life, ritual, and the performance of class, gender, race, and ethnicity. As a discipline, performance studies is often also associated with the radical, political, and avant-garde. The ideas set out in this book may have application to all three fields of study. I have chosen to foreground 'theatre' in the title of this book because the three case studies are arguably the most widely covered theorist-practitioners in theatre studies (although it is certainly relevant to drama and performance studies too). The evidence presented here comes from dramatic texts, manifestos, real and imagined theatre processes, and those writers' own reflections of theatre theory. While these case studies were revolutionary at the time, they have very much become part of mainstream pedagogy.

I Can See Clearly Now: Truth or Fiction

Theatre-practitioners often talk about finding the truth of a text, or being truthful in performance.[10] It would be a mistake to take this surface resemblance of vocabulary and argue that theatre-makers are positing a correspondence, coherence, or pragmatic theory of truth in the same way as philosophers debate the issue.[11] Truth in the 'theatrical sense' has just as much to do with feeling as it does with logical argument – probably a bit fuzzy for scholars from an analytic tradition. The danger is that practitioner statements about the truth of a moment, action, or choice assume a fundamental transparency of those concepts and may descend into relativism (implying 'it is true for me'). All theatre is necessarily of its time and creative choices are always relative to the audiences for which it is made and the conventions that are widely practised in any given era and culture. But a phenomenological view of truth as an 'Event' (*Ereignis*) – a movement towards un-hiddenness, Heidegger's appropriation of the ancient Greek word αλαθεία (*aletheia*) – seems to capture something more of a creative sense of truth. So throughout this book, keep this word *aletheia* in the back of your mind and I will return to it in the conclusion. Playwright and philosopher Aldo Tassi also suggests that theatre can be understood through a play between concealment and unconcealment drawing on the phenomenological tradition (Tassi, 1995, p. 472; 1998; 2000). Such an argument requires a shift away from truth as 'correspondence' towards truth as a process or 'Event'.[12]

Truth-revelation of this sort may not suit all historical worldviews, political ideologies, and particular socio-economic class interests. The dangers of performance and its power to convince audiences of certain ways of thinking has been the careful subject of censorship and regulation throughout the centuries and across cultures (Kohansky, 1984; Wikander, 2002). Theatrical representation has been labelled as potentially damaging to our concept of reality and truth in the first place – what theatre historian Jonas Barish labels 'ontological queasiness' (1987, p. 3). Alongside the potential moral corruption demonstrated in the theatre, so the theory goes, it may be physically dangerous for actors, and degrading of the ability to distinguish the real from the illusory in everyday life: theatre unsettles our perception of reality. I suggest the opposite: theatre can bring ontology into view as much as it can conceal it.

Krasner and Saltz also note the common link of seeing (2006, p. 3). Both philosophy and theatre aim at clear sight. One warning I would offer to this suggestion, and one that I will develop in conjunction with Heidegger's philosophy, is that a certain metaphysical understanding of sight might lie hidden here. The metaphor of sight may suggest that the world is that which can be seen in material terms. Heidegger's existential thought suggests that we don't just see material things but possibilities. If, in chapter 9 of *The Poetics*, Aristotle (1996) is right in suggesting that theatre too is about seeing possibilities – the way things *might be* – then the metaphor is not merely in a regular sense perception, but a kind of existential sight. Aristotle claims that in this sense, poetry is more philosophical than history. But theatre is not just a seeing place (*theatron*), it has also been known as a place for listening (*auditorium*) and for action in drama (following the etymology of the Greek *dran* – 'to do, to act'). And as I will discuss in the conclusion, it is also a place for feeling and being touched.

On the one hand, the practical insights of actor-preparation and performance might well shed light on philosophical-theoretical understandings of human experience. On the other hand, phenomenology may be useful in devising new techniques and approaches to performance. An awareness of the structures of experience may be useful to the art of the actor. If nothing else, such a study might also offer actors a way of better articulating elements of their experience. My argument is not that Stanislavski, Artaud, and Brecht explicitly understood themselves as phenomenologists, but rather that they sought a practical understanding of Being in the context of theatrical creation and the art of acting. Placing their work in a phenomenological context makes explicit, and to a certain degree explains, how the world reveals itself to consciousness in different ways and how these are uncovered through some acting processes. In other words, phenomenology and acting could be considered as mutually informing discourses: philosophy might reveal something about theatre-making and performing might reveal something about the nature of conscious experience. The extent to which phenomenological description accurately captures 'the lived experience of the world' could therefore provide an inspiration for theatrical process. The art of acting might be one way to examine phenomenology in a practical context. If a phenomenological description or model is faithful to the experience, then it has the potential to be useful in practice.

Exercises and Topics for Discussion

1. Consider a play with which you are familiar and discuss how it asks and answers the types of philosophical questions in the opening paragraph of the introduction to this book. Perhaps it doesn't give a specific answer. If not, why not?
2. To what extent do you think that theatre must be experienced in order to be understood? Is it enough simply to read a play text in order to apprehend its philosophical significance?
3. Pick an everyday activity. Describe the difference between 'knowing how' to do the activity and 'knowing that' it works in a specific way – facts about the activity.
4. Select a performance practice or period of theatre history. Think about the 'implicit' philosophical underpinnings behind that practice [as Joseph Roach (1985) does in relation to Western understandings of passion and emotion in performance]. You might need to research contemporary scientific and philosophical worldviews dominant in the period to make sense of it. How does this research help you to understand philosophical elements of the text that you may have previously overlooked? What are some of the underlying philosophical assumptions in the world of the play or practice? How could you make these relevant to a contemporary audience and overcome these assumptions?
5. Choose a performance that you have seen recently. What truth does it uncover? Is it possible for art to reveal truth at all? How do you think the work or production relates to 'existence as a whole'? What does it conceal? Are these questions too broad or general in approaching the text? How might you hone in on the philosophical nature of that play or performance?
6. Think of another cultural practice that you think is philosophical. It might be something like a religious ritual or artistic practice. What makes it philosophical and what effect does it have on its participants?

Notes

1 An excerpt from Lucian's text is also reproduced in Nagler (1952).
2 See Austin (1962) for a discussion of performative utterances.

3   See Cartledge (1997) for an extended discussion of the role of theatre in reflecting upon the Greek life-world. Also see Beistegui and Sparks (2000) on tragedy and philosophy. It is worth noting that Martin Heidegger gives a philosophical account of drama in section two of his piece, 'Hölderlin's Hymn, "The Ister"' which provides an interpretation of Sophocles' *Antigone* (Heidegger, 1996, pp. 71–122).
4   As an example of Film Philosophy, see Marks (2000). See Nussbaum (1990) for a discussion of the philosophical nature of literature more generally.
5   For a discussion of philosophy in Chekhov, see Whyman (2011).
6   For a useful overview and selection of writings on these themes, see *The Foucault Reader* (Foucault, 1984).
7   In this book, I will capitalise Being (*Sein*) in contrast to the being of specific beings. Heidegger calls this 'the ontological difference'. We should be wary of thinking of Being as a mystical metaphysical presence behind reality. It is simply meant to signal that which makes the being of things intelligible in the first place (see Sheehan, 2001). Following the convention of John Macquarrie and Edward Robinson's translation of *Being and Time* (Heidegger, 1962), I will also leave 'being' lowercase when used as a verb. I will also capitalise terms such as Being-with, Care, Temporality, and Historicality to indicate that they are being used in their technical Heideggerian sense. The intention is that this will signal Heidegger's special use of these words.
8   Note J. Lowell Lewis' (2013, pp. 43ff) criticism of the liminal-liminoid binary. He suggests that there needs to be a third term 'not-liminal' or not very ritual-like.
9   For a useful introduction to the distinction between these terms, see Shepherd and Wallis (2004).
10 For example, see Cole and Chinoy (1970).
11 See Grayling (1998) for a general introduction to some of these theories of truth.
12 Also see Badiou (2013) for a similar discussion of truth in theatre as experiential and potential, especially in relation to Racine and Corneille.

3

Setting the Stage: Phenomenology in Context

Tying the Knot: Knowledge in your Fingertips

When introducing phenomenology, I usually ask my students to describe what a shoelace is and how to tie it.[1] But then I add in that they need to do so as if they were talking to an alien. Perhaps you could do the same thing? Pretend that you are trying to communicate the meaning of this object and action to a Martian who has no understanding of the concept of wearing shoes at all – in fact, no understanding of anything that is familiar to our environment. Most students find it a curious activity. But in the task, I often note that the communicators tend to mime or demonstrate the action of tying a shoelace. The object of inquiry is not simply a thing to be described but, rather, an operation to be grasped in the doing: the knowledge is in the fingertips, so to speak. When prompted a little further, the students explain what a shoe is, what its parts are, what it is for, the activity of walking, what it means to protect a foot, what a foot is, what material the lace is made of, and so on. In other words, this tiny object holding footwear together reveals a world of shoe-making, walking, and more generally, the day-to-day world of human existence. All of these elements are important to what a shoelace is, but none of them individually encapsulates the matter. A further dilemma arises when the students realise that even the words that they are using are probably incomprehensible to this imaginary interlocutor from outer space. The exercise emphasises the idea that the world 'hits us all at once' rather than as discrete properties of an object, qualities of an action, or words and phrases with intrinsic meaning.

The word 'phenomenology' tends to evoke a variety of connotations to do with the study of one's conscious (and possibly unconscious) embodied encounter with the world.[2] It simply means the study of phenomena. The trick comes in describing what phenomena are, as we have seen in our alien shoelace exercise. Most commonly, it is used with reference to the philosophical movement calling for a return to experience as a basis for describing the nature of consciousness and how it grasps the world within which it exists. Nevertheless, we should be wary of oversimplifying the phenomenological project or even suggesting that there is *one* project. Some see phenomenology as a series of beginnings and interruptions rather than a coherent doctrine (Glendinning, 2007, p. 1). This self-interruption is characteristic of the movement itself – it is continually 'rebooted' in order to clear away misapprehensions, false-starts, and misguided assumptions.

In general, phenomenology emphasises lived experience and attempts to reveal the structure of our engagement with the world. The movement accuses traditional Western philosophy of disconnected abstraction and unfounded bases in 'thought', 'ideas', or 'rationality'. Many philosophical systems of the past mistakenly maintain 'dualistic' ontologies (any theory that posits there is more than one type of substance that makes up the world, most famously in the Cartesian mind-body split propounded by René Descartes [1596–1650]). But we should be careful of categorising phenomenology as simply concerning sensory and mental phenomena. Danger lies in characterising this approach as 'all inside one's head'. Terminology is important here: even the word 'consciousness' can bring with it a dualistic understanding of encountering the world. The point is not to emphasise mental, physical, or material phenomena, but to ask how we come to experience them in different ways to begin with.

There are several features that broadly characterise the phenomenological approach. Firstly, phenomenologists take a unique epistemological position (a theory of how we *know* the world) by 'bracketing off' the question of objective reality. There is no way that we can jump outside of our own heads and see the view from nowhere so to speak (or perhaps the view from no-one). Secondly, phenomenology seeks to grasp the modes of experience or 'givenness' of the world (how we encounter different objects and things that are there in the world). Rather than claim that reality exists independently of perception (objectivism) or conversely that it exists solely within the mind (subjectivism), phenomenology demands rigorous attention to 'the things themselves' (the object as it is actually experienced). In some forms, phenomenology focusses on critiquing the history of philosophy by interrogating and exposing dualist theories of reality. The movement also encourages us to question how certain metaphysical conclusions (i.e. theories of the types of things there are) have been formed in different periods of history. The point is not whether the world exists outside or inside the mind but how we can experience an outside or an inside in the first place. And, thirdly, phenomenology (in some incarnations) emphasises the *essence* of our experience of the world. In this sense, the movement bears similarities to empiricism (gathering evidence based on experience and the experimental method) aimed at uncovering the nature of our consciousness of the world. As such, it is not necessarily a science of 'facts' but an inquiry into how we apprehend facts at all.

Part of the problem with beginning to study phenomenology is that one quickly realises that its key concepts are inextricably linked. Philosopher Maurice Natanson notes:

> If we ask what phenomenology is in a searching, genuinely attentive manner, then we may begin to recognize that we can understand essence only by comprehending the status of intentional objects, that intentional objects are rendered available for inspection and analysis by way of reduction, that so long as we restrict ourselves to the psychological origin and actuality of thinking we can never attend to structural features of phenomena, that opening up the phenomenological field is, ultimately, to inquire into the conditions, a priori, for the possibility of there being a field at all, that the mundane world of our daily, taken for granted activity itself harbors the most complex philosophic commitments, and that the naive life we live as common sense men possesses an infinitely rich logic upon which the whole of reality is founded. (1973, p. 5)

Phenomena (the objects of study in phenomenology) are not merely the way that things *appear*.³ The approach focusses on the way things *are*: so if things *are* other than they *appear*, their manner of appearance *is* illusion, dissimulation, or deception – their *manner of appearing*. In this way, phenomenology offers a different way of thinking about the term 'truth': it attempts to break with mistakes in the history of Western philosophy by returning 'to the things themselves'.

It might be more appropriate to think of phenomenology as a *practice* rather than a system or doctrine. The approach aims to describe phenomena – the things that appear in the way they appear (Moran, 2000, p. 4). Husserl's reductions are meant to clear away the misconstructions that the perceiver brings in advance, and to get at the phenomena understood from within. Phenomenology is also largely a rejection of congealed tradition and dogmatism in philosophy, preferring rather to develop methods from the manner in which phenomena present themselves. In this way, the movement also rejects the metaphysical bases of knowledge that had been presented in the historical philosophical tradition. Instead, the practice returns to the lived human subject rather than an abstract floating being hovering over the world. In other words, phenomenology abides by Brentano's adage, 'experience alone is my teacher' (Moran, 2000, p. 30). As mentioned, the movement might be considered to be a transformation of empiricism that rejects the separation of the perceiving subject and the object perceived.

If seen as a practice, we should also be wary of apprehending phenomenology as a *single* method or approach to consciousness. In his later writings, Heidegger claims that 'there is no such thing as the one phenomenology' (1982, p. 328). However, the movement might be best encapsulated by Husserl's famous call for a return to 'the things themselves' (Husserl, 2001, p. 252; Heidegger, 1962, p. H24). Both Husserl and Heidegger reject the representationalist view of consciousness in which the mind contains a copy of the outside world. In this sense, phenomenology might well be seen as a reaction against idealism (although Heidegger later criticised Husserl for adopting a form of idealism).[4] Instead, they posited that consciousness engages directly with the world. Phenomenology thus entails a description of the way that things appear to consciousness. So, in another sense, it is also a reaction against externalism (the philosophical worry about the existence of the external world is overcome by reduction). Again, phenomenology also seeks to explain why this worry arose in the first place. The Cartesian view of experience in which the human subject is separate from the world (exemplified in Descartes' distinction between thinking things and material things – *res cogitans* and *res extensa*) is subsequently up-ended by Martin Heidegger and his transformation of phenomenology. Heidegger's philosophy asks the fundamental question of what Being means and claims that the history of philosophy has overlooked its relationship to Temporality. Not only are human beings inextricably linked to the world in which they live but they are also thrown between possibility (the way things might be) and actuality (the way things are) (see Chapters 6 and 7 for further discussion). The meaning of Being, including human existence, is only sensible in so far as being is always within time – the fact that life begins at birth and ends at death gives meaning to what happens in between. Maurice Merleau-Ponty (1962) later modulates phenomenology to emphasise the importance of embodiment in shaping human experience. Subsequently, other phenomenologists went on to thematise different aspects of experience such as ethics, the demands of the others there in the world, hermeneutical interpretation, and even the aesthetic experience. In short, the phenomenological movement seeks to uncover the deeply intertwined relationship between of lived experience and the world, to describe the way the world presents itself to consciousness, and to gesture towards the meaning of existence.

Typically, phenomenology acknowledges subjective experience as an unavoidable part of describing the full nature of knowledge and understanding. But this new science seeks 'to reinvigorate philosophy by returning it to the life of the living human subject' (Moran, 2000, p. 5). This does not necessarily mean solely emphasising the subjective point of view but, rather, takes intentionality as key to understanding any mode of access to the world. More broadly, the movement formulates a critique of naturalism (a view that rejects subjective experience and seeks an explanation of the world purely in natural, objective terms). Likewise, Husserl points towards the practice of phenomenology as a critique of historicism and relativism because of the process of reduction (although Heidegger and Merleau-Ponty both reintroduce a consideration of the historical conditions of the subject and subjective truth personally). Emmanuel Levinas focusses on the importance of the 'Other' as the foundation of the human subject, and Jean-Paul Sartre later introduces politics and ethical decisions into phenomenology (Moran, 2000, pp. 17–18). So while the movement is far from homogeneous, it contains a common task of getting to the truth of the things themselves.

Husserl: Return to the Things Themselves

Although the word had been used before in different senses (by Immanuel Kant and G.W.F. Hegel, among others), as a philosophical movement phenomenology is widely acknowledged to have been inaugurated as a distinct approach by Edmund Husserl (1859–1938) in his *Logical Investigations*. Husserl attempts to provide a foundation for science by concentrating on the essence of rational experience in the first place – specifically, the experiences of thinking and knowing (Husserl, 2001). His works contain a dense expression of philosophical ideas and almost all of his writings were an attempt to *introduce* phenomenology (Glendinning, 2007, p. 32). Husserl is partly restricted by the language of natural sciences that is not readily equipped to describe the 'thought-stance' of unnatural reflection.

Husserl was inspired by psychologist Franz Brentano (1838–1916), who introduced the concept of 'intentionality' – the idea that all psychical acts are *about* or directed towards some object regardless of whether or not it actually exists (Brentano, 1977). Brentano proposes that consciousness is characterised by this 'aboutness'. Mental acts cannot be empty or without an object: they are always directed towards something regardless of the actual existence of that thing. In other words, psychic acts are always transitive. So when I love, I love *something*; when I think, I think *something* – whether or not there really *is* the thing that I think about or love, the psychic act has content. There may be a secondary moment where the subject of the act can become conscious of itself. Following Descartes, Brentano suggests that such content in all conscious acts is undoubtable because the intending subject cannot be performing an empty act of intention. Husserl elaborates upon the notion of intentionality and is concerned with getting to the *essence* of psychic experiences. This method thus diverges from the positive sciences' relation to empirical facts.

Husserl employs the term 'givenness' to describe the idea that all experience is given to someone *in a manner of experiencing*. As opposed to empirical facts in the natural and physical sciences, this givenness is the highest form of evidence upon which to found philosophy (Husserl, 2001). His concept of phenomenology later develops into a transcendental science of consciousness (what might be said about consciousness *a priori*) by looking for the conditions for the possibility of any conscious act and by describing the laws binding those acts and their contents.

Husserl's method of observing consciousness involves stepping back from what he calls the 'natural attitude' (our everyday engagement with the world through involved activity). He wants to clear away all world-positing acts involved in intuition and suggests that the existence of the world should be taken as given. Such a suspending of judgements about the existence or nonexistence of the world is part of called the phenomenological reduction or *epoché*. For Husserl, this new science of phenomenology is to focus on transcendental subjectivity (the conditions for the possibility of the perceiving subject separate from the act of perception). In what he understands as a transcendental science, the conscious subject aims to apprehend the world stripped back of extraneous and accidental features and boiled down to its essential structures. The reduction also brackets away all knowledge other than that which appears in the thing by resisting the temptation to assume specific properties and explanations of the thing being observed. Husserl thus formulates the 'transcendental' and 'eidetic' reductions as fundamental to the phenomenological method (2001). The transcendental reduction suspends judgement about what we think we know and looks simply at the object itself by stripping back any psychological or everyday interpretations. This allows us to get at the sense in which we can say that the object exists and the way in which it is given to consciousness. The eidetic reduction boils down the experience to that which makes it unique and distinct from other similar experiences. In other words, it singles out the unity of meaning in the thing itself as pure phenomenon. The result of this method and object of investigation is the thing's *essence* – the proper object of phenomenology in Husserl's system.

Sartre, Merleau-Ponty, Levinas: Existence, Embodiment, Ethics

Jean-Paul Sartre (1905–1980) advanced his version of phenomenological thought by merging it back into the existentialist movement.[5] He expands upon Husserl's assertion that consciousness is neither a natural thing nor an object in any usual sense. Sartre also acknowledges the fundamentally situated being-there of the human subject, its temporal basis, together with a dialectical relationship between consciousness and Being. His most famous philosophical work, *Being and Nothingness*, explores this dialectic (a two-way interaction between thoughts, concepts, or points of view) by positing the *pour-soi* (for-itself) which approximates to consciousness and the *en-soi* (in-itself) which can be understood as Being. For Sartre, the *pour-soi* and *en-soi* have a mutually reciprocal relationship because neither is primary nor reducible to the other. But the *pour-soi*, by the fact that it is not a thing, is a 'no-thing-ness' which always aims to become Being – to become a complete thing. The en-soi, by contrast, is not directly accessible to consciousness and can only be thought of in terms of that which is opaque, dense experience, or absurd (Stewart and Mickunas, 1990, p. 74).

According to Sartre, although the human individual has no essence in itself, it strives to become what it is through enacting its own free will. This thought is expressed in Sartre's famous statement that 'existence precedes essence' (Sartre, 1992, pp. 565, 725). Developing Heidegger's thematic of Temporality, Sartre understands a person's existential situation as transcendent in that it projects itself into the future. A failure of responsibility for one's own choices is called 'bad-faith'. By referring to one's environment and circumstances as the cause of one's behaviour, for instance, one denies or abrogates responsibility. Authentic humans take on responsibility for their choices by exercising open possibilities of a future project. In other words, freedom 'is not what you do gratuitously.

It is what you do with what's been done to you' (Gerassi, 1989, p. 47). But caught up in this striving towards Being, the *pour-soi* is structured by a negativity – a 'not-yet', rendering it continually incomplete. Likewise, a person is not who they were in the past – a person is also a 'no-longer' – a doubled negativity with a perpetual loss of self. Somewhat paradoxically, Sartre also argues that who one *is* – as ego – is the sum of one's past choices and possibilities made concrete. He further melds existential phenomenology with Marxism, although he denies any simple material determinism in one's social and economic circumstances. He sees capitalism as shutting down possibilities of human choice in that it forms a treadmill for the individual to earn more money in order to partake in lifestyle choices and experiences. Consumerism also closes down thought about other possible ways of living and serves to limit free will and choice for the individual.

Maurice Merleau-Ponty (1908–1961), Sartre's sometimes friend and colleague, has become one of the most cited phenomenologists in theatre and performance studies primarily because of his emphasis on the body as a central feature of Being-in-the-world (*être au monde*). In particular, his work seeks to come to terms with prereflective and prepredicative experience: perception before we have thought about it and formulated it into the structures of logical meaning and language. His thought was seen as an alternative existential phenomenology set against Sartre's, especially in its criticism of dualism in the *pour-soi* and *en-soi*. Moreover, for Merleau-Ponty, consciousness itself can be seen as a continuum of self-awareness including animals (Moran, 2000, p. 396). The behaviour of an animal (including humans) is not simply an automatic response to external stimuli. Instead, the organism is a dynamic and fluid system of forces that interacts with the environment (Moran, 2000, p. 414). In particular, he draws on Gestalt psychology and emphasises the mutual relationship between whole and the parts of human bodily experience, consciousness, and perception. As with Husserl and Heidegger, Merleau-Ponty attacks the traditional scientific tendency towards objectification of the world and turning away from the world that we experience in our everyday dealings with it. One of the most famous examples of destabilising of this binary opposition between subject and object appears in *Phenomenology of Perception*, in which he contemplates the unique example of touching oneself – one hand touching the other (Merleau-Ponty, 1962, p. 92). He notes the way one's perception flips between the toucher and the touched – but never both at the same time. The two are deeply intertwined with one another as different modes of perception as is the visible world that surrounds us.

At the heart of Merleau-Ponty's philosophy is an attempt to understand the nature of corporeal experience in a new light – not unlike the way artists are able to foreground the material qualities of perception. In a sense, the challenge is to return to the preconceptual experience of a child while at the same time emphasising the inseparability of self and world. He uses the remarkable phrase 'the flesh of the world' to describe this bodily encounter with its environment and sees our own body (*le corps propre*) as akin to the heart of an organism, breathing life into it and forming part of a delicate system. Extending a different metaphor, the world is a closely woven fabric rather than a series of perceptual acts integrated together through consciousness (as Immanuel Kant and David Hume thought). More importantly, the world hits us all at once, complete with meaning and content, rather than a series of perceptual packets. In this way, our bodily intentions already lead us into a world that is constituted for us before we think about it. When engaged in activities in the world, we are able to explore our environment virtually before carrying out that task. So when reaching for a pair of scissors, we see the possibilities of movement beforehand with our 'phenomenal body' (*le corps phénoménal*). At times, Merleau-Ponty uses marginally mystical and metaphysical language as he writes about the 'mystery' of the world and the way in which the body is 'incarnate' in the world. He also notes the temporal and historical basis for human existence and rejects the idea that we can view the course of history from the outside: historicality is also closely interlinked with thought and language.

Emmanuel Levinas (1906–1995) studied under Husserl and Heidegger at Freiburg and later brought his teachers' thought to France where he was to become one of the most influential thinkers of the modern era. He produced the first translation of Husserl's *Cartesian Meditations* but became known for his own thought in *Totality and Infinity* (Levinas, 1991). Early on, Levinas was impressed by Heidegger's thinking about Being-with-others Anxiety, Care, and Being-towards-death. But upon

Setting the Stage: Phenomenology in Context 37

learning of his teacher's involvement and support of the Nazi movement, he came to reject that view as self-centred, individualistic, and privileging of Being over human freedom. Levinas was imprisoned in Germany during the war and survived the Holocaust although many members of his family did not. It is unsurprising, then, that his major contribution to phenomenology places an emphasis on morality – comportment towards others there in the world with us – which he thought was the true first philosophy (not fundamental ontology).

As with other phenomenologists, he seeks to unsettle the foundations of traditional thought – in this case, ethical egoism (that posits one's relation to oneself as the primary structure of social and ethical engagement). Instead, Levinas argues that our responsibility to the Other is primary: we should not treat others as mere objects but, rather, as human beings – by their proper name. Language is crucial to engaging with the Other as 'who they are' rather than reducing them to knowledge or objectification. The first step, however, is to see the Other 'face-to-face' a concrete person there in front of us. But the face of the Other is not 'given' in the same way as other things in the world. It stands in for the personhood, culture, and society of the being standing before us. In experiencing the face of the Other we are thus able to transcend our own being. Yet at the same time, the face is also fundamental to our own existence as we are confronted by others in our everyday life. In this respect, the face of the Other is an ethical demand on our own behaviour – the outstretched hand of a beggar or the thief threatening violence. The task of the philosopher is not so much to construct an ethics as it is to find its meaning. But in describing this meaning, Levinas' work issues ethical demands in so far as it gestures towards how we should relate to the Other. At times his work also strays into the mystical as his writing exhibits a difficult texture to penetrate. He takes on themes such as the Absolute which he saw as transcending the totality of History. He also sees human beings as exceeding Totality (the all-encompassing drive to representation) and totalising knowledge which he conceptualises this excess as our 'exteriority'.

As one of the most influential movements in twentieth-century philosophy, phenomenology has (for some time now) been a theory buzzword in the humanities and social sciences (as we will explore in the next chapter). In the disciplines of theatre and performance studies, Merleau-Ponty in particular has been widely invoked because of his interest in the corporeal experience of the world as being inseparable from the human subject.[6] However, I have chosen to concentrate on Heidegger's phenomenology because he tries to lay out the relationships between Being, time, and human existence – more broadly than simply the body's encounter with the world. One of the major claims of Heidegger's philosophy is that human beings possess a unique form of existence different from other things in the world, such as stones and trees. We humans have the ability to direct ourselves towards our own being (1962, p. H15). Heidegger is the main philosopher called upon in the chapters that follow in order to head off the danger of thinking that the (material) body is all that we 'are'.[7] Shifting the emphasis too far towards the body would be a mistake in phenomenological terms. Phenomenology seeks to overcome the metaphysical distinction between mind and body. As I will mention in the next chapter, many students mistake phenomenology for the description of subjective experience, stream of consciousness, or the mere outward appearance of things.

Heidegger: The Question of Being

We go back a little bit here to Husserl's most influential disciple who came to betray his teacher both in philosophical thought and political action. Martin Heidegger (1889–1976) was born in Messkirch (the son of the parish sexton), briefly entered training to become a Jesuit priest, and received church funding to study theology at Freiburg in 1909. At this time, he encountered Brentano's work on Aristotle, Husserl's *Logical Investigations*, and the hermeneutics of Friedrich Schleiermacher. In 1911 he left his religious training behind to complete a doctorate at the University of Freiburg. His *habilitation* (the thesis that qualified him for teaching at university) was on 'meaning' in the work of medieval philosopher Duns Scotus. Heidegger taught at Freiburg and after military service in 1919 returned to become Husserl's personal assistant and then an associate professor at Marburg.

Even before he had produced a major publication, Heidegger was well known for his charismatic, convincing, and magnetic teaching style as 'rumours of a hidden king' teaching new philosophical thought circulated through the academy. Husserl had noticed his talents and helped him to publish. No doubt Heidegger also influenced his teacher's thinking, although the two later fell out both intellectually and socially. When he became Rector at Freiburg, Heidegger began to implement the Nazi policy of weeding out any academics identified by the Nazis as Jewish and stripped his mentor of emeritus status in the University. Heidegger's philosophical thought shares much in common with Merleau-Ponty, who also studied under Husserl. With such students throughout his lifetime as Hans-Georg Gadamer, Herbert Marcuse, and Hannah Arendt, Heidegger had a direct impact on some of the most prominent thinkers of the century – as they too rebelled against the ideas of their teacher.[8]

Heidegger became a radical transformer of the phenomenological project into 'fundamental ontology' focussing on Being as the central topic of his thought. He shifts emphasis away from mere description of intentionality and the structures of consciousness as set out by Husserl and Brentano (and rarely actually uses the word 'intentionality' in his writing). Instead, he formulates what he calls 'the question of Being'. His thought is characterised by a rejection of dualism in its many forms. Instead, he emphasises the involved nature of the human subject in the world and the impossibility of isolating that subject from its world. For Heidegger, it is a mistake to abstract 'the subject' in an attempt to get to an objective viewpoint (essentially, his criticism of Husserl's approach to phenomenology). Heidegger also rejects 'representationalist' and 'correspondence' accounts of truth. He understands human beings as also fundamentally temporal: just as it is impossible to conceive of the subject without taking the world into account, so too is it impossible to consider time from an external point of view. The failure of past philosophy has been in its inadequate account of time and its connection to Being. *BT* is an attempt at uncovering the intrinsic relationship between these two concepts (1962, pp. H19–27).

Heidegger's phenomenology differs from Husserl's substantially because he claims that getting to the things themselves cannot simply be achieved by describing conditions for the possibility of intuition or consciousness. For him, such an investigation must take into account the position of the enquirer too – or rather, the type of being that can inquire in the first place. Phenomenology for Heidegger is not simply a description of what the perceiver intuits but is also an *interpretation*. In this way he draws on the tradition of hermeneutics as a model for investigating human existence through textual elucidation. For Heidegger, the core of philosophy is questioning – or rather finding an authentic way of formulating *the* question in the first place – the question of the meaning of Being:

> Do we in our time have an answer to the question of what we really mean by the word 'being'? Not at all. So it is fitting that we should raise anew the question of the meaning of Being. But are we nowadays even perplexed at our inability to understand the expression 'Being'? Not at all. So first of all we must reawaken an understanding for the meaning of this question. (1962, p. H1)

Heidegger's thinking can largely be understood as a reaction against what he called 'metaphysics'. This is a term used somewhat uniquely to mean any philosophy that has failed to take into account or give a proper explanation for Being especially by overlooking its relation to time.[9] Incidentally, the term metaphysics (via Jacques Derrida) has been adopted by contemporary literary and critical theory as perhaps one of the biggest insults to any system of thinking (indicating that it is based on false or unfounded assumptions). Perhaps the most prevalent usage of the word metaphysics now holds connotations to regions of mysticism, astrology, and the supernatural. Ancient problems in metaphysics include the question of why there is something rather than nothing. Traditionally, metaphysics is the branch of philosophy that deals with Being. Aristotle's *Physics* – about the nature of change in the world – then the *Metaphysics*, deal with concepts such as time, space, and causality. Metaphysics for Heidegger has a tendency to conceal fundamental ontology and therefore takes on negative connotations.

The most influential of these metaphysical systems in the history of Being have been based variously in the absolute creative power of God; a detached, objective subject controlling and viewing the world; the transcendence of rationality; and (from the Enlightenment onwards) the all-pervading spirit of scientific investigation. As it happens, these foundations for the conditions of knowledge are precisely those rejected by the phenomenological movement and its transformation into post-structuralism. Both Derrida and Foucault acknowledge the key influence of Heidegger's thinking in their own work. Foucault's emphasis on the historical nature of subjectivity and Derrida's deconstruction were both born out of Heidegger's destabilising of metaphysics. And even today Heidegger's thought is gaining a new importance in his influence on the post-structural movement in general and his radical rethinking of human subjectivity.

Heidegger defines the phenomenological method of inquiry as 'letting things show themselves in the way that they show themselves from themselves':

> We must rather choose a way of access and such a kind of interpretation that this entity [*Dasein*] can show itself in itself and from itself'. (1962, p. H16)

So rather than begin his investigation into Being by examining objects, our material body, or the potentially mistaken content of our perceptions, Heidegger starts by thinking about the entity – the type of being – that could have access to the world and its own being in the first place.

Being and Time: Another Starting Point

The origins of *BT* can be traced to at least three major influences on Heidegger's early thought: *Lebensphilosophie*, Husserl, and Aristotle (although he critiques and reinterprets their ideas; Moran, 2000, p. 223). Heidegger criticises fellow phenomenologist Karl Jaspers' *Lebensphilosophie* for its inadequacy of concepts in dealing with 'factical life' (everyday experience) and its connection to the metaphysical tradition. Heidegger argues that human life in a philosophical sense cannot be approached directly, although it can be seen through acts about which humans have anxious concern (*Angst*) and a renewal of self-concern (Heidegger, 1962, p. H184ff). Furthermore, Temporality must not merely be thought of as an appendage to the present moment and requires a hermeneutic of the historical mode which cannot be universalised (1962, p. H372ff). In his attempt to interpret factical life, Heidegger also draws on Christian writings such as those of St. Paul Augustine, Luther, and Kierkegaard. He views Facticity as both contingent and concrete. Human life is also preoccupied with meaning and is founded in the structures of Care (*Sorge*) and Concern (*Besorgnis*) (1962, p. H301ff). Time is never encapsulated as an objective passing of a series of instants. It can only be apprehended by a transfiguring moment (*Augenblick*) – something out of the ordinary. Heidegger suggests that we need to uncover the way that lived experience interacts with the environment (*Umwelt*) in its living fluidity, specificity, and concreteness.

In his lectures on the phenomenology of religion (1920–21), Heidegger interprets the terms 'Care' and 'Concern' as central to Aristotle's notion of practical knowledge (*phronesis*). In this interpretation of the fundamental structures of human existence, Heidegger sees humans as fundamentally becoming what they are. Humans must embrace their finitude in 'resoluteness' (*Entschlossenheit*) towards their own death. Heidegger interprets Aristotle in terms of the search for articulating factical human life in the *Physics*, *Metaphysics*, and *Nicomachean Ethics*. The crucial structure of Care involves Circumspection (*Umsicht*) (1962, p. H69). For the most part, humans are caught up in their everyday concern with practical engagements with the world. Humans are generally in a state of Falling concern (*Verfallen*) (1962, p. H57). In order to cope with the world, we generally try to smooth things over and settle our anxiousness towards existence and specifically to our own death (1962, p. H75ff).

Heidegger therefore transforms the task of phenomenology as getting to the things themselves to include both everyday life and the meaning of existence as a whole. He also thoroughly rejects Husserl's dualism. However, he does draw upon Husserl's concepts of world and environment (*Umwelt*) and maintains a special interest in the problem of Being in Aristotle and Brentano. This leads to the idea that in perception we do not only grasp objects but their being. We can grasp their being because we have a special access to the world characteristic of our own type of being. Heidegger also draws on Bergson, Scheler, and Dilthey in their thoughts about being human with an emphasis on the historical, lived nature of factical experience (1962, p. H45ff). The conclusion is that we humans primarily encounter the environment through practical engagement. The manner of engagement also needs to be uncovered. Descriptive phenomenology needs to take into account both the historical understanding of Being and the active apprehension of Being within the context of the practical world. So not only does Heidegger reject dualism but also all intellectualist accounts (that see our psychic acts alone can account for the way we encounter the world).

BT begins its investigation into the meaning of Being by considering the conditions necessary for factical life. The verb 'to be' can be used in many different senses and it is not clear that there is *one thing* it means. Heidegger surveys various explanations as to why this is so: (1) the meaning of 'to be' is *obvious* – we already know what it means, so there is no reason to investigate it; (2) the term is *indefinable* under a single meaning; (3) being *is not a real predicate* that can be added to something (1962, pp. H2–4). The task is to find a way to break into the question which has been so easily dismissed: none of these explanations seem satisfactory. Moreover, Heidegger suggests that there are twin *reasons* why we have become so forgetful of Being: (1) we have been seduced by an encrusted and mistaken philosophical tradition, and (2) our everyday practical concerns in the world distract us from the question (as one might fail to see the spectacles on the end of one's nose because when one is looking through them).

The core premise of Heidegger's most famous work is that human beings have a different kind of being from mere things or material objects in the world. We have the ability to inquire into our own being. Furthermore, human existence is not simply actuality or presence as had been assumed in previous philosophical investigations dating back to the ancient Greeks. Being is *possibility* more than *actuality.* In other words, 'who we are' is more than simply 'what we are' at any point in time. Who we *are* is also who we *might* be – which is to say that we are most properly our possibilities. This is also borne out in the way that we direct ourselves to the world in projects that we undertake: our outlook is futural. In other words, we are concerned with how things *will* be rather than just how they are *now* and this directs the way that we act. In this sense, Heidegger also stresses *praxis* (involved human activity). This does not mean that *theoria* (detached contemplation) is inferior or derivative; it is simply another possible way of being. Instead of blindly accepting the traditional understanding of man as a rational animal, or as a being created by God, Heidegger attempts to think about human existence on its own terms.

In order to clear away the many misinterpretations of Being throughout the history of philosophy (the history of metaphysics), Heidegger appropriates a term 'Dasein' (Being-there). This word had been used by Kant and Hegel to indicate uniquely human existence. Dasein is that which is 'closest', but in this closeness, remains hidden (1962, p. H42). In trying to get at what is closest, you might suggest we begin with our body – our materiality. However, this falls into the trap of thinking that we are mere things like other objects in the world – precisely the kind of interpretation that Heidegger wishes to avoid.

Part of the reason that we have interpreted ourselves as mere things is because we are in the world (*Welt*). Our world is that which surrounds us in our everyday practical concern (*Besorgnis*) or behaviour (*Verhalten*). The tendency has always been to interpret ourselves in terms of mere things there in the world because they are what we encounter daily. Furthermore, Heidegger argues that our understanding of Being has *decayed* over time. He suggests that the original meaning of Being (forgotten since the dawning days of philosophy in ancient Greece) must be recovered. The historical interpretation of Being – how people understand what it means to be – also reveals something about the nature of Being itself. Being covers itself up.

For Heidegger, phenomenology is the only proper way forward for philosophy. Everything else is metaphysics and congealed tradition. As mentioned, he defines phenomenology as letting things be seen in the way in which they show themselves from themselves (1962, p. H34). Philosophy, then, is not a meaning imposed upon the world in advance, but the practice of letting the world be seen as it is. Furthermore, it is an investigation of the *way* in which things show themselves. As such, Heidegger claims that phenomenology does not have any discrete subject matter or object. Phenomenology is the proper mode of *access* to beings rather than a discrete science (as Husserl and some other philosophers had thought). Unlike other sciences with the suffix 'ology' such as anthropology, psychology, sociology, or biology, phenomenology does not just look at different aspects of Dasein but, rather, gets to its 'primordial existentiality' (1962, p. H45). Without a discrete object for study, Heidegger realises the need to focus on *something* in order to set the investigation on the way. Dasein – the being that has special access and concern for its own being – is therefore the proper object for his enquiry in *BT*.

The project of *BT* is not meant to be exhaustive in its description of all possible modes of human existence. And even though Heidegger thinks that this study of Being underpins other social sciences this does not mean that other social sciences should not proceed with investigating their specific areas of Being (1962, pp. H51–52). The phenomenological project he hoped for would provide the proper foundation for the social sciences (as opposed to what he saw as the spurious metaphysical tradition that had served as a basis up until the advent of phenomenology).

Temporality is the key to this rethinking of the meaning of Being. Heidegger believes that traditionally time has been interpreted with respect to space (1962, pp. H18–19). In *BT*, he approaches time as it is lived through experiences (*Erlebnisse*) (1962, p. H48). Death, in particular, serves as a clue as to how we experience time. Life is stretched out between birth and death as we attempt to achieve certain projects in between. But Dasein is always 'outstanding' in the sense that it is never finished: there is more to come (1962, p. H241ff).

What Heidegger calls the Destruktion of metaphysics is a reinterpretation of Being with time as its horizon (1962, p. H15ff). All human experience is from a definite standpoint in time, looking to the future, and in a distinctive historical period that will enable its own understanding of Being. Being too has a history and this is to be found in the way that peoples have understood the term throughout the ages, as mentioned. However, the task of Destruktion is not entirely negative but, rather, looks to the past and salvaging the truth in different understandings of Being that have been held throughout history (1962, pp. H22–23). For Heidegger, there is wisdom to be recovered from ancient Greece.

So instead of turning to Husserl's definition of phenomenology, Heidegger reaches back to the Greek etymology of the term in search of an older meaning. The word φαινόμενον (phenomenon) comes from the verb 'to show', and is related to bringing something into the daylight or showing that which is bright (1962, p. H29). But things can show themselves in many different ways, depending on how we have access to them. In order to counter the argument that we might be taken in by 'mere appearance' in this task, Heidegger proposes that dissimulation, illusion, and seeming are derivative of the primary showing of something: in order for something to seem it must be showing *something* and the way that it shows itself is precisely what is up for investigation. So phenomenology not only encounters intuition and perception but also *how* things show themselves. Space and time, for instance, need to be able to be seen as they are, not as objects in the world. The *manner* of showing of things needs to be the sort of thing that we can apprehend.

Heidegger translates λόγος (*logos*) – the root of the suffix in 'phenomenology' – as 'discourse', although he acknowledges that it could also mean reason, judgement, concept, definition, ground, or relationship (1962, p. H32). He thinks that rather than binding two things together, the concept of logos is the making manifest of what one is talking about in discourse. Logos has the character of pointing something out, and can mean letting things be seen together rather than joining them artificially. By defining logos in such a way, Heidegger moves away from the idea of something as true or false because of correspondence between perception and reality. He conceives of truth as 'letting be seen'. *Aletheia* (unconcealment or unhiddenness) is thus the original meaning of truth (1962, p. H33). In this sense, logos is not mere perception, nor is it judgement but, rather, an uncovering of the manner of appearing.

Heidegger's *magnum opus* was rushed to publication in 1927 in order to qualify him for nomination to the Chair of Philosophy in Marburg. Initially, he was turned down for the position when the Education Minister declared the publication inadequate, although he soon went on to gain a full professorship and then took over as Chair at Freiburg when Husserl retired. Only the first two sections of the first part of the projected two-part text appeared in print (although through lecture notes and subsequent writings it has been possible to glimpse what might have been the content of the missing parts). Even by this time, his thinking was changing.

The Turn: From the Being of Beings to Being Itself

After the publication of *BT*, Heidegger had already begun the 'Turn' (*Kehre*) away from examining the being of beings to concentrate on Being itself. Instead of continuing his analysis of the structures of human existence and its relation to the world and showing how previous philosophy had failed to come to such an account, he turned to art, architecture, and history in order to think through the meaning of Being. Heidegger ceased to refer to his own work as phenomenology (at least in explicit terms) although he retained the notion of truth as disclosure and unconcealing. This retains the goal of getting to the things themselves. He also turned from the transcendental project of describing the conditions for the possibility of human existence and Being which motivates *BT* towards the notion of truth as Event (*Ereignis*).

His later writings introduce an anti-subjectivist, anti-aesthetic understanding of the ontological status of the work of art which he saw as connected to the idea of world-founding. He also distanced himself from humanism (including Marxism), which he saw as yet another metaphysical system. Towards the end of his career, he changed from indicating that Being was to be recovered simply from Greek thinking towards the idea of Being as a futural promise; it is not a matter of Dasein freeing Being, but rather Being itself revealing and concealing itself. He sometimes also mysteriously uses the archaic form 'Seyn' (translated as 'Beyng') to denote his search for elusive origin of Being. He also moves towards poetry as a potentially revealing pathway to understanding Being. But dissatisfaction with everyday life in the modern world persists in his thinking – especially the way in which technology (and technological frameworks) threatens uniquely human modes of existence.

Heidegger has long been shrouded in controversy and criticism for his involvement in National Socialism as mentioned earlier.[10] It is still up for question whether his political beliefs so infect his philosophy that they form a case for ruling him out of consideration in any serious theoretical debate. Nevertheless, his influence on the development of twentieth-century philosophy both in Germany and internationally is still significant even today and his contribution to reforming the concept of phenomenology is substantial. Heidegger has also been attacked for his dense style of philosophical writing (along with many other phenomenologists and post-structuralists since, as I note later). His work is replete with neologisms coined to achieve descriptive precision. He constantly employs word-play and often places great significance on (his interpretation of) etymology. His difficult language might be seen as an attempt to overcome what he saw as the mistaken pathways of the philosophical tradition that has appropriated certain vocabularies. Heidegger might be criticised for privileging German language, culture, and supposed national destiny in his view of the development of philosophy. Later in his career, in an attempt to reach new modes of thinking, he departed from more structured philosophical discourse towards a 'poetic' speaking of Being (*Dichtung*).

It's All in Your Head: Criticisms of Phenomenology

A number of criticisms have been launched at phenomenology. The most widely expressed concern is that phenomenology places undue emphasis on subjective experience. Lacking any consistent methodology, fundamental concepts, structure, or object of study, one might say that it doesn't really even constitute a philosophical movement at all. It may therefore be futile to reduce experience, consciousness, and the lived world into philosophical treatment. One could say 'that's just life'. The proposition that the philosopher's task is to return to the things themselves could be seen as a philosophical truism in this sense. By uncovering or rather stating the obvious one might even ask whether the approach offers anything new to our understanding of existence. Phenomenologists might agree and argue that is the point – the aim is to show the world as it is. The world is both unremarkable yet astounding and we have forgotten how to question the obvious.

As we have seen, the movement has constantly attacked, refuted, and criticised its own foundations. Husserl had first proposed phenomenology as a rigorous science, opposed to life-philosophy and worldviews, although he later changed this view (Moran, 2000, p. 20). Heidegger reintroduced attention to the Historicality and Facticity of human living in his analysis of Dasein. He also focussed on the importance of the lived experience of time and the importance of inter-subjective experience as opposed to Husserl's concentration on individual experience. Husserl's original project of a descriptive science of phenomenology was doomed to failure together with its aspirations for objectivity (because even a description is an interpretation). Every description of experience takes place within history and in specific conditions enabling its experience in the first place. Both Heidegger and Merleau-Ponty rejected the transcendental ego as a basis of experience as metaphysical. Heidegger himself drifted away from phenomenology in his poetic approach to Being, although he was still very much concerned with the way things show themselves as the object of his thinking. As I will return to in the next chapter, Derrida (1978) attacked the possibility of pure presence with his term 'différance'. He also suggested that in Heidegger's thought the term 'spirit' was merely another form of metaphysics (Derrida, 1989).

Attacks also came from outside phenomenology: the Frankfurt School including Jürgen Habermas criticised Heidegger's involvement in the Nazi movement. Theodor Adorno rejected Heidegger's project of fundamental ontology in *Negative Dialectics* and questioned the jargon of authenticity as open to ideological and political misuse and abuse. Max Horkheimer saw phenomenology as the epitome of 'traditional theory' from which his philosophical school rebelled. Proponents of analytic philosophy such as Bertrand Russell attacked Heidegger for lacking any substantial meaning in his work. It was dismissed as meaningless pseudo-metaphysics by philosophers such as A.J. Ayer who rejected all forms of phenomenology. Criticism also arose from positivists and the Vienna Circle (Moran, 2000, p. 21). From these perspectives, phenomenology was attacked for its emphasis on intellectual intuition. From a Marxist position, phenomenology was a fundamentally bourgeois philosophy, forming the epitome of individualism with its overemphasis on the self. Structuralists attacked phenomenology for its naive trust in the evidence of consciousness and argued that hidden unconscious structures underlie our experiences.

Apart from anything else, the difficult language in which phenomenological texts are often written is an obstacle for many.[11] It could be countered that such difficulty is part of the process because it slows the reader down, emphasises the difficulty of thinking, displays the complexity of the theoretical ideas that are at hand, emphasises the playfulness of language in its mediation of philosophy, and invents a new vocabulary in order to brush away the errors of traditional metaphysics.

The term 'postphenomenology' has also gained currency especially in relation to scholarship surrounding technology. Don Ihde (2003), for instance, hopes to move away from a subject-centred view that he sees as characteristic of phenomenology (again, specifically Husserl's 'transcendental ego'). More broadly, the approach emphasises materiality over textuality, acknowledges the independence of objects from any human experience of them, and places 'alterity' as fundamental to our Being-in-the-world. Arguably these features represent a continuation of the phenomenological movement (as a set of disruptions) rather than a surpassing of it. The prefix 'post' in this context signals the intention to bring phenomenology into conversation with postmodernism and post-structuralism – approaches which themselves were reaching their peak of influence at the time.

Whether or not the age of phenomenology has ended, its key concepts still exert considerable influence in the intellectual landscape. Part of the usefulness of phenomenology is in its aim of bringing the obvious to attention – it bothers to question what we take as given and transparent. It may also aid in stimulating rich description of our experiences of the life world replete with its subjective window on the world (drawing attention to the frame that makes the vista possible). 'Return to the things themselves' is a maxim that still bears relevance in the study of theatre as we will also see in the next chapter. It may also be that theatre offers an important perspective in the poetic speaking of Being.

Exercises and Topics for Discussion

1. Choose an image that you think conveys a sense of Being. Talk about why you chose that image and what you think it communicates about the nature of existence.

2. Deprive yourself of one of your senses – hearing or seeing, for instance. Think about how this deprivation radically changes your perception of the world. How do your other senses come to the rescue and alter the way that you apprehend the being of things?
3. Pick an object to observe. Write a one-page description of that object merely present-at-hand that you experience primarily in its materiality rather than function. Do the same with a tool (something that you regularly use to complete a practical task). What philosophical assumptions do you bring to observing the thing? What prior knowledge affects the way that you observe it? What do you think the essence of your apprehension of the thing is? Now use your observation of that object to create a short one minute performance. How did you communicate the object to your audience? In what way was the communication inadequate?
4. Write about a celebrity that you have read about or seen in the news. Now write about someone you know intimately – a close friend, family-member, or partner. What are the differences in the language you use to describe each object or person? Is it possible to describe each simply as a thing, tool, or person?
5. Choose a character from a play. How might you think about that person in terms of existence, embodiment, and ethics? What terms from Sartre, Merleau-Ponty, and Levinas are useful in approaching and understanding the role?
6. Pick a concept from a phenomenological text. You might choose the *epoché*, the Other, or the Uncanny, for example. How might you use this as a stimulus for a short devised performance? What form would your presentation take – a physical movement piece, a text-based dialogue, a task-based performance, an event of performance art?

Notes

1　Interestingly, in his phenomenology of comedy on stage and screen, Shaun May (2016, p. 58) uses the example of tying a shoelace to think about the involved referential world of everyday life. But rather than stop at the equipmental context, I point towards the existential context of Dasein as revealed in this simple piece of string here.

2 For two useful overviews of the movement, see Dermot Moran's (2000), *Introduction to Phenomenology* and David Stewart and Algis Mickunas' (1990) *Exploring Phenomenology*. For the more advanced, see Herbert Spiegelberg's (1971) *The Phenomenological Movement: A Historical Introduction*.
3 For Heidegger's explanation of this point, see Heidegger (1964, pp. H28–31). All page numbers in *Being and Time* referred to here are in the original German pages as included in the margins of Macquarrie and Robinson's translation and marked with 'H' to indicate this.
4 See Moran (2000, pp. 226–33) for a discussion of Heidegger's rejection of Husserl's view of consciousness.
5 For an engagingly written account of existentialism for a popular audience (with reference to phenomenology), see Sarah Bakewell's (2016) *At the Existentialist Café*.
6 For example, see Fraleigh (1987), Garner (1994), and States (1985).
7 It should be noted the Merleau-Ponty (1962) does make a distinction between the material body (*Körper*) and the lived body (*Leib*). There is a danger of falling back into a dualistic ontology if these terms are not applied rigorously, however.
8 See Jones (1998), 'Heidegger the Fox: Hannah Arendt's Hidden Dialogue'. Arendt presents a parable of Heidegger as a fox who is not able to discern traps in his path. He builds himself a den which is, itself, a trap, and invites all the other foxes to visit. Unable to get out of this trap he built for himself, he also claims to be the best of all foxes given the number of others who fell into his trap.
9 Heidegger's understanding of existence also draws on concepts such as Falling, Guilt, and the Call of Conscience – terms that come from sources such as Kierkegaard and Meister Eckhart.
10 See Victor Farias' (1989) *Heidegger and Nazism*, Collins' (2000) *Heidegger and the Nazis*, Young's (1997) *Heidegger, Philosophy, Nazism*, and Sherratt's (2013) *Hitler's Philosophers*.
11 See Blackburn (2000) for a scathing review of the obscure language in Heidegger's (1999) *Contributions to Philosophy: From Enowning*.

4
Revealing the Scene: Doing Phenomenology in the Theatre

Back to the Old Drawing Board: A Philosophy of Beginnings

One problem with 'doing' phenomenology is that it is very difficult to know where to start. In a way, that is a significant point to start with in itself. As discussed in the last chapter, the world hits us all at once. So to isolate particular elements of the world is to lose sense of their meaning in the larger context of our involvement in particular tasks. So where can we begin? Many phenomenological investigations begin by asking the question of what phenomenology is and proceed to redefine it – a point that Glendinning (2007) makes when he describes phenomenology as a series of beginnings. Many phenomenologists do not attempt to describe specifics directly because they aim at a level of abstraction in their focus on essence. Heidegger often begins by asking what is thinking, what is questioning, or what is dwelling. His start point is often the self-reflexive task of inquiring into what an inquiry is in the first place – a phenomenology of phenomenology. Stewart and Mickunas (1990, p. 141) make the distinction between pure and applied phenomenology where the former is primarily aimed at elaborating the phenomenological method while the latter aims to investigate and describe a particular phenomenon or set of phenomena. But they also note that the distinction between the two is not entirely clear and that it may simply be a matter of emphasis.

When I am trying to explain the process of phenomenological research, another task I ask students to carry out involves simply going outside and taking a walk. Why don't you do the same thing? Walk up your street or somewhere nearby outside and pay attention to the way in which the world reveals itself to you. My students report back that they feel strange throughout the task. Divested of their bags, books, and study paraphernalia, they often feel a little bit naked and ill-equipped to deal with their environment. You might notice the soft breeze on your face, the warmth and light of the sun, or the dull drizzle of rain. You might become aware of noises in the environment, the laughter of people sitting on benches, the sounds that your feet make as you step on down the footpath. You might start to feel the weight of your clothes and how your garments brush against your skin. Or you might become aware of the colours and shapes of the built human environment and surrounding natural world. Because you aren't walking to a particular place for a particular purpose (other than to observe the world and how it shows itself to you) you might notice that you are a bit disoriented and time doesn't seem to progress at its usual tempo. You might notice that you are walking at a different pace from when you are going to class, or rushing to a meeting, or on the way to catch up with an old friend.

This practical exercise involves stepping out of the natural attitude or immediate Care structure of your regular involvement with the world. You begin to encounter aspects of experience in a different way by paying attention to the way in which they present themselves to your conscious experience. But when I ask students to write about their experiential walk, I notice that they often produce a kind of stream-of-consciousness prose in return focusing on their preoccupied thoughts and emotional response to the task. Each element of perception that the students describe is often detached from other elements and the experience as a whole. And I find that most responses pay little attention to how each moment of awareness offers itself to consciousness. The question remains as to how such observation and description of experience can be taken further. As I will suggest, the answer will be 'tacking' between observing individual experiences and the context of the world that makes consciousness possible. And it will depend on which phenomena you are letting come to light.

What does it mean to 'do phenomenology', then? In part, it is searching for the ineluctable qualities of experience: pinpointing what it is about a particular cognitive or perceptual event that makes it what it is. When it comes to answering this question about your walk up the road, it is difficult to boil the experience down to a single essence. The type of answer that you might give could be relative to what has happened to you today, what is happening to you at this time in your life, and your family context, culture, and society. If your legs are arthritic, perhaps the walk would reveal a sense of loss of mobility and pain. If your ex-lover used to live up the top of your street, then the walk might reveal deep unrequited love and sense of rejection from the world. Each is a different experience though it may be directed towards a similar material object. Likewise, if you draw on concepts from a particular phenomenologist then your attention will be inflected to a particular thematisation: the body (Maurice Merleau-Ponty), consciousness and free will (Jean-Paul Sartre), the face of – and ethical responsibility towards – the Other (Emmanuel Levinas), the mystery of existence (Gabriel Marcel), the human (Hannah Arendt), or the meaning of Being (Martin Heidegger). The simple act of walking up the road might reveal each of these phenomena. The task of the phenomenologist is to show how. Your perception of the street will present itself in its materiality, but also takes on a wider significance in terms of your lifeworld, the context of your broader existence, and the historical moment.

On the other hand, if you are viewing a theatrical production (or analysing a performance process/play text), that object (the performance, creative activity, or text) may direct the audience and performer towards particular thematisation of Being as mentioned earlier. The work sends forth a call from and of existence. Depending on the performance or text, it may also be directed towards certain elements of worldhood. The various aspects of Being that might be relevant to your walk up the road might not be so open when you view such a work. By attending to 'the thing itself', you are led by the object of enquiry towards uncovering the essence of the performance or text. The approach differs from other methods of analysis – for instance, New Criticism, which involves a close reading solely of the text itself, perhaps looking for evidence of neurosis in the work and traces of the author's autobiography. A truly phenomenological approach will see a dramatic-, creative-, or performance-text as closely intertwined with the wider world of its creation and reception. There is no definitive 'reading' to be reached outside of the dynamic intersubjective exchange of the performance event. In this sense, the approach does not fall into the intentional fallacy (locating meaning in what the author *meant* to convey). Nor does it isolate the text from the world in which it is created and performed. Whatever the focus of analysis, the danger is to impose meaning beforehand – or, even worse, to apply a preconceived theory about the phenomenon blindly and without question.

In this book, I have emphasised comparative inquiry over any conceptual dissection characteristic of pure phenomenology.[1] The goal here is to draw theatre and philosophy into critical dialogue. Most theatre doesn't explicitly reflect on the history of philosophy, but rather aims to show something truthful about life and the way that we encounter it in the here and now. As I will discuss later in this chapter, focussing phenomenological awareness also has the advantage of developing capacity for descriptive writing about performance process. Such a task is to capture a sense of experience by vivid description and therefore to understand theatrical practice in a new way. As I will suggest, the focussed attention offered by phenomenology may also feed into artistic practice and generate theatrical ideas and practices. In fact, the key chapters in Part II look at how theatre practice itself is already engaged in phenomenological questioning. In this sense, I am setting out a 'comparative phenomenology' by allowing tension and conversation between philosophical theory and artistic practice. The next step is to see theatrical performance as philosophical in itself and let it talk back to more formal philosophy. This is giving art a voice to speak back to philosophers. But again we might ask where to begin.

Maurice Natanson distils the essence of what it takes to practise phenomenology:

> What is needed is rather simple: to learn what is meant by the natural attitude, to practice the *epochē*, to attempt descriptions of presentations without prejudicing the results by taking for granted the history, causality,

intersubjectivity, and value we ordinarily associate with our experience, and to examine with absolute care the fabric of the world of daily life so that we may grasp its source and its direction. (1973, p. 8)

Thinking Outside the Box: Phenomenology in the Humanities and Social Sciences

It is difficult to think of an area of the humanities and social sciences that has not been influenced by philosophical phenomenology in some way. The broad investigation of the relationship between individual and society, meaning, language, texts, art, and how we come to know the world are fundamental to many aspects of social and cultural experience. As discussed above, phenomenology offers an alternative to a positivist conception of objective knowledge and stresses the interconnected and interrelated nature of self and world. Since its inauguration by Husserl, phenomenology has instigated the rethinking of fundamental principles in many disciplines, questioning their presuppositions, and showing the limitations and scope of each field of study (Stewart and Mickunas 1990, p. 118). A quick (but by no means exhaustive) survey of some relevant and related disciplines shows the variety of contexts within which the approach has been adapted.

Phenomenology has always been closely related to psychology in so far as Husserl developed the descriptive project of Franz Brentano (1838–1917). Brentano's approach attacks behaviourism and its focus on the physical expressions of consciousness rather than experiential content. From the perspective of behaviourism, psychological explanation is based only on observable aspects of the human response to its environment. The danger with this way of thinking is that it reduces mental events to mechanical material reactions. Such a model overlooks meaning in conscious experience and may deny the possibility of meaningful explanation in psychological discourse itself: if all human behaviour is simply a response to external stimuli, then so too are the psychologists' statements about those stimuli. In contrast, for Brentano psychology must take the 'lifeworld' into account and give a full account of meaning in context. In the 1920s, Ludwig Binswanger (1881–1966) later drew upon phenomenology in his technique of psychoanalysis called 'Daseinsanalysis' (*Daseinsanalyse*). In what he initially thought of as phenomenological anthropology, Binswanger (1963) adapted Heidegger's investigation of Dasein and emphasised the tension between Being-with-others and being alone as the heart of the human existential situation.

In a similar way, phenomenological sociology seeks to emphasise the mutually generating relationship between social agents and their environment. Alfred Schütz (1899–1959) refused any attempt to align the study of the social world with the natural sciences and their emphasis on objective observation and classification (Schütz, 1967). Instead, he argues that the object of study is human conduct. For him, an interpretation of the social world necessarily involves a subjective orientation. The social participants being observed in such study have their own understanding of their social world and are engaged in an ongoing process of making sense of it. The social scientist, however, is not involved in the social world in the same way, and attempts to take on the role of disinterested observer (stepping out of the natural attitude in Husserl's terms). The task of the researcher is in part to unpack the 'taken for granted' behaviours of social agents in developing models of human action. Furthermore, those models should be understandable by the social actors themselves and remain consistent with the common-sense experiences of the social world.

A little later in the discipline of anthropology, phenomenology altered the study of culture by emphasising a co-constitutive relationship between individual and community, the crucial role of cultural practice in societal formation and development. Through the work of Clifford Geertz (1926–2006) via philosopher Gilbert Ryle (1900–1976), the discipline began to rethink conceptions of self by taking the 'insider's point of view' into account. This perspective contrasts with an imperialist/colonial model of anthropology observing 'primitives' from a culturally superior standpoint. In practical terms, phenomenology has influenced ethnography (a process which involves a period of fieldwork during which the researcher observes the activities, interactions, communication, and practices of a particular group of people in order to understand what it means to be an insider). Traditionally, the 'informant' for the ethnographer was from a 'foreign' culture, but more and more, ethnographic practices have been taken up in 'familiar' social groups. The danger with studying one's own culture is that the 'taken for granted' in social interaction needs to be held at arm's length, described, and analysed objectively (where phenomenology seems to help). By immersing themselves in a cultural way of life, ethnographers become 'participant-observers' – never wholly separate from the cultural phenomena that they witness. They also acknowledge that their mere presence affects the nature of the practices that they are attempting to study. The period of fieldwork is followed by a stage in which the researcher tries to make sense of what they experienced through writing it down – ethnography. This may involve looking for structures of practice, patterns of interaction, and even theory as to why the people behave in the way that they do. Contemporary ethnography is wary of imposing a final interpretation claiming to be totally objective and warns against dismissing the participant's point of view. As inflected by phenomenology, the aim of ethnography is to get as close to the participant's understanding of their own lifeworld as possible through a process of 'thick description' in 'experience-near' terms (Geertz, 1973, pp. 3–30, 1983, pp. 55–71).

Pierre Bourdieu (1930–2002), one of the most frequently cited social theorists of the twentieth century, was also heavily influenced by phenomenology, although he presented a staunch critique of Husserl's work. Bourdieu's most well-known term '*habitus*' refers to an internalised structure or set of structures through which an individual acts and reacts to the environment. Arising out of both the physical world and pre-existing structures of social experience, *habitus* operates in such a way that the social agent does not consciously follow a set of rules. Its structures generate specific practices, perceptions, and dispositions towards the world. Bourdieu argues that *habitus* is durable (it lasts over a period of time) and is transposable (can be adapted to different situations) (1977, p. 72). In other words, an individual's attitude and behaviour is predicated upon the social environment in which it has been formed, and generates that social environment through social practice – it is the mutual interaction between habit and habitat. *Habitus* is therefore historical (although it tends to forget its own history) and bodily in that it is performed and expressed through practice. Bourdieu uses the term *body hexis* to indicate the socially formed mode in which individuals move, hold, and position themselves in the social world through a series of movements, gestures, and postures – the organisation of one's own body. Social agents also have a particular sense of reality or *doxa* which they see as natural, self-evident, and taken for granted. These belief systems are only seen when competing discourses come into conflict (in cultural, political, and economic crises, for example). Not unlike later phenomenologists, Bourdieu launched a critique of subjectivist and objectivist traditions (and saw phenomenology as part of the former). In fact, it is Husserl's transcendental phenomenology that he criticises and his approach shares much in common with subsequent perspectives on phenomenology. For Bourdieu, consciousness co-constructs the world of objects it perceives and is formed by each individual's practice in a world of objects sharing those same structures (1977, p. 91).

Phenomenology has had a profound influence on the study of space and place (through the work of Yifu Tuan, Michael Jackson, Ed Casey, Michel de Certeau, to name but a few).[2] Philosopher Gaston Bachelard developed a phenomenological reflection on architecture in literature and the built environment emphasising personal experiences elicited by buildings and spaces rather than aesthetic rationales (Bachelard, 1994). The co-creation of self, lifeworld, and environment are central to understanding the spaces we live in, work in, play in, and travel through. Rather than interpret space as a set of Cartesian coordinates, such approaches emphasise the cultural reverberations of practices, events, persons, and history in creating a sense of space. Although there is some variation in terminology, human geographers often distinguish two senses of spatiality: (1) a geometric, scientific abstraction (sometimes called 'space'); and (2) a lived, en-cultured, historical, embodied concept of that which surrounds us (sometimes called 'place'). Drawing on the phenomenological tradition, the latter is primary and the former secondary in that we bring a social understanding to our environment bound up with our own personal history. In fact, there may be some debate as to whether we could ever experience pure geometric space devoid of any cultural inflection at all.

Hermeneutics (the study of interpretation) has also been deeply interconnected with the study of culture and phenomenology through such thinkers as Paul Ricoeur, Merleau-Ponty, and Hans-Georg Gadamer (Sauter, 1997). From its origins in the exegesis of biblical texts, hermeneutics expanded to the broader interpretation of human nature through the study of verbal and paralinguistic communication. In particular, Gadamer became a central figure of hermeneutics through his text *Truth and Method* which approaches topics of language, questioning, conversation, historicality, and more generally, the nature of human understanding. He also investigates myth, art, and religion as storehouses of human meaning. Ricoeur, on the other hand, emphasises human capability and vulnerability in the context of one's actions, life, and world. Later he came to see that self-interpretation is always carried out through a system of language which itself requires interpretation – thus combining phenomenology and hermeneutics.

On the subject of language, it is almost impossible to overlook one philosopher who engaged with phenomenology to rethink the way we understand communication and discourse. Jacques Derrida (1930–2004) is considered a phenomenologist by some philosophers because of the centrality of temporality in his thought and an engagement with the phenomenological tradition as a basis for his own work and method (Moran, 2000, p. xiv). His philosophy is often seen as yet another beginning of phenomenology. Derrida offers a critique of Ferdinand de Saussure's structural linguistics and the relationship between the 'signifier' (the material vehicle of communication such as the written word or spoken sound) and 'signified' (the meaningful content conveyed by the word). Saussure claimed that the relationship between a word and its meaning is arbitrary (merely a convention agreed by a community of speakers) rather than having any intrinsic or innate connection. Such arbitrariness accounts for different words standing for different things in different languages. Furthermore, particular words can only take and convey content because they operate within a system of differences: particular words are meaningful only in so far as they are distinguishable from others. For example, the word 'bat' and 'cat' have meaningful phonetic difference intelligible to an English language speaker (you can hear and see that they begin with different sounds). But for Derrida, the meanings of words are constantly shifting with each utterance and there is no ultimate meaning to be arrived at in interpreting language because the field of written and spoken discourse is always moving on. He coins the word *différance* to indicate the deferred nature of meaning operating within this system of difference. Thus following the phenomenological tradition, Derrida asserts that there is this essentially temporal element to language and its interpretation.

Over and above the processes of signification, Derrida is also interested in speech and writing as discourse (a system of power that operates in different ways of speaking). For him, language is not simply a dynamic system of meaning, but also a subtle vehicle for operations of power within social relationships. Many discourses tend to hide such power relationships by reference to a stable metaphysics (universal truths) underlying the discourse. Derrida coins the term *logocentrism* to draw attention to legitimating discourses of the spoken word over the written word in validating such metaphysics. These discourses are premised upon *logos* – a fixed meaning or rationality behind its worldview (such as the soul, truth, and essence). And such grounding has a system of value in operation such as to privilege certain terms over others – most notably in terms of binary oppositions: male/female, Western/non-Western, white/black, and so on. One of the terms is considered to be foundational and positively valued, and the other derivative and negatively valued. The technique of destabilising such binaries and unmasking the systems of power that they enable is what Derrida calls 'deconstruction'. Such an attack on the operation of power in language and social discourse is common to many postmodern theories of culture and society.

With an approach similar to Derrida's, Judith Butler (1956–) offers a phenomenological account of the way in which gender is performed, within the framework of feminist analysis (Butler, 1990). Butler argues that gender is constructed through a series of iterative acts rather than through an innate category grounded in physical/biological features. Mundane bodily movements and gestures create the illusion of a stable gendered identity always situated within a social temporality. In other words, the features of gender are culturally and historically contingent (as Simone de Beauvoir argued) and there is no stable 'I' or subject that precedes these acts.

Unsurprisingly, history and historiography have also taken up some of the same ideas in relation to how we can know the past, and even what sorts of knowledges are privileged in a traditional writing of history. Michel Foucault (1926–1984), for instance, admits that he was a secret reader of Heidegger (Legrand, 2008). His post-structuralism draws on phenomenology in its rejection of essences and emphasis on bodily and material practice by which cultural meaning is perpetuated. For Foucault, power and knowledge are constructed by embodied processes throughout history. Many of his descriptions of the micro-practices of power have a distinctly phenomenological flavour.

More recently, Bruce Smith (2000) used the term 'historical phenomenology' in his analysis of premodern sexuality. He focuses on the study of sense experience from a first person point of view during the specific historical past. The upshot is that feeling and sensing are not simply biological process, but are historically relative and themselves have a history. The approach has been useful in Shakespeare studies (Smith, 2010; Curran and Kearney, 2012). The way that we feel sad or smell perfume is very different from Shakespeare's time. But feeling and smelling are not historical artefacts as a text or archaeological relic, they involve subjective processes. Historical phenomenology stands at the intersection of sensory history, cultural history of emotion, and the 'affective turn' in the social sciences.

It is worth taking a sideways glance to consider a parallel tradition to phenomenology set out by Charles Sanders Peirce (1839–1914). Initially overlooked, Peirce has become an important figure in semiotics (or as he refers to it, 'semeiotics') for his relational system of signs (Houser, 2010). He argues that philosophical logic as a science should study representation, inference, and argument. The objects of such study should be signs and sign-operations. The realm of sign activity (semiosis) is human thought (although he infers that even the laws of nature are semiotic products). This science can be seen as the basis for studying language, communication, and information processing more broadly. Peirce suggests that three elements are present in the development of the natural world: chance, law, and habit making. These elements map onto Peirce's categories: *firstness*, *secondness*, and *thirdness*. Firstness is the non-relational aspect of a sign or phenomenon – the redness of red, or the twinge of pain in itself. Secondness is the relation of that sign to something else – the contrast of red to white, the area of pain to nonpain. Thirdness is that which mediates the first two – the code of colours as understood by flag-makers, the meaning of pain in medical diagnosis. For Peirce, these three categories provide a structure for every disciplinary field. He believes that it is possible to classify all sciences in relation to one another in a systematic way. Peirce advocated philosophical pragmatism (the idea that knowledge is only that which is useful and makes progress as opposed to foundationalism which appeals to a fundamental indisputable ground for truth). Later, he came to see mathematics as the fundamental science grounding phenomenology, normative science (aesthetics, ethics, and semiotics), and metaphysics.

Phenomenology for Peirce is the study of the different elements of experience that we can feel, conceive, or talk about, together with the different classes of experience. For him, semiotics contains sub-branches studying grammar (what constitutes a sign and syntax), critic (the relation of signs to what they represent), and rhetoric (relating signs to their users and the effects of signs). In contrast to Saussure's dyadic semiotics (the signifier and the signified), Peirce posits a triadic system relating (a) the sign, (b) the reference of the sign to objects (referent), and (c) the interpretation and effects of signs on a user (interpretant). Importantly, all signs including experience are mediated by this third term for Peirce. The most famous terms of his semiotics are the three classes of sign – icon, index, and symbol. An icon bears resemblance to the thing it represents (a photograph, for example), an indexical sign has a relationship of causality to the thing is represents (smoke signalling fire); and a symbol which bears a relation to the thing it stands for by virtue of a symbolic system agreed by a community of interpretations (such as the ink marks you are reading on the page now, or the internationally agreed flag a system). The task of metaphysics is to study the general features of reality and real objects independent of the mind, with respect to their *thirdness*. Peirce thus provides a phenomenological basis for understanding signs pragmatically.

The point is that there is no single all-encompassing phenomenological method in the study of sociocultural practices. It is not clear that a silo-approach in the humanities and social sciences is either helpful, or possible. Different disciplinary and theoretical perspectives will reveal something different about the phenomenon in question. There are obviously many more points of contact than I could possibly deal with here.

Phenomenology tends to challenge the theoretical underpinnings and fundamental principles of each discipline by shifting emphasis towards the interconnected and co-creating relationship between self and world. Phenomenology need not be the method to replace all others, but to supplement them.³

Interdisciplinarity itself has become a feature of many areas of study in the humanities and social sciences. Various methodologies are adapted and borrowed between disciplines as noted by Geertz in his essay, 'Blurred Genres: The Refiguration of Social Thought' (Geertz, 1983, pp. 19–35). The plurality of perspectives sometimes promotes complementarity and other times contradiction. Interdisciplinary is engendered in theatre and performance studies with the result that phenomenology has passed through these other disciplines and exerted secondary influence. Willmar Sauter (1997) notes, theatre studies has gradually freed itself from the study of drama as literature towards the wider social processes and practices involved in the production of meaning. Research in the field typically combines anthropological, hermeneutic, or deconstructionist methodologies applied to cultural interactions by observing theatre-making processes. In the context of such borrowing and sharing, it is difficult to know exactly where phenomenology ends and where other disciplines begin.

Thinking Through Your Body: Phenomenology and Theatre Studies to Now

Clearly, phenomenology has an extended influence beyond the discipline of philosophy in conceptualising culture, meaning, and language, especially in the second half of the twentieth century. In each academic field, the approach supplements the 'host' discipline by emphasising the interconnection between the lifeworld and individual experience. It also challenges any subjective/objective binaries that act as fundamental principles for each subject area. Almost all of the theorists mentioned above have been invoked in the study of theatre. As a mode of performance analysis, phenomenology is of particular importance in reconnecting research and interpretation with actual experience of the theatre. Interestingly, most approaches to studies in theatre and phenomenology to date have focused predominantly on texts or formulating an ideal spectator's perspective rather than the actual experience of the event.

Phenomenologists have been interested in theatre for over a century, beginning with Max Scheler (Husserl's pupil) who approached tragedy in terms of the structures of consciousness in 1915 ('The Tragic Phenomenon') (Garner, 2001, b2). Subsequent studies in literature and aesthetics (Mikel Dufrenne and Roman Ingarden) adopted a phenomenological approach, taking particular note of drama in aesthetics and literature respectively. One possible reason for the rise of phenomenological studies of theatre can be traced back to the concerns of modernism and postmodernism. Bodies, places, temporality, historicality, consciousness, and presence have become primary concerns of theatre-makers and theorists alike: one is tempted to say that theatre itself entered a phenomenological period. The so-called Theatre of the Absurd, for instance, was interpreted in terms of existentialism of the mid-twentieth century (Esslin, 1961). Playwrights such as Beckett raised questions with parallels in philosophy concerning meaning, language, identity, freedom, and temporality. And subsequent avant-garde theatre has continued this exploration in what has come to be known as postdramatic theatre (Lehmann, 2006).

One of the first formal examinations of phenomenology and theatre in philosophy can be found in *Role Playing and Identity: The Limits of Theatre as Metaphor*, where Bruce Wilshire (1982) interrogates the relationship between theatre as a representational art and the mimetic characteristics of identity in social life. He sees the theatre as an examination of human identity formation (a process which is theatrical in a sense). But humans don't take on 'roles' in the same way as actors: there is no 'unmasked' self behind social reality. On this point, Wilshire critiques of Erving Goffman's (1956) use of theatre as metaphor in *The Presentation of Self in Everyday Life*. According to Wilshire, identity is formed by the roles that one takes on rather than resting in a true self offstage. Theatre thus exhibits the intersubjective nature of the social self, together with the embodied world of the theatre as a medium. Wilshire suggests the limits of understanding social life in terms of theatre thus formulating a philosophy of identity.

Bert States (1985) was the first to apply a phenomenological approach from within theatre studies in the seminal book, *Great Reckonings in Little Rooms: On the Phenomenology of the Theater*. He contrasts phenomenological and semiotic approaches by arguing that to reduce the experience of theatre to 'signification' misses out on the rich perceptual experience of the spectator's engagement with the medium. But rather than posit that these two modes of analysis are incompatible, States suggests that they can complement each other in a 'binocular vision': theatre studies can and should tack between the meaning-making processes of theatre as a sign, and an embodied engagement between scene, actor, and spectator (1985, p. 8). The actor – as a nodal point between the play text, the stage, and the audience – attends to phenomenal presence in a unique way by engaging in what States labels self-expressive, collaborative, and representational modes. At certain moments, the instability of these modes is foregrounded – in the curtain call, for instance. For States, the purpose of his book is to awaken the reader's own experience of going to the theatre and as such he uses imagined examples to illustrate his ideas. He does not pretend to be conducting a thorough and scientific analysis of every aspect of theatre through phenomenology. But he does look broadly at theatrical signification on the stage, the creation of world through Shakespearean language, naturalistic depictions, expressionism, and Brechtian dramaturgies. Each mode invites a shift in phenomenological attention. He then goes on to investigate the actor/text and actor/audience relationships. Ultimately, he dwells on the collusive artifice of the theatre as 'transcendental hypocrisy' – a spell that ends with the actor's bow.

Not long after States' book, Janelle Reinelt and Joseph Roach (1992) included one of his essays under a section entitled 'hermeneutics and phenomenology' in their collection of essays in critical performance theory, thus cementing phenomenology in the theoretical armoury of the discipline. It is worth noting, however, that both semiotics and phenomenology were subsumed into an opening section on 'performance analysis' in later editions.

In one of the seminal works in theatre phenomenology – *Bodied Spaces: Phenomenology and Performance in Contemporary Drama* – Stanton Garner (1994) pays particular attention to space, its interaction with bodies, and its co-creation of corporeal experience. The theatre occupies a special place in this regard as it is both inhabited as a lived space and a place created to be seen by an audience. Garner notes that in Samuel Beckett's plays theatrical bodies are materially grounded in the performance space, yet they also represent flux, absence, and loss in their theatrical reception. Bodies disclose themselves and disappear in the moment of performance in a range of phenomenal modes (especially in contemporary performance). But rather than witness such revealing/vanishing in a disembodied way, the audience too inhabits theatre space in a material and corporeal way in order to perceive the signifying body of the performer. Garner draws upon a range of examples from modern drama to explore the visual field, movement, scenography, props, the relationship between language and place in subjectivity, the political body in representation, violence and trauma, gender, pain, and traces of the past – all from a phenomenological perspective.

Alice Rayner's (1994) *To Act, To Do, To Perform: Drama and the Phenomenology of Action* begins with Shakespeare's unpacking of the meaning of the word 'action' from *Hamlet*'s Gravedigger in order to investigate intentionality, materiality, and performativity. For Rayner, phenomenology is an antidote to reductive binaries including self-object, text-performance, thinking-doing, and mind-body. Her study attempts to capture the meaning of 'action' not through an analytic focus on structures and essences in the abstract but by examining action itself. For Rayner, theatre offers a window into action. Again, Beckett appears here as an example of the breakdown among agency, plot, and action. By considering dramatic action ('virtual' action) we can begin to understand action in everyday life. In the case of *Macbeth*, for instance, the temporality of action in the present becomes radically visible as cut off from the past and the future. In Chekhov, by contrast, the very unity of the social subject and its life-project is collapsed by a radical interiority. The meaning of action is inevitably tied up with language. In some cases, words structure the way we encounter the world; in others, there is an unbridgeable gap between expression and actuality of experience. And finally, Rayner argues that action entails an ethical responsibility in that it is drawn into a discursive social world through public time, and historical convention. In the theatre, action can take the form of self-reflexive game-playing through an interplay between Hamlet the character and the actor playing him, for example.

Phillip Zarrilli (2002, 2004) undertakes a descriptive phenomenology of the way in which the body appears from the perspective of the psycho-physical actor in performance. He describes four modes – mediated respectively by flesh, blood, breath and appearance. Drawing on Merleau-Ponty and Drew Leder, he notes how the 'surface' or 'ecstatic' body also opens up the world to us through sensory experience, yet the body of the actor often recedes into absence. We also experience the body viscerally through internal organs and autonomic processes. We can engage with the body aesthetically by subtly attuning ourselves and focussing awareness in the act of artistic creation and training. The aesthetic body has both an inner and outer focus. More broadly, he thinks about how we can know and theorise the actor's body (2001). The originality of Zarrilli's writing lies in its engagement with the conscious experience of the involved actor; it is not satisfied with merely analysing abstract theatre spectatorship, the implied body of a dramatic text, or the general notion of action and the human subject.

There has also been considerable debate as to how phenomenology should fit into theatre and performance analysis. Stuart Grant (2012) suggests semiotics and other ideologically driven approaches tend to disconnect the actual experience of performance from its analysis. Such approaches may be attempting to transcend experience and sidestep the materiality and affective power of theatre. Grant claims that in theatre and performance studies, there is

> growing frustration with the predominance of discursive and political approaches to the understanding of theatre and performance; approaches which obscure the object itself in a primary concern with the social context from which it emerges as an expression of a power structure, culture or system of signification. (2012, p. 9)

In other words, Grant is calling for a rigorous phenomenology focussing on 'the thing itself' on stage in contrast to the study of signs and social discourse. He argues that under the influence of analytic philosophy there has been an active rejection of phenomenology in theatre studies on the grounds that it is 'essentialist'. He suggests that in performance studies there is a lack of first-hand knowledge of phenomenology (having come predominantly via Butler and Derrida). In theatre and performance studies, Grant sees the major contribution of phenomenology to theatre studies in its critique of presence – a cornerstone of theatrical ontology. But even though the field has noted the importance of phenomenological themes such as the body, there is relatively little phenomenological investigation of embodiment in itself.

For Cormac Power (2008), phenomenology is one possible methodological solution to the problem of the metaphysical 'presence' as the basis and essence of performance. Building on a post-structuralist critique of presence, he revises the bases of fictional and literal presence, together with the aura of the work and artist. He also looks at debates in liveness and emphasises the importance of technology in analysing stage presence. The indefinable magic of theatre offers an environment in which to stage the appearance and disappearance replete with potential to challenge traditional forms of perception and understandings of consciousness. In the next section below, I will make a similar claim by invoking phenomenology to defend at least some forms of theatre from such post-structural assault.

Pannill Camp (2004, p. 83) notes that phenomenology is often invoked as a critical approach to account for specific and recurring objects of interest in performance, namely: animals, open flames, and the bodies of actors. Judged by such repeated invocation, the conclusion may be reached that some objects are more phenomenological than others. In such cases, the objects do not primarily stand as signs for something else: the materiality of the stage is emphasised rather than a fictional world evoked through mimesis. Camp suggests that we can forego talk of phenomenology and simply focus on rich description of the material elements of such phenomena.

More recently in *Performance and Phenomenology: Traditions and Transformations*, Maaike Bleeker, Jon Foley Sherman, and Eirini Nedelkopoulou (2015) attempt to bring the tensions between performance and phenomenology into the context of early-twenty-first-century theory and practice. They begin from the foundations of performativity for perception and cognition and cover a range of different case studies from actor training, dead animals on stage and the legal implications of phenomenological interpretation. Both performance and phenomenology

> are modes of thinking and embodied engagement with the world that invite ambiguity instead of identification, and that locate the stakes of grasping that world in our urgent and inconclusive contact with others. Both performance and phenomenology engage with experience, perception, and with making sense as processes that are embodied, situated, and relational. These aspects have become increasingly important with the transformations referred to as the end of the grand narratives (Lyotard), the performative turn and the experiential turn, as well as with the emergence of new, experimental forms of theater, dance, and other performances. (2015, p. 1)

Performance is a privileged object for phenomenological investigation from the traditional to technologically cutting-edge pieces. Perception of the world, in this sense, is seen as a (series of) performative acts and now more than ever technology has altered the way that we see and interact with the world. Moving into the broader realm of performativity, the authors note that phenomenology has influenced performance theory from digital performance (Susan Broadhurst), technology (Jon McKenzie), gender (Elizabeth Grosz, Rosalyn Diprose, and Sarah Ahmed), and normative notions of the body especially in relation to disability (Petra Kuppers), and in body based events of performance art (Amelia Jones). Each of these perspectives privileges involved practice:

> The world must be done in order to be experienced. The repetition of socially conditioned and located perceptions produce a world that can in turn be further transformed by acts of performance that address and disrupt the action of perception. (2015, p. 8)

The scope of my book here is obviously narrower in focus than the broader topic of performance and performativity. More specifically however, phenomenology has also been invoked to interpret various playwrights, genres, and performance styles. Shakespeare, Beckett, stand-up comedy, and dance, for instance, have all received the phenomenological treatment.[4]

Demolishing Tradition (While Fossicking for Truth)

Each of these phenomenologically inflected works in theatre studies has a slightly different focus in terms of object, method, and goal. Each is slightly different from how I engage phenomenology in the chapters that are to follow – inspired by Heidegger's task of Destruktion. As mentioned in the previous chapter, the Destruktion of metaphysics is not a process of destroying, but a 'loosening up' of history to discern the 'original experiences' that gave rise to historical understandings of Being (Inwood, 1999, p. 95). It is a process of showing the merits as well as the failings and limitations of those traditions and providing a reinterpretation especially with respect to Temporality. In turn, the approach is also meant to rethink Being in our own time unencumbered by encrusted traditions. In some instances, Heidegger seems to understand history as the linear unfolding of this meaning of Being through its various epochs. Dreyfus and Wrathall (2005, p. 11) note that in his later works, 'Heidegger came to argue that the philosophical history of the West consists of a series of "epochs" of different total understandings of being, and that the unconcealment of beings varies according to the background understanding of Being'.[5] At other points, Heidegger notes the way in which different notions of Being spring up. The Greek word ἐποχή (*epokhē*) is related to 'restraint'. Philosophy in the past has tended to hold back Being through a process of withdrawal (Inwood, 1999, p. 96). Metaphysical thinking focusses on individual being rather than the abundance of Being as a whole – compounding a tendency in Everydayness. New epochs begin when ordinary time-reckoning stops – constituting a 'moment of vision' (*Augenblick*). And phenomenology is intended to help this process along.

In Heidegger's later writings, the history of Being becomes intertwined with his discussion of art and language (Young, 2001).[6] For Heidegger, great works of art throughout history can be seen as paradigmatic of (and for) our understanding of Being (and how it should be). In other words, art can depict the world itself and incite change by reconfiguring the world and the way that we see it (Dreyfus and Spinosa, 2002). Great art gives a push to history and its understanding of Being so that it either starts up or starts again. In this way, from out of the past new worlds have arisen and opened up a place for truth to reveal itself:

> This foundation happened in the West for the first time in Greece. What was in the future to be called Being was set into work, setting the standard. The realm of beings thus opened up was then transformed into a being in the sense of God's creation. This happened in the Middle Ages. This kind of being was again transformed at the beginning and in the course of the modern age. Beings became objects that could be controlled and seen through by calculation. At each time a new and essential world arose. At each time the openness of what is had to be established in beings themselves, by the fixing in place of truth in figure. At each time there happened unconcealedness of what is. Unconcealedness sets itself into work, a setting which is accomplished by art. (Heidegger, 1975, p. 74)

Thus art can be crucial in the process of unconcealment in successive epochs of Being (Young, 2001, pp. 25–37) and it is not a stretch to see theatre as participating in this opening-up of the world. For the ancient Greeks, truth was founded in essence, in the medieval period by createdness, and in the modern world by the objective scientific measurement. The point is not to dismiss these conceptions altogether, but to provide an interpretation that uncovers the essence of truth they contain.

Critical perspectives attacking various theories of acting as 'foundationalist' (in the sense that they rely on a false conception and locus of the actor's self as the authenticating object of truth on stage) fail to take this preserving element of Destruktion into account. Rather than accuse approaches to acting of harbouring false metaphysical systems, we might interpret them as potential 'opening up' of truth. The task is to demolish the metaphysical system while fossicking for flecks of truth.

Philip Auslander's (1995) widely read essay, '"Just be Yourself": Logocentrism and difference in performance theory' contains just such an indictment of theatre. Auslander appeals to Derrida's concept of logocentrism in order to critique various theories of acting that posit 'presence' as the foundation of meaning in performance. As discussed,

Derrida's deconstruction is a transformation of Heidegger's Destruktion adapted to critique foundationalist concepts of language and meaning (Schrift, 1990, pp. 115–16). Derrida expands upon the idea that language as a system of differences – although difference *itself* is inaudible. The 'productive non-presence' is what he calls *différance* – meaning is both deferred in the sense that there is no ultimate meaning nor is there an originary source that guarantees what something means. Auslander argues that various theories of performance

> implicitly designate the actor's self as the logos of performance; [they] assume that the actor's self precedes and grounds her performance and that it is the presence of this self in performance that provides the audience with access to human truths. (1995, p. 52)[7]

Auslander deconstructs three theories of the most iconic twentieth-century theatre theatre-makers for falling prey to foundationalism. Firstly, he considers Stanislavski's view of the actor's art and artistic meaning with 'inner truth'. Because the artistic process involves dealing with 'subconscious truths' that cannot be known or perceived, true self-presence is impossible. Stanislavski's famous metaphor of searching for a bead of memory within a house in the mind also draws attention to the way in which memories can change and separate from actual events in the past. Auslander concedes that Stanislavski understands the self as produced by the psycho-technique of the actor. Nevertheless, he claims that the subconscious self is the legitimating object in Stanislavski's system. Next, he considers Brecht who emphasises a distance between actor and character. In this case, the personal social experience of the actor and their rational presentation of a role is equally logocentric with the view that a political or social dilemma is solvable (from a Marxist dialectical perspective). In his interpretation, the Brechtian actor is guided by the basic meaning of the play. Finally, for Jerzy Grotowski, a truthful inner self can be revealed in performance as a kind of therapy for actors and audiences whereby the text becomes a tool of exposure of true self by way of the *via negativa*. The truthful inner spiritual self is revealed by the actor on stage by stripping away social and cultural confinements with respect to being.

But is Auslander right to indict artists such as Stanislavski, Brecht and Grotowski of such a metaphysical misdemeanour?[8] If they saw Being or the Self as a 'thing', then the accusation might be warranted, but it is not entirely clear that this is the case. These performance-makers were not operating within the confines of philosophy but theatre – with a strong emphasis on process and reflection. The metaphors and models of selfhood they employ are not intended to be theories of the self, but aids in the pursuit of creativity. And, finally, extracting a theory of acting from its historical context also overlooks the intertwined relationship between self from its world. In defence of Auslander, he does signal that it is not his intention to discredit these theatre-makers, but rather to 'indicate their dependence on logocentrism and certain concepts of self and presence' (1995, p. 58). Nevertheless, he criticises the view of actor-presence grounding meaning in a performance and takes a semiotic perspective on performance and emphasises the production of meaning – and more to the point – the process of 'writing' of self:

> In discussion, we often treat acting as philosophers treat language – as a transparent medium which provides access to truth, logos or a grounding concept which functions as logos within a particular production. (1995, p. 53)

It is not entirely clear that these approaches to acting treat language as transparent. In fact, the problem might be solved if we decouple this critique of practitioners to the way that they have been interpreted in the past – or at least acknowledge a gap between their theory and practice. When theatre-makers talk about actors revealing their soul, are they making a metaphysical statement? In many ways, witnessing a performance in the theatre is more than understanding what it means, but also feeling through the body (or body-mind). I would argue that it is not possible to exhaust the meaning of acting as merely a 'sign' nested in a system of differences. Notwithstanding the metaphysical discourse in terms of Being (spirit, hidden reality, physical impulse and *via negativa* aimed at revealing a truthful inner self, or the authentic social and political relations of actors and characters) we might ask what truth these practices reveal about worldhood. Then we are beginning to do phenomenology.

One Size Doesn't Fit All: Theatre Phenomenology

Having briefly surveyed the terrain then, I propose that there are various ways you might 'do' phenomenology in theatre studies (although again, this list is not necessarily exhaustive). Your approach might:

- examine performance as a way of understanding elements of Being-in-the-world (for example investigating the meaning of 'action' in Rayner) – regional ontologies;
- appropriate theatre as a means of understanding human identity and Being while acknowledging the limits of this metaphor (Wilshire and Goffman) – examining the performative self;
- approach and interpret different phenomena of theatre-making and reception (States and Garner) – formulating a phenomenology of the theatrical event;
- draw upon phenomenological concepts to generate a faithful description of theatre processes and events (Zarrilli and States) – descriptive phenomenology;
- construe theatrical practice as a form of phenomenology (Wilshire, States, and Garner) – theatre as phenomenology;
- find a productive tension and dialogue between philosophical practices and theatrical processes (as I am attempting here) – comparative phenomenology; and
- utilise phenomenological research in order to generate and develop different forms and artistic processes (a topic for future research) – creative phenomenology.

Again, it isn't an either/or proposition when it comes to these approaches. Other theoretical perspectives can supplement or thematise the phenomena of theatre, Being, and the creative state. The important thing is not to bring any preformed assumptions or interpretations of the object of inquiry and to let the thing show itself.

At the beginning of this chapter I suggested the task of simply walking up the road and observing the way that the world presents itself to your consciousness. To a large extent, the exercise focuses on Being as revealed to the observer and brings out self-awareness in an unusual way. A lack of purposeful action in this perambulatory reflection shows something that is missing: a separate *reason* for the jaunt (for example, to buy some milk, to return a book to the library, to visit a sick friend, and so on). At the same time, there *is* a task being carried out: the observation of how the world presents itself to consciousness. The exercise begins to take note of different aspects of Being.

The next task would be to think about how the world presents itself to us in specific involved activities. This is often more difficult because we are *doing* those tasks. A colleague of mine often points out how dancers can be 'put off' or 'lose their flow' when they become self-aware and begin to analyse what they are doing at any given moment in a dance. Many types of performers experience an anxiety of analysis – stand-up comedians, actors, public speakers, and sportspeople. Even lovers of art and literature might be afraid of over-analysing the experience of the artwork because it will ruin it. But in certain circumstances, this type of analysis can enhance the experience and make us aware of elements that would normally go unnoticed. And furthermore, we might equip ourselves with new tools useful for creating art. So in order to describe the structures of experience of artistic creation, one may need to describe in retrospect, or practise immersing oneself in a task and switching to observing in turn. This is a process of tacking between the experience, its meaning, and being involved in creative process. This dual (or multiple) consciousness of self and world experienced when carrying out an activity is not dissimilar to what the eighteenth-century philosopher-critic Denis Diderot (1957) called 'the paradox of acting'.[9] And as it happens, the double-awareness of an actor's self and the part is at the heart of Stanislavski's thinking about acting, as we will see in the next chapter.

Exercises and Topics for Discussion

1. Try the experiential walk suggested at the beginning of this chapter. Produce a piece of writing based on what you observed and share it with a partner. What similarities do you notice in the resulting texts? What differences do you notice?

2. Take an everyday interaction and describe it in as much detail as possible. For instance, you could reflect on making a purchase at your local café. Try doing one small thing differently and perhaps against social custom. For example, stand slightly off balance when you are ordering a coffee or use a slightly higher voice than normal when you meet and greet someone. Observe the reaction. Try to unpack how your changed action affected the phenomenon.
3. Make a visual representation or map of what you think it means to be a 'self'. Share it with a partner. What strikes you about the other person's representation that you had never thought of before? Now try to draw the same representation of a self, engaged in a specific activity. What did you do differently here? Draw another map or picture of your selfhood at age 12. How is that selfhood different? Why?
4. Here are some topics for discussion: What sorts of assumptions do we make about the nature of reality? Do you think that there are any 'dualist' tendencies of thought in our everyday interactions? What are they? In what sections of society and life are metaphysical assumptions rife? Why do they flourish in certain contexts?
5. Try to write a phenomenological description of a particular moment in a theatre production that made an impression upon you. What difficulties do you have in describing the experience itself? What strategies might you adopt to get at 'what it was like'? How does that moment fit in with what you see as the 'essence' of the production? Think about what a phenomenological approach might *not* do so well in analysing a performance process. How might other methodological and analytical approaches ask different but complementary questions?
6. Create a two-minute performance for your class. Try to write up your experiences of rehearsal and performing from a phenomenological standpoint. Did you find yourself tacking between observing your process and engaging in it? How did that affect what you were doing?

Notes

1 Comparative Literature generally looks and compares works of literature across cultures, nations, and disciplines. A parallel might be found in studying theatre. As we will see later in this chapter, performance studies itself is already inherently interdisciplinary.

2 See Cresswell (2004) for a useful overview of conceptions of space and place from a range of different theoretical perspectives.
3 For a fuller discussion of phenomenology and its influence in this regard, see Maurice Natanson's (1973) *Phenomenology and the Social Sciences*.
4 In relation to Shakespeare, see Curran and Kearney (2012) in their special issue of *Criticism on* Shakespeare and Phenomenology, and Smith (2010). For Beckett and phenomenology, see Garner (1994) and Maude and Feldman (2009). On Heidegger and stand-up comedy, see May (2016). There are many works on phenomenology and dance, but two significant studies are Sheets (1966) and Fraleigh (1987).
5 Guignon notes: 'In contrast to such a familiar conception of history, Heidegger proposes an approach he calls "historical reflection," a form of reflection on sense (*Be-sinnung*) aimed at understanding a happening (*Geschehen*) in which we are now immersed and which gets its point from where it is going as a whole. In Heidegger's words, "reflection is looking for the meaning [*Sinn*] of a happening, the meaning of history," where the word "meaning" refers to "the open region of goals, standards, impulses, decisive possibilities and powers" that "belong essentially to happening"' (Guignon 2005, p. 393).
6 For a later work concentrating specifically on the world-revealing nature of art, see Heidegger (1977): *Basic writings: From Being and Time* (1927) *to the Task of Thinking* (1964).
7 It is notable that post-structuralism also attempts to deconstruct discourses of 'naturalness' – discourses that are prevalent in the theatre and acting too (Counsell 1996).
8 My work on phenomenology and theatre has argued that because acting and performing are practical arts rather than abstract reasoning, they embody a certain resistance against a 'dualistic' understanding of the world (Johnston 2008; 2011a, b).
9 Diderot articulates what he sees as a paradox of emotion in acting: that one must necessarily feel emotion when portraying the actions of a dramatic character, yet also be free from emotion in order to control the performance.

Part II

5

Stanislavski's Phenomenology of Being-in-the-world: Action and Involvement

Theatre for Disclosing a World

How can the act of creativity show the world as it is? What do you do when creative inspiration fails? There was something that happened at the turn of the twentieth century in Russia that made these questions possible. Rather than rely on stock-in-trade methods learnt on the job through an apprenticeship in acting, new forms were emerging that required a different kind of precision. This involved understanding something about the creative artist as organism and the world of the text as set down in the work. No longer was it possible to rely on spontaneous inspiration for the moment of performance. This led one artist to write down his thoughts and investigations of the sources of creativity for the theatre actor. That person was, of course, Constantin Stanislavski.

This chapter offers an interpretation of *An Actor's Work: A Student's Diary*, drawing attention to phenomenological aspects of the acting process described.[1] Specifically, I will focus on 'Year One: Experiencing' – from Stanislavski's renowned fictionalised account of actor education – through the lens of Heidegger's analysis in *BT*. The approach to actor training and role preparation set out by Stanislavski bears some striking connections with what we might call a *practical* philosophical exploration. Notwithstanding the absence of phenomenological terminology,

Stanislavski is detailing an acting process that requires an embodied understanding of the way that the world presents itself to human consciousness in its rich, lived experience. This understanding is developed not for its own sake but rather to produce controlled artistic presentation on stage, while avoiding the inconsistencies of an untrained intuition. In this sense, the actor's art can be seen as an embodied philosophy that makes different ways of Being-in-the-world manifest and ultimately gestures towards the meaning of Being.

Of course, there are also fundamental differences between the respective projects of Heidegger and Stanislavski. The former was attempting a radical revision of philosophy which challenged the idea that 'knowing' is the fundamental way in which human beings experience the world (a premise that entails a split between mind and body endemic in Western philosophy). The latter was attempting to articulate different ways actors might avoid a reliance on fickle inspiration in performance and to foster maximal conditions for creativity through self-awareness and detailed understanding of the fictional and actual worlds of the performer. The conceptual territory between these two thinkers constitutes a third space where a fruitful dialogue might be possible between the practical understanding of the actor and the theoretical project of phenomenology.

It is worth noting that *An Actor's Work* and *BT* both consciously employ language as a tool to investigate being, though in very different ways. For Stanislavski, the meaning of the actor's being necessarily exists outside of the fictional diary itself in actual self-discovery, exploration, observation and training. The language he uses is simple and intended to incite a curiosity for readers to experience the meaning of the exercises for themselves. Heidegger, on the other hand, deliberately uses difficult language that causes the reader to progress very slowly, noting etymological connections in terms employed and indeed newly coined vocabulary designed to overcome metaphysics (unfounded assumptions about the nature of existence). The work is a dialogue with a dense philosophical tradition and is not meant as a practical guide, but as a challenge to arguments from previous philosophical treatises. Still, it is the being of Dasein that stands outside of the work and holds it to account in terms of truth. For Heidegger, the language that we use to describe the world is essential to our experience of Being.

As I will discuss later in this chapter, it is not merely the 'doing' that is important on stage, but an explicit awareness and understanding of action worked out in preparation and performance. One might well argue that in order to perform convincingly the actor need not have *actual* knowledge of the relationship between self and world but only a reliable way of producing an intended behaviour. A mental image, for example, might be useful in bringing about an action, though it does not coincide with the physical reality of that action. But what is unique about Stanislavski's investigations is that his attention to science and pursuit of self-knowledge constitutes a 'return to the things themselves'.

Stanislavski's 'topography of the self', in his account of the actor's creative engagement, overlaps with a phenomenological conception of selfhood and discovers aspects of Being through a parallel pathway: he articulates the deeply intermeshed relationship between self and world; he is not so much concerned with objective reality as the way in which the world presents itself to consciousness; he presents a holistic understanding of selfhood in its engagement with objects, other people, mood and emotion, history, and engaged activity within the world; and rather than conduct a philosophical 'reduction of the natural attitude' (stepping outside everyday involved activity in its lack of self-awareness), he notes how theatrical presentation on stage already highlights the structure of human action. In short, rather than pinning the nature of Being down to a specific and concrete system, his approach arrives at what I argue is a phenomenological openness to different modes of being. Of course, his discoveries were made in the context of theatrical creation and driven predominantly by his search for the elusive sources of creative inspiration rather than in formal philosophical investigation. Yet it may be that profound truths about existence are not found in abstract systems of thought but in a renewed understanding of everyday existence and experience. Such a rediscovery and awareness of the quotidian is central to Stanislavski's actor training – an awareness centred around truth:

> The actor must first of all believe in everything that takes place on the stage, and most of all he must believe in what he himself is doing. And one can believe only in the truth. Therefore it is necessary to feel this truth at all times, to know how to find it, and for this it is unescapable to develop

one's artistic sensitivity to truth. It will be said, 'But what kind of truth can this be, when all on the stage is a lie, an imitation, scenery, cardboard, paint, make-up, properties, wooden goblets, swords and spears? Is it all truth?' But it is not of this truth I speak. I speak of the truth of emotions, of the truth of inner creative urges which strain forward to find expression, of the truth of bodily and physical perceptions. I am not interested in a truth that is without myself; I am interested in the truth that is within myself, the truth of my relation to this or that event on stage, to the properties, the scenery, the other actors who play in the parts with me, to their thoughts and emotions. (Stanislavski 1980b, pp. 265, 266)

An Actor's Work

The central question in *An Actor's Work* concerns how actors might consistently and reliably reproduce the conditions for creativity.[2] The fundamental problem for the actor in the theatre is how to generate 'truthful' performances night after night and not merely by fickle flashes of inspiration. The meaning of theatrical truth in this sense is developed through exercises, discussion, self-observation, and study. The hidden premise behind Stanislavski's way of posing the problem is that acting can be communicated, taught, and learned. Importantly, although Stanislavski's writing on actor-preparation has become known as the 'system', it is not 'systematic' in the sense of providing just one method for fostering the creative conditions for the art of the stage; rather it points to a range of approaches that he changed and developed throughout his theatrical career.[3] Nor are these approaches simply for use in naturalistic performance aimed at presenting 'life as lived' on the stage. For Stanislavski, the system is useful for understanding the creative organism in a range of different theatrical styles. The problem is twofold: to be able to understand the creative mechanism and control how that mechanism works (the actor's self) and the imaginary life of the creation (the actor in the part) (Merlin, 2003, p. 20). So not only is this an investigation of the performing subject ('the self') but also a developing understanding of the structures of action within the environment of that imagined world ('the character').

While *An Actor's Work* presents an approach to acting predominantly situated within a text-driven, character-based, narrative form of the Western theatrical tradition, its fictional account is based on Stanislavski's real-life theatrical investigations and outlines improvisation and self-examination exercises for approaching a role. In this process, play scripts serve as a starting point for the exploration of potential 'ways of being'. As I will elaborate upon later in this chapter, the script offers 'given circumstances' for the role. So the text provides a basis for launching the direction, though by no means wholly predetermines the outcome of the exploration.

Rose Whyman's (2008) *The Stanislavsky System of Acting* delves into the scientific, social and political context of Stanislavski's writing together with a detailed analysis of his theoretical influences. Her study returns to the archives, extant notes and transcripts, surveys his library collection and trawls his published works, offering a conceptual archaeology of his influences. Without doubt, Stanislavski lived through an age of sweeping change including the upheavals of the Russian Revolution, the proselytising of Soviet aesthetic policy and the installation of socialist realism as an official style for the arts. From a literary point of view one should note the importance of Tolstoy's theory of art and expression of emotion. Theatre itself was undergoing great change and the influences of Gogol, Shchepkin Chekhov, Ibsen, the Duke of Saxe-Meiningen Company are all seen in his approach to acting. More specifically, in his articulation of the problem of acting, Stanislavski looked back to Diderot and the 'paradox of acting': how can an actor both be experiencing the emotions throughout their performance and yet at the same time observe their own actions so as to coolly control them?

The *épisteme* (to borrow Foucault's term) of the late nineteenth century wrested itself from the philosophical idealism of Fichte, Hegel, Schelling and a concern with man's relationship to nature.[4] A new set of ideas emerged including empiricism, a focus on material conditions of existence from Marx, Engels, and dialectical materialism in the social sciences. At the same time, humanity's relation to animals was radically rethought with regard to Darwin's theory of evolution. Whyman also suggests a close connection between William James' 'associationist psychology', the related concept of 'stream of consciousness' and Karl von Hartmann's notion of the 'unconscious' (Whyman, 2008, p. 263). Pavlov's behaviourism was of crucial importance to contemporary science and research into the role of human reflexes as championed by official state science, although evidently Stanislavski's own approach to acting is better explained by his reading of psychologist Théodule Ribot.

Although the metaphor of 'the human being as machine' was prevalent at this time, Stanislavski did not simply look to science for sources of inspiration. Yoga fed into Stanislavski's actor training technique perhaps introduced to him by his assistant, the well-travelled jack-of-all-trades Sulerzhitsky, or perhaps from other sources at the Moscow Art Theatre. In any event, Stanislavski appropriated the concept of 'prana', a life force that emanates in 'rays' transmitted between human beings enabling communication.

As discussed in the previous chapter, Philip Auslander (1995) accuses Stanislavski of 'logocentrism' (presenting the self as an original source of truth). I would argue that *An Actor's Work* takes into account the intertwined nature of self and world, environment and body not with an origin, but as an entity continually in the process of becoming within temporality. Elusive moments of inspiration are difficult precisely because the self (conscious or unconscious) is not a stable material origin of truth. And although Stanislavski divides his approach into 'experiencing' and 'incarnation' (which one is tempted to read as 'mind' and 'body') he is not falling into dualist metaphysics, but focusses on different modes of experiencing the self without necessarily claiming that they are separate.

In addition to the influences on Stanislavski noted by Rose Whyman, theatre scholars such as Robert Leach and Mark Fortier note similarities between phenomenology and Stanislavski's work. They are not, of course, implying that Stanislavski drew on phenomenological writings and certainly would not go so far as to suggest that he was actually *doing* phenomenology. Leach writes, 'Stanislavski's phenomenology has much in common with Heidegger's, with its interest in individual consciousness and how lived experience interacts with the "real" world' (2004, p. 50). Fortier suggests that 'what might be called phenomenological concerns figure prominently in the work of Constantin Stanislavski' (1997, pp. 32, 33). Yet I argue that the connection pushes beyond metaphor in the sense that philosophy and theatre can jointly elucidate the question of Being.

The bringing together of phenomenology and acting is not so clearcut, however. Stanislavski unequivocally denies that his approach to acting, known as the 'system', is a philosophy. He expresses his fundamental conviction that acting is only ever discovered through embodied knowledge and personal exploration, and never through purely intellectual theorising over the true nature of the world and existence. He warns:

> The 'system' is a guide. Open it and read it. The 'system' is a reference book, not a philosophy. The 'system' ends when philosophy begins.
> Work on the 'system' at home. Onstage put it to one side. You cannot act the 'system'. There is no 'system'. There is only nature. My concern throughout my life has been to find ways to get nearer what we call the 'system', that is, to the nature of the creative act. (2008, p. 612)

The word 'philosophy' here refers to an abstract theoretical system detached from practical activity. Such an understanding of performance is never apprehended 'in general', but only ever in the practical pursuit of creativity. But by taking phenomenology as an interpretative lens here, the emphasis is precisely upon a radical interrogation of the experience. Although Stanislavski was not directly influenced by phenomenology as a philosophical movement, he independently arrived at many connected conclusions, as I will examine. This might be explained by the broader *épisteme*, the discursive structures that allow for certain types of knowledge to arise in any age. In particular, I am interested in the actor's uncovering the way things show themselves to the consciousness of the actor: action for a purpose, the magic 'if', the given circumstances, imagination and attention, bits and tasks, emotion memory and communication. Each of these displays a phenomenological insight into the relationship between the self and world in the context of actor preparation. And so I now turn to a closer investigation.

Action and Inauthenticity

At the beginning of their studies, students from the fictional acting school of Stanislavski's narrative fall into a range of faults typical in the untrained actor: mechanical, external, conventional, self-indulgent, egotistical, superficial performance (2008, pp. 5–15). Kostya, the protagonist and first-year acting student, has a few flashes of inspiration in his first attempts at scenes from *Othello* on stage but on the whole is seduced by the allure of the audience and exhibitionism. This tendency is also evident in his fellow-student Marya's exercise of just sitting on stage: instead of actually doing something, she 'demonstrates' what she thinks will convey the exterior attributes of such an action (2008, p. 37). She repeats this tendency to signal performance rather than execute real action in a later exercise of finding a missing brooch in the acting studio. Unable to understand both the actor and character's purposeful action within the world, the inexperienced pupils resort to a disconnected, disjointed and distracted series of actions. These errors are practical examples of straying from experience as the basis of performance.

Rather than view these failures of acting as idiosyncratic to the stage, a phenomenological interpretation might suggest that they are symptoms of a wider misapprehension of the nature of Being. The pull towards external acting is an expression of the lure of metaphysics – a term used negatively in critical theory to denote the tendency to misinterpret what 'to be' means based on false assumptions about the nature of reality. The 'bad' actor will resort to exterior representations and received notions of reality rather than 'returning to the things themselves' (the famous catch-cry of phenomenology, articulated by Husserl). The challenge of the 'truthful' actor is to reach an authentic and complex understanding of selfhood. The untruthful actor will be left with a 'passed down', second-hand, reductive interpretation of being that is not based upon experience. Marya's errors of disconnected gesturing and externality, for instance, fail to recognise that the living human subject exists within a surrounding context of involvements. Such a superficial reproduction forgets that action can never ever be understood in isolation, but only ever in relation to involvement. This mistake of practice is, on this reading, a symptom of ontological blindness: what Heidegger calls 'inauthenticity'. The task of actor training is to develop an understanding of Being in the creation of a role. This is not simply picked up without effort but requires a great deal of attention, concentration, self-discovery, and practice.

Rather than make grand claims about absolute truth and universal authenticity here one needs to keep in mind the theatrical conventions of Stanislavski's time. His own experiments in acting technique were a reaction against a rhetorical-declamatory style of acting (though, of course, what is received as a realistic performance has changed from generation to generation depending on current worldviews and scientific discoveries).[5] Various social and cultural practices such as acting reflect their own contemporary understanding of the nature of reality and may well be prone to metaphysical error (misapprehension of being).

Both the actor and the phenomenologist are required to return to that entity which is 'most their own' as the start-point – that 'thing' which possesses the quality of what Heidegger calls 'mineness' (1962, pp. H15, H16). As suggested by Stanislavski, to begin with anything other than this quality of 'mineness' will result in exterior, insincere acting. In Heidegger's phenomenological jargon, this is a tendency towards a 'falling' understanding of the world (1962, pp. H175–180). Rather than perform actions with a grasp of their purpose in context, the students display a 'non-self' and this inauthenticity is instantly recognisable. In this sense, truthful performing is much more than contemplating one's own being; it is recognising and manipulating one's own being in order to create the life of the character through the actor in the part.

This ability also involves having some understanding of the structures of Being more generally in order to be able to analyse and embody different characters in different contexts and situations that may be quite dissimilar to the actor's own life. One of the fundamental aspects of action – either in the circumstances of the character or the actor as he or she inhabits the stage – is that action is always for a purpose (Stanislavski, pp. 45–48). In phenomenological terms, action is set within the 'involvements' and 'assignments' of a particular life-world and to forget this point is to lose sight of the structures of Being. Furthermore, individual agents act because the world *matters* to them, not only because actions are nested within a structure of purposeful action. In phenomenological terms, such a concern for the world is called Care (Heidegger, 1962, p. H15). The world is 'an issue' for individuals and action is a means of expressing that concern. When the fledgling student actors neglect such concern for action, they are criticised by their teacher.

Being-in-the-world and Dasein

Acting is 'an art' for Stanislavski when there is logical coherence of action within a scene and where the characters act with purpose (Stanislavski, pp. 45–48). In order to reach an understanding of the character (and approach the state of 'the actor in the part') Stanislavski introduces the now-famous magic word 'if' (Stanislavski, p. 65). The task of living though the part is projecting life's involvements and concerns into the imaginary life of the character and exploring the structures of that care. And although Tortsov, the teacher in this fictional acting school, introduces the idea to his students in terms of a child's game he plays with his niece, he is actually articulating the key principle to this revolutionary approach to acting. In phenomenological terms, the 'if' is none other than the demand for the creation of a 'world' in its rich lived experience not as actuality, but as *possibility* on stage. The truthfulness of the performance will be judged in the actor's capacity to flesh out the structures of the world that would be experienced by the character. The teacher's instruction never to act 'in general' is recognition of the necessary and specific contexts of human experience and action within the world. Indeed, any attempt to tackle the problem of what 'being in general' means is doomed to fail, as Heidegger came to realise.

From a phenomenological standpoint, of course, a self and the world in which it dwells can never be understood in isolation; self and world are co-constitutive. Stanislavski's exercises involving 'the given circumstances' are an exploration of the interdependent relationship between subjects and their environment. So when the students are invited to take gradual steps away from the reality of the situation of the 'here and now' – being asked to act *as if* it were another time of day, or another season and so on further away from the present reality – they are actually exploring aspects of the interconnection between world, self and temporality (Stanislavski, 2008, pp. 66, 67). The justification of action is always connected to the thick weave of self and surroundings at a particular point.

This interwoven performance of self will break down if not fleshed out in its completeness. For example, when Kostya tries to imagine the given circumstances of his own room at home, his imagination dries up and he describes the melodramatic and unbelievable action of going to hang himself in the closet (Stanislavski, 2008, pp. 69, 70). He is able to picture the details of the physical room, but without a sense of purpose – what he is doing in the room – his imagination falls short. If the self is constituted by its activity within the environment, then any acting exercise that fails to take such purpose into account will result in failed authenticity. A superficial approach to 'the way things look' in acting neglects to reach an understanding of being: involved activity in the given circumstances. This is evident when the director remarks,

> In our vocabulary, 'I am being' refers to the fact that I have put myself in the centre of a situation I have invented, that I feel I am really inside it, that I really exist at its very heart, in a world of imaginary objects, and that I am beginning to act as me, with full responsibility for myself. (Stanislavski, 2008, p. 70)

In Heideggerian language, such an understanding of 'I am being' is an artistic experience of the phenomenological unity of Being-in-the-world. Incidentally, the word for 'I am being' apparently has religious overtones from Slavonic orthodox terminology, and of a spiritual state equivalent to inspiration (Whyman, 2008, p. 254). The point is not merely to signal appearance, but to find a way of penetrating being and find a mysterious unity in duality.

Spatiality and Involvement

The structures of such Being-in-the-world are not understood in totality by recognising action within the environment, however. A human subject does not exist in a world of mere activity but lives 'concernfully' alongside objects within its environment. In phenomenological terminology, surrounding objects are 'ready to hand' in so far as they are of use in activity or tasks one wishes to achieve (Heidegger, 1962, pp. H67–72). Stanislavski sets up a series of exercises to explore the students' connections with objects – both in the real world of the actor on stage and in the imaginary given circumstances of a play or scene. More specifically, he uncovers the way in which objects in the environment reveal themselves to individuals. Yet, strangely, an understanding of human relationships towards things in the world goes mostly unnoticed, and needs to be explicitly thematised in order to develop further: 'In a nutshell,' according to Tortsov, 'we have to learn to look and see' (Stanislavski, 2008, p. 91). This demand applies both to reality and the imagination.

So when the student Pasha tries to imagine himself as a tree, he initially lacks creativity and specificity (Stanislavski, 2008, pp. 77–82). But when pressed he chooses an oak tree in the Alps. Again, deficient of detail, he needs to be prompted by the teacher to fill out the environment: an old castle nearby, the rustling of leaves and a bird's nest in its branches. In the next lesson, Pasha fleshes out the world of his imagination adding bells, the lowing of cows and the gossip of women after work in the fields. He then chooses the medieval time period in which to envision his tree. He constructs a story of a courtier in love with a married woman and the mortal combat of two sworn enemies and a baron who clears the surrounding land to protect his property. Excited by the prospect of a quarrel, Pasha imagines an ensuing battle and is unable to protect his branches from flying arrows.

The point of the exercise, according to the teacher, is that these imaginative details of space (or 'place', we might say more correctly) help to springboard the desire for creativity and action.[6] In phenomenological vocabulary, the world is not experienced as merely present-at-hand (sheer material objects in the environment without use-value) but as spaces invested with meaning because of the activities of the subject within the environment (Heidegger, 1962, p. H42). The vividness of individual objects comes to life when the totality of the scene is developed more and more though practice. Of course, physical exercise, dance and gymnastic classes, fencing lessons and other aspects of the total actor's training are key to giving an embodied experience of being in space and the ability to manipulate and control the body for the purposes of artistic practice (Merlin, 2003, p. 46). Such an understanding of objects in the environment never sees them isolated simply in their material properties and their merely being present; they are invested with the two-fold significance of the world of the character and the activity of the actor on stage.

This 'learning to see' on stage is a result of the fact that in regular everyday engagement with the world, human beings are mostly unaware of their own activities while doing them. The structures of the world and the use of objects in the environment seem largely transparent. But a strange thing happens when the actor enters upon the stage. Any ordinary engagement with objects and environment suddenly becomes 'uncanny'.[7] As a result, such minute attention to detail in the analysis of the given circumstances aims to make the structures of action explicit and break down tasks and goals in context. At the same time, the actor needs to be aware of her or his own 'real' circumstances on stage and motivate her or his actions according to the surrounding environment. Stanislavski's emphasis on the 'why', 'where', 'how', and 'when' of action are provocations to the practical exploration of being in a world – both real and imagined. And in a sense, the heightened awareness of the structures of being on stage is a practical manifestation of the phenomenological 'reduction' (bracketing off the question of the existence of the external world and attending to the way in which the world is given to consciousness). This is true of both performers attending to the way they perform and the audience member judging the action. Attention is directed towards the mode of 'givenness' highlighted for both in the act of performance.

Action and Involvement

Not only is it a requirement that actors relearn to see; they must also analyse the relationship between things in the world and modes of human action. As noted above, Stanislavski's actors need to observe their own actual actions (on stage and in their own life) and analyse the fictional actions of the character in the scene or play. A set of tools is needed for observing and analysing action. The idea that actions cannot be performed 'in general' is central to Tortsov's lessons. And just as the students of the acting class need to 'learn to see again' with respect to objects in their surroundings (both real and imagined) so too do they need to step back to notice the structure of actions in a given situation.

Stanislavski introduces his famous image of carving up a turkey as an analogy for analysing a play. It is impossible to digest the whole bird at once (2008, pp. 139, 140). But sliced up into pieces it can be served out and eaten more easily. Similarly, it is difficult to comprehend any role in its totality without understanding the different bits of that part in the context of the play. So ideally, an actor will get an overall sense of the direction, action and movement of a work as a whole and gradually break down individual scenes and actions within a scene. In practice, this can be done in textual analysis or, as Stanislavski later favoured, on the floor and through improvisations. The actor thus divides their part up into bits and gathers an understanding of the different tasks undertaken to achieve various goals at any one point.

Such an analysis of action in the fictional scene can also be applied to 'real life'. Kostya reflects upon his trip home to bed and thinks about the many different tasks and actions that constitute this journey (Stanislavski, 2008, pp. 137, 138). Whilst every bit of action has its own goal, each feeds into a through line of action aimed at getting home to sleep. At this point, Tortsov draws another analogy of a ship sailing down a channel and sticking to the fairway pass. The ship executes subtle shifts in direction but always with the overall movement in one direction. In a sense, this movement of action within the environment uncovers the human subject's 'concernful' behaviour within its world. The arrangement of action is ultimately aimed back towards the being of the human subject itself and its own continuing existence. The 'involvement structure' of the world and the 'towards-which' of behaviour are analysed in the 'bits' and 'goals' of action (in life and within a scene).

And, indeed, just as objects within the environment are apprehended in many different ways, so too is action understood in different respects. By analysing a simple action such as a handshake, Tortsov breaks the action down into its elements: the mechanical action itself (the physical act); a rudimentary psychological action (e.g. shaking a hand in order to show gratitude); and a psychological action (e.g. shaking a hand to apologise for something). In this way, different senses of 'being' are not only to be applied to objects, but also to action. The being of objects changes according to the activity of the involved human subject within the context.

It is not merely enough to *observe* the structure of life action in the art of acting, however. Actors must *use* this structure from within to create a role. For Stanislavski, the actor's own 'supertask' is creative expression in performance. Incidentally, playwrights also have their own supertask that is seemingly borne out in the thematic pursuits of their writing. Chekhov, according to the teacher, is concerned with the triviality of bourgeois life, Tolstoy the struggle for self-perfection, or Dostoevsky the lifelong search for God (Stanislavski, 2008, p. 307). Actors, on the other hand, are faced with the challenge of engaging their own supertask in a bodily way. Actors need to be aware of their own being on stage and find a way to execute this goal of artistic expression. At the same time, each moment in the performance should be moving towards the overall supertask of the text. Each of these carries a constant reflexivity towards action in context and the involved nature of the human subject within a life's goal.

State of Mind

Humans live in a world surrounded by objects and engaged in practical activity within that environment. But the world does not simply present itself as a mechanistic task-related back-drop. In phenomenological terms, one always brings a 'state of mind' to an interpretation and understanding thereby 'colouring' (my term) the way one sees the world (Heidegger, 1962, p. H164). The immense emotional and situational complexity with which individuals filter the world is central to Stanislavski's approach to actor preparation. One might argue that the American adoption of these writings and the subsequent development of the Method overprivilege the emotional and psychological. It is worth noting Stanislavski's holistic approach to the physical, the mental and the spiritual. Alongside involved activity and encountering objects within the world, emotions are also mostly an invisible feature of everyday experience. We always have a 'mood' that we bring to the world; it is 'the way we find ourselves to be'. Most of the time, however, we are unaware that we have a mood. In fact, it is only ever by mood that we become 'attuned' to the environment and encounter the world in the first place.

On stage, it is not merely a matter of observing one's own mood, but being able to create and control it. Many of Stanislavski's emotion memory drills require a rich storehouse of experiences from which to draw in the creation and performance of a role. But rather than directly accessing the emotions, the actor is meant to lure them out of the subconscious by conscious means. One needs to entice the emotions into the open like a hunter catching woodfowl: there is no way to force them into the open (Stanislavski, 2008, p. 225). By remembering the given circumstances of a past emotional experience – the physical surroundings and context – powerful emotions that could not be accessed otherwise become available. It is important to note that such a technique resists direct conscious control and requires subtler means of engaging the self.

There are a number of difficulties in taming the emotions for use in the creative process, however. One problem is that past memories tend to be unreliable and subject to distortion. In a sense, it is merely the memory's capacity to draw out an emotional response rather than being an actual representation of the past that is important. Another problem is that actors need to access these emotions more or less on cue. As a result, careful preparation and deep internal control are needed to produce a reliable source of emotion. Such a process might well be described as attuning oneself to mood and context. Stanislavski compares the actor's body in comparison to a piano, for instance (2008, p. 131). Attunement is possible because the human subject is not a fixed and stable 'thing' but rather an evolving and changing self throughout time intermingled with the world. Such volatility to change and context draws attention to the fact that human subjects always exist within what we might call the structure of temporality and from a certain point in historical, social, and cultural conditions.

In this way, the actions of an actor are never simply aimed at the universal communication of human emotion but always arise from a very specific cultural viewpoint. The actor's craft is always situated in relation to an audience with a capacity to interpret and understand the circumstances of their own performance. The audience's perception of mood conveyed within a scene is also enhanced and inflected by other elements of the theatrical presentation such as props and décor (Stanislavski, 2008, p. 212). Theatre is a collaborative effort, after all – a point that should not be forgotten despite Stanislavski's emphasis on the art of the actor. So mood or 'the way that we find ourselves to be' is also relevant to the audience on a communal level (think of how one describes the 'house' as having a certain 'temperature'). On a broader view, society as a whole also 'finds itself to be' in relation to historical events. Individuals have moods, but so too do historical epochs.

Communion and Being-with-others

Not only do human beings exist in a world of objects, actions, involvements and moods, they also share that world with others who have the same kind of being as their own. Other people are always 'there' in the world. In Tortsov's classes, the way that one exists in relation to others is through 'communion' or 'communication'.[8] For the teacher, this word does not merely denote verbal communication, but also the many different ways of connection with others – physical, mental and spiritual. Early on in one class, the students learn that they are always in communication with someone or something. Although Kostya believes he finds a moment when he is not (as his mind floated off at a music concert and as he became fixated with a chandelier fixed to the roof of the auditorium) the teacher points out that even this object brings the tradesman who made this light fitting into presence. The maker is visible in the made object. Such an observation of communion with others can provide an endless source of interest and inspiration. Elsewhere, Kostya's attention turns to a lamp that the teacher reveals to be full of relations to human activity (Stanislavski, 2008, pp. 229–31).

Heidegger arrives at a parallel conclusion regarding human relations to objects and the environment. Others are always 'there' with us in the world, even if we are alone (1962, p. H118). In travelling around the perimeter of a field, for example, the owner of the field is 'there' in my action in that I am impelled not to trespass upon that owner's land. If I am alone, I experience others there with me as an absence. For instance, an object that I associate with a close friend brings that person close to hand. These are examples of the wider phenomenon of 'Being-with' – the crucial role that 'others' play in the constitution of 'self' through intersubjective experience. Objects in the environment draw human relationships into the way they are experienced. Rather than simple materiality or equipment, 'things' in the world summon 'others' to presence. This is an important factor in the way that emotion memory works by conjuring up past experiences. Moods in relation to others are useful in finding the inner life of the character. A broad understanding of others there in the world also helps with the concentration of attention to 'the present reality' of actors on stage and their communication with others in ensemble with the audience.

Tortsov explains that there are three aspects to developing communion: self-communication (between the intellectual and emotional parts of the self, for instance), communicating with an imaginary object (people and things) and communicating with many people (the public audience of the theatre, for instance, or a mob in a scene) (Stanislavski, 2008, pp. 247–51). Each of these contains external and internal elements of communication. The overarching goal of Tortsov's instructions is to find an 'inward source of action' rather than to fall into the habits of external acting. Initially, the students might learn from observing the exterior effects of interacting with others. But the mere outward representation of communion is not good enough to produce a believable performance. The teacher points out that it is much easier to actually be in communion with one's acting partner than to pretend to be. Even observing such truthfulness in oneself is quite difficult. Kostya actually thinks that he is quite good at it, but is brought down to earth and criticised by the director.

In the ensuing exercises, Tortsov's students are made aware of the physical means by which they communicate feelings and senses with one another. After he asks the class to stage an argument with one of the other class members, the teacher points out how much Kostya uses his hands and wrists to communicate his point. In order to draw attention to the fact, Kostya has his arms bound and repeats the exercise. Then, one by one, his torso, facial gestures, and eye movements are denied in the exercise, and he is left with nothing but his own internal psychological presence. Kostya complains that he requires his whole self in order to communicate his emotions and the teacher agrees that this is the principle of the art of acting. He also describes communication as emitting rays or streams that emanate from our eyes and both give and receive communion with others (Stanislavski, 2008, p. 250). The teacher points out that it is not good enough in a scene merely to have flashes of communion, but rather a coherent flow of awareness, response and reception to others is required. Once again, this communication and awareness is something that needs to be trained and developed.

Heidegger also notes how our communication with others in an environment fades into the background in regular life because of our focussed attention on involved activity. But in the phenomenological reduction, as on stage, the philosopher withdraws from the natural attitude of involvement, and requires a special attention to the relationship between self and others (if investigating the phenomenon of 'Being-with'). For the most part, we overlook the way that Being-with others makes up our own concept of self (Heidegger, 1962, p. H118). Others 'there in the world' are not encountered as differentiated subjects, but rather as those in the 'with-world'. In this sense, the being of others in the world is always part of one's own being. Stanislavski similarly draws explicit attention to the ways that we are 'with' others and ourselves through these communication exercises. In fact, this is at the very core of living through the part or, more broadly, experiencing.

Stanislavski the Phenomenologist

This is merely a preliminary survey of some ways in which 'world' gives itself to 'experience' that are explicitly explored through Stanislavski's approach to actor preparation and performance. If we follow a phenomenological interpretation, the failures of 'bad' acting are symptoms of a flawed 'metaphysical' understanding of the world. Such a misapprehension of what Being means can only be overcome by training and repeated practice of the art. Each actor training exercise is a return to the 'mineness' of experience overlooked in everyday activity. Far from being a free-floating self or mind in a vacuum, the human subject mutually creates and is created by action within time, place, and objects in the world. Not only must the actor learn to see these modes of being-in-the-world again, but also to analyse and use them in the artistic endeavour of performance. This is made all the more difficult by the elusive role of emotion or mood, together with the complex weave of others there in the world that creates lived experience. But rather than simply analyse these aspects of being in abstraction, the actor explores them through performance by developing an awareness and indeed a way of seeing the world that is quite different from the everyday human agent.

In this way, Stanislavski's actor can be thought of as adopting a phenomenological viewpoint towards the world. An 'existential sight' is borne from the way in which the performance space (whether it be the stage or the rehearsal room) makes the world uncanny and forces the performer to look twice, to think, to act and to be. And as a nodal point between fiction and reality, Stanislavski's actor must at once have developed an understanding of their own complex relationship with the world while simultaneously incarnating the artistic creation of a new being – the person in the part. In this sense, the actor is the site of intersection between possibility and actuality of worldhood.

In summary, several observations about the nature of consciousness that can be drawn from *An Actor's Work* include:

- that the world reveals itself only through involved action within an environment;
- that the given circumstances of the world open up possibilities of action for human beings;
- that presentation on stage 'makes strange' and thereby draws attention to the actor's intrinsic involvement with the world and the nature of action;
- that while it is difficult to grasp the structure of life 'as a whole' an appreciation of the 'involvement' structure of the life-world can be gleaned by considering smaller tasks of action and objects in context;
- that the world is always coloured by particular 'moods' of the engaged subject; and
- that 'others' there in the world are an essential part of the experience of any life-world.

This list, although not exhaustive, parallels some major disclosures of phenomenology emphasising the interwoven experience of self and world through involved activity. More importantly, each observation is not merely uncovered by intellectual effort but through vivid practical experience. In a sense, because acting is a practical art, it is a natural ally of any phenomenologist who posits that knowing is not the primary way in which humans experience the world. Indeed, Descartes' famous statement in the *cogito*, 'I think, therefore I am', may well be an impediment to the actor, as many theatre practitioners would attest!

Above all, the actor's art for Stanislavski is not merely a detached mental act or theorising, but a 'manual philosophy' that returns 'to the things themselves'. This type of philosophical understanding does not provide a systematic and comprehensive account of the conditions for the possibility of being. It is, however, an explicit and embodied awareness of the way in which the world presents itself to consciousness and a presentation of world on stage. At the very least, it is clear that Stanislavski aspired towards a system of acting that entails both a practical understanding and truthful showing of the state of being. In his own words:

> The general opinion is that every moment in our acting should unfailingly be grand, complex, exciting. But you know from your previous work that the smallest action or feeling, the smallest aspect of our technique acquires enormous significance if onstage they are pushed to the very limit. There it ends and living, human truth, belief and the 'I am being' begin. When that happens, then the actor's mental and physical apparatus starts to work according to the laws of human nature, exactly as it does in life, notwithstanding the artificial situation we find ourselves in, having to be creative in public. (2008, p. 330)

Exercises and Topics for Discussion

1. Watch an episode or scene from your favourite soap opera or heightened comedy. In what ways do the actors 'demonstrate' rather than base their performance on 'truthful' experience? Note how the conventions of genre highly influence acting style in these instances. What do you think are the markers of 'truthfulness' in performance?

2. Choose a 'world' and describe in detail the objects, elements and actions of that world. So for instance, you could choose the world of rugby, of politics, or Japanese calligraphy. How do these elements reflect back upon and understand the being of participants in that world? Think about the 'towards which' of actions within that world. In other words, consider the chain of purpose in that action. For example, passing a rugby ball points towards team-work in moving the ball to the opposition's goal line, which is for scoring a try, which is for playing within the rules of rugby, which is for the entertainment of players and spectators, which is for … and so on.
3. Choose a public space and observe the people, objects, and behaviours that constitute it. Try to create a theatrical interpretation of that space through rhythms, directions, magnitudes, heights, movements, forces, sounds, and atmospheres. How do these elements relate to the involvement structure of Being?
4. Think about the others 'there' with you right now. How do you encounter others in your environment? How might absent people also be present for you? Consider the same of a character in a scene of your choice. Play the scene emphasising the Being-there of different people 'there' for your character.
5. How might we treat others as mere objects in the world? What does it mean to engage authentically with others there with us? Is it possible to be authentic at every moment?
6. What is 'the way in which you find yourself' now? Why? In what way do we avoid being aware of our mood? How might moods be useful? When do they get in the way? Now choose a scene from a play you are studying. What is the 'state of mind' of your character in that scene? Play the scene with different temporal focusses. So for instance, play a character with a view to the past, and then again with a view to the future.

Notes

1 In English, the widely known earlier translation is Elizabeth Reynolds Hapgood's *An Actor Prepares* (Stanislavski, 1980a). This chapter refers to Jean Benedetti's more recent translation, *An Actor's Work* (Stanislavski, 2008).

2   For a useful introduction, see Jean Benedetti's (2004) *Stanislavski: An Introduction*. Of course other works in Stanislavski's oeuvre and accounts of his actual creative practice might also contain insights into the relationship between theatre and phenomenology yet I focus here on this text because of its widespread popularity, accessibility, and clarity.
3   Bella Merlin's (2003) *Konstantin Stanislavsky* also provides a concise summary of parts of the system which may be of use to readers.
4   For his exposition of the term *épisteme*, see Foucault (2002, p. 211ff).
5   For an investigation of the scientific worldviews behind Stanislavski's theory of acting, see Joseph Roach's (1985) *The Player's Passion* and Jonathan Pitches' (2006) *Science and the Stanislavsky Tradition of Acting*.
6   For a short introduction on this concept of place-world, see Edward Casey (2002).
7   See Heidegger (1962, pp. H188–190) for further discussion. It should be noted that the word 'uncanny' in Heidegger's usage relates to a special mood of anxiety that reveals the world.
8   Note that Hapgood's translation of *An Actor Prepares* (Stanislavski, 1980a) uses the term 'communion' which has a religious and spiritual dimension that seems to be extinguished somewhat in Benedetti's *An Actor's Work* (Stanislavski, 2008).

6

Artaud's Phenomenology of Anxiety: Language and Being-towards-death

Theatre for Metaphysical Transformation

Can you think of a time when you didn't really feel like yourself? It might have been when you were sick or delirious. It might have been when you were travelling in a foreign country and you weren't able to speak the language. It could have been when you were engaged in an activity or task with which you were deeply unfamiliar. It might have been when you were swept up by some group activity or joined in with a crowd and found yourself doing things that you usually wouldn't do. When did words fail you in a moment of extreme grief? What about when you were intoxicated or under the influence of some other substance? Think about what it was about your state that estranged you from your regular mode of existing.

Most of the time, we think about 'who' we 'are' as something relatively stable. I am the entity that exists from moment to moment and that somehow rests 'underneath' our conscious awareness of the world. But is this right? The common link between the unusual states mentioned above is that they exist in situations where the connectedness of the world seems to break down. But in this moment of dysfunction the world as it usually exists comes into stark view because of its absence (Leder, 1990). What if you were in such a state permanently? This was seemingly the case with our next practitioner.

Antonin Artaud experienced something profound when he saw a Balinese dance troupe at the Paris colonial exhibition in 1931:

> In the Oriental theater of metaphysical tendencies, as opposed to the Occidental theater of psychological tendencies, the whole complex of gestures, signs, postures, and sonorities which constitute the language of stage performance, this language which develops all its physical and poetic effects on every level of consciousness and in all the senses, necessarily induces thought to adopt profound attitudes which could be called *metaphysics-in-action*. (1958, p. 44)

For him, this was the perfect physical example of metaphysical thought made manifest by challenging and transforming selfhood through the theatrical encounter. He ceaselessly tried to replicate the ritual-like revelatory experience he felt when he saw these exotic dancers. Artaud maintained that this type of performance offers hope for an authentic existence lost in everyday life. Later he claimed: '[w]hen I live I do not feel myself alive. But when I act, it is then that I feel myself exist' (Artaud, 1998, p. 275). He saw something in the theatrical experience that allows privileged access to the question of existence. Peppered throughout his writings is the proposition that theatre is not merely theoretical contemplation of the world, but a metaphysical return of Being to one's ownmost self. Although we might criticise Artaud for his misunderstanding and appropriation of non-Western theatrical traditions (Patke, 2013, p. 40), there is no doubt that he was profoundly influenced by this Balinese encounter.

Conversely, few artists in the history of theatre have been so misunderstood as Artaud. He was a self-confessed failure in his attempts to articulate his encounter with life. At the same time he transformed this failure into the content of his essays and art. His manifestos have exerted influence on some of the most significant practitioners in contemporary theatre and performance art in the last century. On the surface of it, Artaud appears to be the quintessential metaphysician in that he continually espouses dualist ontology by positing a reality beyond the physical world and the debased nature of words, language, and the flesh.[1] Instead, we might understand Artaud as subverting a subject – object binary that forms the limit of understanding. His ideal theatre is itself a *Destruktion* of metaphysics. It should be stressed here that my interpretation here does not emphasise historical analysis pointing out the context of Artaud's theatrical practice although such an understanding is important. He is attempting to stand outside of history. In this sense, Artaud seemingly falls into a metaphysical trap in his mysterious pronouncements about hidden forces behind the appearance of Being. But if we dig a little deeper, we can see the Theatre of Cruelty as 'showing the things themselves in their manner of appearing'. Artaud's theatre is phenomenological because it attempts to lay bare the world in its lived experience and structure through performance. We should interpret this philosophical theatre not in terms of rationality and thought but as a radical reinterpretation of mind – body and material existence as mutually intertwined. The question is not so much whether audiences witnessing the Theatre of Cruelty are subjected to totalitarian violence or liberation from constraining norms (Vork, 2013), but how such an experience reveals existential truth. The task then is to read Artaud at his limits as Jacques Derrida suggests:

> If the 'destruction' of the history of metaphysics, in the rigorous sense understood by Heidegger, is not a simple surpassing of this history, one could then, sojourning in a place which is neither within nor without this history, wonder about what links the concept of madness to the concept of metaphysics in general: the metaphysics which Artaud destroys and which he is still furiously determined to construct or preserve within the same movement of destruction. Artaud keeps himself at the limit, and we have attempted to read him at his limit. ('La Parole Soufflée', Derrida, 1978, p. 194)

This chapter is an attempt as such a reading. Just as Heidegger sees phenomenology as a pathway to revealing authentic Dasein, so too does Artaud see theatre as a way of smashing our everyday understanding of existence and bringing forth a fullness and plenitude of Being. Such a comparison risks conflating the ideas of these two figures. Indeed, Jane Goodall notes the temptation of using Nietzschean-Heideggerian frameworks in Derrida, Foucault and Deleuze where Artaud's ideas are invoked because they are terms that these writers were more comfortable citing (Goodall, 1994, p. 210). Because Artaud's theatrical project remained unrealised it has been seen as the perfect canvas upon which to project an array of theoretical perspectives (Puchner, 2013). But I argue that in so far as Heidegger's exploration of selfhood faithfully outlines the conditions for the possibility of being a 'Self' in the first place, it is useful. In fact, in Heidegger's estimation we humans are mostly 'not ourselves' but handed over to Everydayness and inauthentic modes of existence. The concept of Authenticity gives an account of what it means to 'be oneself' and elucidates Artaud's writings. The question to hand is not to debate whether Heidegger was right or wrong but an exploration of such terms in relation to Artaud's project. In a sense, Artaud's theatre is incomprehensible in so far it cannot be encapsulated by ordinary expression: his project can be thought of as a search for a new language of Being from the point of view of a deep ontological Anxiety. It is in this sense that he has something to offer phenomenology.

Appropriating Artaud through phenomenology performs a kind of symbolic violence to his theatrical manifestos. He saw performance as a means of uncovering Being. Yet the matter does not simply rest at the point of ontology. Both Heidegger and Artaud eschew Everydayness and yearn for a more essential, primordial experience of authentic existence. It is telling that both drifted towards poetry as a means of such an experience. Ultimately, both attempt to create a poetry of Being. If we can interpret Artaud as performing a Destruktion of metaphysics, it is useful to remember that Heidegger shows the difficulty of destroying tradition whilst simultaneously preserving any position from which to conduct that destruction. Both have been accused of being metaphysicians themselves: Heidegger in his quest for the essence of Being and Artaud in his mystical ontology. But the former hopes phenomenology would avoid metaphysics by attending closely to experience; the latter attempts to destroy tradition not by intellectual analysis and argumentation, but by bodily means – a 'philosophy of the flesh'.

In what follows, I think about Artaud's famous imagery of the plague itself as a Destruktion of tradition in theatrical practice. His theatrical concept of Self can be understood in relation to *das Man* (Heidegger's term for the 'They' of everyday existence). His rejection of literary conventions and forms stems from a disgruntlement with surface forms of language. I will go on to suggest that his Gnostic understanding of Being can be reinterpreted in terms of Heidegger's term 'Falling' (the tendency for Dasein to understand itself in terms of the world). Rather than view Artaud's Theatre of Cruelty as a psychotic perversion or simply the manifestation of a dissociative disorder, he expresses the existential mood Anxiety in that he hoped to channel it into a form of theatre with the potential for world-revelation. The violence of what he calls cruelty can be seen as an articulation of Being-towards-death and Authenticity. In fact, cruelty represents an attempt to *transcend* Being-in-the-world which also points towards its necessary failure. Let us survey the terrain.

La Peste as Destruktion

The first philosophical connection between Artaud and Heidegger resides in that both assert Western tradition has failed to reach an adequate understanding of the nature of reality. In his preface to *The Theatre and its Double*, Artaud identifies a modern obsession with culture 'which has never been coincident with life, which in fact has been devised to tyrannize over life' (1958, p. 7). He goes on to declaim the separation between things and ideas, between life as we experience it and philosophical systems that don't seem to match up with that experience:

> All our ideas about life must be revised in a period when nothing any longer adheres to life; it is this painful cleavage which is responsible for the revenge of *things;* the poetry which is no longer within us and which we no longer succeed in finding in things suddenly appears on their wrong side [...] (1958, p. 8)

For Artaud, theatre is one way in which this separation of ideas and life can be overcome. To break through language and touch life is to create theatre (1958, pp. 12–13).

Heidegger also sees philosophy as the means of unmasking erroneous conceptions of being endemic in the Western tradition. In fact, the task of the phenomenologist is to show how these traditions have passed themselves off as self-evident. As discussed in Chapter 2, the phenomenological method enacts a Destruktion of the history of ontology. In contrast to the English word and false friend 'destruction', however, Heidegger's term is not simply a negative toppling of tradition. Past understandings of Being may contain within them a germ of truth that should be preserved. Yet at the same time, the philosopher should be wary of assumptions about the world and the nature of reality.

The plague (*la peste*) is perhaps one of the most well-known and vivid images that Artaud uses to describe the 'doubles' of life and theatre.[2] Citing the story of the eighteenth-century Sardinian Viceroy, Saint-Rémy, who had a premonition-dream in which he succumbed to the plague, Artaud dwells on the strange effects of this epidemic (Artaud, 1958, p. 15). Heeding this dream, the Viceroy turns away the *Grand-Saint Antoine* that had sought to dock in the port. The ship subsequently sailed on to Marseille where it spread the 'Oriental virus'. It is significant for Artaud that the disease originated and drew its power from the East. For Artaud, the Viceroy has a psychic connection with the plague – although not a strong enough one to actually be infected. For those who are contaminated by the full force of this mystical power, Artaud believes that there is a psychic as well as physical overcoming that takes place. For him, historical instances of the plague (from the Egyptian plague in the Old Testament onwards) stem from the same metaphysical origin (1958, pp. 17–22).

The social effects of infection are also a manifestation of the plague's power: a breakout of immorality in affected towns, acts of incest, and all manner of crimes amongst the ever-rising piles of bodies burning in the streets (Artaud, 1958, pp. 23–25). Artaud even suggests that those who survive the plague are drawn back to the stinking, infected cities. But the plague is neither just a metaphor nor biological phenomenon. For Artaud, words and symbols have the ability to summon real forces and produce physical effects. His ideal theatrical encounter is a channelling of the actual metaphysical forces of the plague (perhaps not unlike the power of the dream that affected Saint-Rémy). This conception of theatre rejects the 'disinterested' theory of art, with its focus on beauty, the sublime, perfection of form, and imperative of moral instruction prevalent in nineteenth-century Romanticism. For Artaud, a new idea of art enacts a visceral, disruptive, and jolting encounter. Nevertheless, the word 'cruelty' should not simply be taken as negative pain and suffering, but the fulfilment of inevitable powers unleashed by the plague. And just as he sought to smash artistic sensibilities and conventions, so too did he think such an encounter could smash stale social customs and superficial etiquette.

The link here is that social codes, conventions, and patterns of behaviour can be thought of as examples of what Heidegger calls Falling. Humans 'fall prey' to tradition as it has taken hold without question (Heidegger, 1962, p. H21). In this sense, tradition is an understanding of the world and a pattern of behaviour that has been passed onto Dasein from the cultural world that precedes it. Heidegger argues that tradition stops Dasein from inquiring into its own basis (i.e. the basis of Dasein in itself) and prevents it from 'choosing' for itself. Tradition also conceals its own origin and transmission:

> If the question of Being is to have its own history made transparent, then this hardened tradition must be loosened up, and the concealments which it has brought about must be dissolved. We understand this task as one in which by taking the question of Being as our clue, we are to destroy the traditional content of ancient ontology until we arrive at those primordial experiences in which we achieved our first ways of determining the nature of Being – the ways which have guided us ever since. (Heidegger, 1962, p. H22)

And where can the clutches of tradition be observed more clearly than in the realm of aesthetics? Artaud's writings seen through the lens of phenomenology are a response to everyday Falling. The task at hand here is performing a Destruktion of his work, while simultaneously interpreting it *as* a Destruktion.

For Artaud, theatre is at the centre of a truthful experience of Being and constitutes a vital encounter between individual and society. In fact, he slips seamlessly between writing about the plague and the theatre by seemingly conflating the two ideas, or rather, intimating that they are 'doubles' of one another. The actor is a chiasmic point in this encounter as metaphor and actuality, sign and materiality, inside and outside. Any distinction between theatre and reality dissolves in the plague. The notion of psychic and physical transmission at a distance is a recurring trope in discourses of emotion throughout history, used to explain the power of actors to affect an audience, as Artaud well knew. But unlike Aristotelian *catharsis* that supposedly purges audience members of *negative* emotions, the plague operates both by destructive and creative forces. It is not simply a matter of transforming the emotions of spectators, but rather performing alchemy upon their Being. In his criticism of the stale dogmas of faith Artaud yearns for the primitive power of belief without the fake social structures of religion (Artaud, 1958, p. 31). At the same time, he also hopes to undercut any rationalist/intellectual view of nature by connecting with the unconscious at a deeper level than can be articulated in words.

Although the plague as a double of life tends to evoke images of violence and suffering, the effects may at times be pleasurable. Humour also has the power of infection. Artaud himself was very fond of the Marx Brothers and the way in which their comic words, language, and symbols were detached from everyday use. Through the turmoil of such physical form of humour, Artaud sees a 'kind of boiling anarchy, an essential disintegration of the real by poetry' (Artaud, 1988, p. 144). Cruelty in this sense is full of feeling and effect through the mechanism of laughter. Presumably, one's body loses conscious control and transcends the boundaries of social norms. The thought contains similarities to Bakhtin's (1984) *Rabelais and His World* in which he outlines the subversive power of laughter. In many ways, his abolition of 'psychological acting' is a reconsideration of 'thinking' as the basis of Being (as claimed by Descartes). In the throes of the plague (and Artaud's theatre), physical reactions (rather than thoughts) constitute existence.

Both Artaud and Heidegger also sought to overcome past attempts at understanding the relationship between the human subject and its world especially as those systems do not seem to match with the way that we experience the world. In such a state, one may even experience self-awareness and self-unity in a way that cannot be encapsulated by words. The plague indicates the possibilities of existence (Artaud, 1958, p. 27). Heidegger calls such a mode Authenticity; Artaud calls it cruelty. Artaud's conception of theatre calls for an authentic mode of questioning Being.

Falling Understanding and the Everyday Falling Self

The second borderland between Artaud and Heidegger is situated in a radical rethinking of self-hood and reconsideration of any rigid distinction between self and world. According to both thinkers, most of the time we aren't really ourselves: we are 'taken over' by the world and barely look into the essence of our own existence. Indeed, self-loss is a constant theme in Artaud's writings, especially in the attempt to articulate that essence in language:

> I suffer from a horrible sickness of mind. My thought abandons me at every level. From the simple fact of thought to the external fact of its materialisation in words. Words, shapes of sentences, internal directions of thought, simple reactions of the mind – I am constantly in pursuit of my intellectual being. Thus as soon as *I can grasp a form*, however imperfect, I pin it down, for fear of losing the whole of thought. I lower myself, I know, and I suffer from it, but I consent to it for fear of dying altogether. (from 'A Letter to Jacques Rivière 5 June, 1923', Artaud, 1988, p. 31)

In this passage, we can see how the vital power and force of Artaud's experience of the world resists any linguistic translation. He seeks a form of expression beyond everyday language in something primordial.

Further frustration with words and their impotent meaning led Artaud to attack the establishments of art and literature for their concern with mere forms and conventions. In defending his rejected poetry, he suggests that the essence of his thought is stolen from him at the moment of articulation. For Artaud, the theft can be overcome by returning to a bodily engagement in performance. More importantly, the language employed in traditional text-based drama deprives actors of self-expression as their own words are 'spirited away' (Derrida, 1978, p. 175). Of course, Artaud didn't completely ignore the dramatic canon in his manifesto for the Theatre of Cruelty published in *The Theatre and its Double*, as evidenced by his proposal for possible productions (Artaud, 1958, pp. 99,100). And it should also be noted that artistic, linguistic, and philosophical circles were beginning to investigate the arbitrariness of words in relation to their meaning at the beginning of the twentieth century (a notable theme of modernist thought). Nevertheless, for Artaud the power of words lies in their capacity to bring about a bodily effect; meaning is secondary to the *force* of words and gestures. He sought to overturn the way in which the meaning of Being is determined by the cultural world beforehand.

Correspondingly, Heidegger develops a critique of Everydayness (*Alltäglichkeit*) and its tendency towards an anonymous, unquestioned understanding of the world presented by society and tradition. This Everydayness also has a manifestation in language, talk, and discourse. In many ways, the difficult and idiosyncratic language that Heidegger employs is in reaction against a language with metaphysical baggage. Not only are language and expression determined by the world; so too is the very possibility of action for Dasein at any given point. An inauthentic mode of existence rests in the way we understand ourselves in terms of the world as merely material things – an understanding that has been passed down through history and philosophy. Whereas Artaud thinks that authentic existence can be achieved through the material truth of performance, Heidegger resists viewing the world solely as materiality; for him such an interpretation also risks inauthenticity.

Authenticity requires Dasein to truthfully grasp itself as 'thrown possibility'. We are 'thrown' into the world in the sense that it is the world that predetermines our language, physical capabilities, and choices for action. Yet at the same time, we can also accept the options that are given to us and choose positively with awareness of the fact that one day our choices will come to an end. In this mode, the possibilities of existence for any individual are simultaneously handed over by the world and positively chosen. Authentic Dasein simultaneously sees the groundlessness of its own existence and seizes the available opportunities with full knowledge of the fact.

According to Heidegger, philosophy in the past has understood the 'who I am' of Dasein as the 'I myself', 'the subject', or 'the self'. This self has traditionally been thought of as a *thing* that is maintained through different experiences and behaviours (Heidegger, 1962, p. H114). In the past, a person's 'identity' was mostly understood as something 'constantly present-at-hand'. The word 'subject' in this sense derives from *subjectum*

– a term that already implies a separation between subject and object of the self and world. Subsequently from the Christian/Aristotelian tradition, 'personhood' is identified with soul or substance that lies beneath manifest change in the physical world. A little later, 'who I am' is taken as given or beyond doubting because of its basis in 'thinking' (as proposed by Descartes). But far from being simply transparent, Heidegger claims that the self has a tendency to overlook itself in everyday life (1962, p. H116). In this mode, Dasein is precisely not-itself because it interprets itself as simply another thing alongside other things in the world (1962, p. H115); Dasein has lost itself to the world. This is the mode of 'Everydayness' in which Dasein fails to ask the question '*who* am I?' and mistakenly asks '*what* am I?' This explains the history of understanding the self as a 'thing'.

Artaud is attempting to bring together these questions of the 'who?' and the 'what?' in his reflections on selfhood. On the surface of it, his complaint of the 'alien robbery' of his true self could be seen as a misrecognising the nature of reality. His claims about hidden forms behind the superficial appearance of the world could be seen as an extreme Platonism (or, rather, Gnosticism). On the other hand, we could interpret his theatrical vision as a rethinking of the binary distinctions of body-thought/the world-self:

> The theater is the only place in the world, the last general means we still possess of directly affecting the organism and, in periods of neurosis and petty sensuality like the one in which we are immersed, of attacking this sensuality by physical means it cannot withstand. (1958, p. 81)

Artaud intimates such an attack can be carried out through the physical means. Cruelty is key in this respect is the 'implacable necessity' of existence that unleashes its reality through true theatre. Such a reality overcomes the blindness of everyday, tranquilised culture because of its absolute imminence. For Artaud, art ceases to be a detached object for contemplation and takes on the role of an immanently approaching threat. The Theatre of Cruelty rages against a dull and anaesthetised passivity of the audience safe from any understanding or impact by the real. In Heidegger's terms, it seeks out the baselessness of its own existence and faces that void directly.

Throughout *The Theatre and its Double*, Artaud calls for the reinstitution of danger into performance. He describes the poetic and balletic scene of a police raid on a brothel where all spectators are implicated in the drama:

> This is really total theater. Well, this total theater is the ideal. This anxiety, this guilt feeling, this victoriousness, this satisfaction, set the tone, feelings and state of mind in which the audience should leave our theatre, shaken and irritated by the inner dynamism of the show. This dynamism bears direct relation to the anxieties and preoccupations of their whole lives. (Artaud, 1958, p. 16)

The point of this quest for immediacy in theatre is to gain his identity back from the disinterested art of dilettantes. For Artaud, mere intellectual engagement with art achieves no tangible efficacy; he seeks a kind of performance that can have a direct impact on life. Again in Heidegger's terms, this shock is aimed at awakening everyday inauthentic existence and coming face-to-face with Being.

In terms of performance, Artaud hopes to address the mismatch between the actor's state and reality. This disconnection with reality is not limited to the theatre audience, but society in general which dupes itself with culture, civilisation, morals and philosophical systems. He also challenges ineffectual theatre – theatre that induces passivity. This detachment is equivalent to an interpretation that is simply handed over to the audience, pre-digested rather than engaging the actors and audience in their own being. Rather than take the fictional situation of characters on stage as objects in the gaze of the spectator, the Theatre of Cruelty forces the question of 'who?' for both audience and performers.

Being-with-others and the They

Here it is useful to consider Heidegger's account of others there in the world with us. When he mentions the Other (*Andere*) Heidegger is not implying that there are isolated and separate entities that linger as present-at-hand for Dasein. The Others are, rather, those from whom Dasein does not distinguish itself. Like 'the ready-to-hand' (things around us that are available for use as tools or to some end), others are discovered through the concerned involvement of Dasein within the world – environmentally and in terms of the projects and activities of Dasein at the time. In fact, just as Dasein can encounter others within the world, so too can it encounter itself: in what it does, uses, expects, avoids – those things in which it is most closely concerned (Heidegger, 1962, p. H119). The important point is that Dasein does not encounter itself or others merely in terms of materiality – the 'present-at-hand' – but rather in terms of its involvements with the world. The world – including objects, tools, others with the same kind of being as Dasein itself – is encountered through structures of Care (*Sorge*).

Most of the time, then, the 'who' of Dasein is not its own self (although this sounds paradoxical). For the most part, Dasein is anonymous, unindividuated and determined by its relation to others there in the world. Heidegger calls this self-given from the outside the 'They-self'. So there is a second misunderstanding in Dasein to interpret itself not only in terms of objects within the world, but also in terms of anonymous others. The 'who' of everyday being enters into a mode in which Dasein is not itself – it is the 'They' (*das Man*). In English, *das Man* might be translated as 'one', the impersonal pronoun, as in 'one does what one can', for instance. In this impersonal mode, Dasein stands in subjection to the Others and to the world. Instead of understanding who it is in itself, Dasein understands itself in terms of what it is *not*:

> And when indeed, one's knowing oneself gets lost in such ways as aloofness, hiding oneself away, or putting on a disguise, Being-with-one-another must follow special routes of its own in order to come close to Others or even to 'see through them'. (Heidegger, 1962, p. H124)

Generally, Dasein does not know itself nor does it really know Others there with it in the world in an authentic way. Mostly, Dasein just passes by Others in 'Publicness' (*Öffentlichkeit*). Dasein also takes on this kind of Being in everydayness in relation to its self-understanding – it does not see itself as unique in its own being (as possibilities). In 'Distantiality' (*Abständigkeit*) Dasein constantly sees itself in comparison to the way

Others are, whether it 'lags behind' or 'forges ahead' (Heidegger, 1962, p. H126). In 'Averageness', Dasein takes on the general opinion of the Others – 'what they say'. In Publicness, Dasein's understanding is 'levelled down' (*Einebnung*). In this state, there is nothing that is new, interesting or unthought except that which has already been interpreted by the They. Artaud's attack on the conventions of art seems to be aimed precisely at this levelled down opinions and tastes of the art world. Such Publicness never gets to the heart of the matter. Everything gets obscured. Everything gets passed off as familiar and accessible to everyone. The They-self is a radically unindividuated self that denies all responsibility, particularity, and visibility. The They are 'alongside everyone everywhere' but they steal away whenever there is a definite decision to be made (Heidegger, 1962, p. H127). The They presents every judgement as its own, and deprives Dasein of every individual answerability. In its everydayness, Dasein is disburdened (*entlasten*) by the They. Dasein has a tendency to make things easy and let them come easily.

In this regard, Artaud's disillusionment with art criticism stems from the 'dictatorship' of They (in Heidegger's terminology). Rather than see the individual self as somehow cut off from the world in a radical duality of existence (the mind-body split), he aspired to dissolve the idle trivialities and sickness of the masses through the force of spectacle. Mind and body are not seen as separate in his proposed Theatre of Cruelty. For Artaud, there is a radical material continuity with existence brought about by the hidden forces of (impossible) unmediated symbols directly acting on the spectators. In the throes of performance, materiality is transcended when the separation between the self and the world is dissolved.

Artaud is also interested in the idea of answering 'who?' (in the sense of an authentic response to the being of Dasein). He constantly maintains that his own existence is unique and untranslatable into words. He seeks to replace past metaphysical systems with new practices of being directly present rather than split off from reality by transferring meaning of the sign. When Artaud writes about metaphysics, he is referring to hidden forces at work in the world, doubles that can be revealed in the theatre, signs which speak of hidden meaning and symbols that conceal the reality that they communicate. In everyday life, we are for the most part asleep and unaware of the hidden connection between material and the true essence of reality that lies behind it. Artaud rejects being interpreted in terms of a literary tradition: the superficial talk of the They that has always been interpreted by the masses; always known and grasped beforehand. He wants to understand himself as a radically individuated and unique being irreducible to mere words.

Heidegger's description of the They is useful for thinking about Artaud's alienation from himself from an existential point of view. Instead of standing in subjection to the world and having possibilities handed over to him by the world, Artaud wants to usurp his own relation to the world drastically together with that of the actor and audience. As Derrida suggests, he wants to step outside the relational structure of the world that constitutes the possibility of representation. By creating performance and controlling the hidden forces behind material reality, Artaud claims that he is able to be himself. In this way, he is not reduced to intellectual or cognitive articulation of Being. This understanding is *existential* in that it sees the self as a total relation to existence which includes feeling, emotion, physicality, and materiality. It aims at an embodied understanding of Being. Artaud's ideal spectator is not lost or disburdened by a sense of anonymity or social norm, but rather is faced with radical transgression of society's conventions, moralities, traditions in an authentic way. His theatre maintains the possibility of overcoming the subjugating/subjecting dominance of the They by reforming continuity between materiality, meaning, and the world. For Artaud, theatre is the way to smash the tranquilised Everydayness of the They – a practical and visceral philosophy.

Moods, Anxiety, and Being-towards-death

The third point of crossing to this Heideggerian frontier lies in the term 'state of mind' (*Befindlichkeit*) that reveals something about the trajectory of human life, its limits, limitations, and totality. State of mind in this sense is how you find yourself / how you are. For Heidegger, Anxiety (*Angst*) is a 'mood' (*Stimmung*) in which the worldhood of the world is revealed; it discloses the structures of human involvement in the world through disengaged absence. As opposed to its meaning in psychological discourse, according to Heidegger Anxiety is the nonspecific fear of nothing, or rather the world itself (1962, p. H188). Existence itself becomes something feared as one's regular Falling understanding of the world is confronted. Artaud sought such a confrontation with the world in theatre. And by drawing on Heidegger's term here, we might interpret Artaud not through the lens of madness but rather through existential Anxiety.

Heidegger begins his discussion of Anxiety in terms of Falling (1962, p. H184). Most of the time, Dasein is absorbed in the They and the world of concern – tasks in a physical environment; it flees from an authentic understanding of its own being and avoids coming face-to-face with itself. In contrast, Anxiety is a state of mind in which Dasein shrinks back from Being-in-the-world in general. 'That which is feared' seems to be nowhere; there is no specific entity in the world that is threatening, but it is not nothing. In this state, when Dasein is anxious it doesn't know what it is anxious about. What threatens is close, oppressive, and stifling. In fact, the object of such angst is the world itself and potentiality for being. In such a state, Dasein recognises that it can choose itself and its own possibilities. Anxiety reveals Being-in-the-world through detachment.

Consider such a mood in Artaud's later writings where he describes his mental state as revealing the very essence of Being:

> It is done. I have really fallen into the Void since everything – that makes up this world – has just succeeded in making me despair.
> For one does not know that one is no longer in the world until one sees that the world has left you ...
> Now no longer existing myself, I see what exists.
> I really identified myself with that Being, that Being which has ceased to exist.
> And that Being has revealed everything to me.
> I knew it, but I could not say it, and if I can begin to say it, it is because I have left reality. (from 'New Revelations of Being', Artaud, 1988, p. 414)

As an existential mode, Anxiety precipitates a sense of the 'uncanny' (*unheimlich*) (Heidegger, 1962, p. H188) – a concept particularly germane to Artaud's condition. This uncanniness brings an experience of not feeling at home in the world anymore: the everyday world of objects in which we are normally absorbed no longer offers respite. In such a state, he comes face-to-face with his own being and possibilities. We might even read Artaud as having transcended the structures of the world altogether:

> It is a real Desperate Person who speaks to you and who has not known the happiness of being in the world until now that he has left this world, now that he is absolutely separated from it.
> The others who have died are not separated, They still turn around their dead bodies.
> I am not dead, but I am separated. (Artaud, 1988, p. 414)

The Theatre of Cruelty can be seen as an authentic 'Being-towards-death' in response to uncanniness. Both Heidegger and Artaud see death as crucial to existence. For Artaud, performance offers a key to recovering the totality of life and Being. He turns to the theatre as an art form because it offers the unrepeatable gestures and uniquely individual moments. In the ephemeral instant of performance lies a cruel death. In the moment of acting, he believes he transcends representation as he recounts in *The Theatre and its Double*:

> Let us leave textual criticism to graduate students, formal criticism to esthetes, and recognize that what has been said is not still to be said; that an expression does not have the same value twice, does not live two lives; that all words, once spoken are dead and function only at the moment when they are uttered, that a form, once it has served, cannot be used again and asks only to be replaced by another, and that the theater is the only place in the world where a gesture, once made, can never be made the same way twice. (from 'No More Masterpieces', Artaud, 1958, p. 75)

For Artaud, the theatrical gesture is an individuating moment of death or what he calls the 'implacable necessity' of cruelty. In fact, his view of this unrepeatability is beyond the structures of life and death, of incomplete existence. The singularity of the Theatre of Cruelty as beyond representation can be accounted for in phenomenological terms.

In Part II of *BT*, Heidegger shifts focus to Temporality. Dasein is constantly 'ahead of itself' and 'outside itself' because it undertakes projects and deals with the world as *possibility*. As such, Heidegger presents a reinterpretation of all the elements of world with respect to time: Dasein is its possibilities. The fact that the continuation of its own being matters for Dasein indicates the totality of the structure of the world in Care (*Sorge*). We care about our projects and continuing existence. Care is a temporal phenomenon because possibilities are always caught up in time and things are left outstanding. Dasein can direct itself towards objects that are ready-to-hand in concern (*Besorgnis*) and towards others there in-the-world in solicitude (*Fürsorge*) in anticipation of what is to come. Care shows that Dasein is always ahead-of-itself. For Heidegger, the problem of the totality of Dasein comes into view in the temporal structure of Care.

The key to this totality lies at the limit of Dasein's very existence: death. Death is also the thing that Dasein is afraid of in Anxiety: the possibility that ends all possibilities. Death is not just the transition of a living thing to a merely corporeal thing present-at-hand. The problem with death is that it never offers direct experience of itself: by the time death comes, Dasein is no longer there to experience it. Death is also a unique phenomenon in that no one else can take it on for a person: 'No one can take the Other's dying away from him' (Heidegger, 1962, p. H240). A person can die for another in the sense of sacrificing their own life, but this is not taking the death of that other away. Death is a unique existential phenomenon; to analyse it in terms of physiology or biology would only describe 'perishing', but not this existential nature of the phenomenon, even though the structures of the present-at-hand seem to be the best way of understanding it. So instead of thinking of death as a thing, Heidegger sees it as a possibility essential to life. As a phenomenon in life then, we can take up a relation to our own death as something that is certain and something that is most our *own*. Heidegger calls this mode Being-towards-death. Death is the point at which Dasein can take up no more possibilities; it is non-relational. Authentic Dasein takes up the possibilities of life in relation to the fact that choices will one day have an end. In Being-towards-death, Dasein can see itself as a whole.

Artaud constantly claims that he lacks such totality. He wants his own past and future generating from himself his own possibilities rather than have them handed over to him by the generational structure of the world.

Not only does Artaud rebel against and reject having the structures of the world, but also the temporality in which those structures are based. He takes the matter even further and describes the physical manifestation of Anxiety, taken over bodily:

> Who in the depths of certain kinds of anguish, at the bottom of certain dreams, has not known death as a shattering and marvellous sensation unlike anything else in the realm of the mind? One must have known this suction-like rise of anguish whose waves cover you and fill you to bursting as if driven by some intolerable bellows. An anguish which approaches and withdraws each time more vast, each time heavier and more swollen. It is the body itself that has reached the limit of its distension and its strength and which must nevertheless go further. It is a kind of suction cup placed on the soul, whose bitterness spreads like an acid to the furthest boundaries of perception. And the soul does not even possess the ability to burst. For this distension itself is false. Death is not satisfied so cheaply. In the physical sphere, this distension is like the reverse image of a contraction which must occupy the mind over the whole extent of the living body. (from 'Art and Death', Artaud, 1988, p. 121)

Artaud attempts to escape Temporality through the power of theatre. By reawakening mystical forces in performance, he seeks unity with himself:

> Big as a conch, it can be held in the hollow of the hand, this secret; it is thus that Tradition speaks.
> All the magic of existence will have passed into a single chest when Time has been locked away again. (from 'The Theater of Seraphim', Artaud, 1988, p. 275)

In such terms, Artaud's theatre and the plague gesture towards seeing life as a whole in the face of the violent effect of social breakdown. Surrounded by disease and impending doom, the victims of the plague are faced with the meaninglessness of their own existence and death becomes present. A radical individuation is experienced in the breakdown of world order and the regular structures of Care. Death is imminent and brings with it a physical feeling for life beyond representation. The Theatre of Cruelty does not hide behind aesthetic forms and literary traditions, but stands face-to-face with the brutality of life; it is a Being-towards-death in facing the physical, social and existential constraints of existence. By witnessing the breakdown of meaning and culture, we simultaneously apprehend the world as it is and experience ourselves as a self. For Artaud, the unrepeatability of the theatrical moment overcomes the individuation of death.

The unity of the moment of performance transcends time for Artaud, uncovering a secret language handed down in tradition but forgotten in everyday language and ways of being. Derrida would perhaps characterise this loss as the deferral of meaning, yet for Artaud it is not simply a matter of words or signification, but existence. His claim of being denied the possibility of totality or self-unity actually reveals the structure of being in time while also being a symptom of a Falling understanding of the world. Rather than simply dwell on the not-yet of existence, Artaud struggled to keep himself whole and resist falling away from himself. This feeling is most manifest in relation to his language and thought:

> I am the man who has most felt the stupefying confusion of his speech in its relations with thought. I am the man who has most accurately charted the moment of his most intimate, his most imperceptible lapses. I lose myself in my thought, actually, the way one dreams, the way one suddenly slips back into one's thought. I am the man who knows the inmost recesses of loss. (from 'The Nerve Meter', Artaud, 1988, p. 85)

Being Oneself: A Theatre of Homecoming

In his article 'Things That No One Can Say: The Unspeakable Act in Artaud's Les Cenci', Robert Vork (2013) offers a reading of Antonin Artaud's drama (more specifically, his adaptation of Shelley's play) in relation to two opposed interpretations. The first stems, on the one hand, from Jane Goodall's (1994) exposition of the 'devouring principle' of Gnostic mythology – the *mal* (evil/sickness) at the foundation of material being which establishes destruction at the heart of all creativity. All existence 'consumes to create and creates to consume', ultimately hurtling being and art towards self-cannibalistic death. On this account, Artaud's Theatre of Cruelty is (at least in principle) the embodiment of this destructive self-consuming creative force resisting all aesthetic forms and social values. On the other hand, Kimberley Jannarone (2010) offers a reading of Artaud's envisaged theatre as an exercise of power and an attempt to carry out his violent designs for mass coercion and control. *Les Cenci* is meant to bring about the same violent effect upon the audience that is depicted in the play itself – the violation of cultural values through incest carried out upon Beatrice (the protagonist) by her father (the count), the ensuing patricide, and her subsequent execution. In theory, the deindividuated audience, having experienced an assault on the senses, rejects the confining boundaries imposed by society together with the material and perceptual distinction between subject and object in the world. Goodall commends Artaud's theatre as liberation from alienating systems of control; Jannarone criticises Artaud's conception of theatre as a totalitarian gesture of violence. Vork notes that both interpretations hinge on Artaud's staging and theatrical effects as an attempt to 'carry out a radical annihilation of subjective experience' (2013, p. 310). But there is uncertainty as to whether this annihilation constitutes either resistance against the totalitarian violence or the triumph of those forces. In fact, Vork argues that both occur at once and this apparent paradox is vital to understanding Artaud's adaptation.

To think about participants in the theatrical encounter as isolated subjects and then claim that the Theatre of Cruelty deindividautes them is to fall back into a metaphysical binary. Quite the opposite is true in that Artaud's vision for performance is to attain a moment of really being oneself. His expression of alienation from the world demonstrates the limits of worldhood and Temporality. The Theatre of Cruelty can be taken seriously as metaphysics in action in so far as it is a truthful uncovering of the being that is overlooked in everyday life as a moment of dysfunction. In phenomenological terms, such a practice would:

- reawaken a sense of wonder at Being by making its incarnation in the body manifest (either through pain or pleasure);
- destroy the metaphysics of traditional philosophy and destabilise assumed concepts of morality and social behaviour;
- challenge rationality and thinking as the basis of Being;
- wrestle awareness away from a Falling understanding of the world and our absorption in Everydayness;

- undermine the dictatorship of the They through the call of authentic individuation; and
- show Anxiety as an existential mood through which Being shows itself.

On one level, Artaud hopes to return to materiality. He sees true theatre as overcoming the cognitive and intellectual understanding of humanity that was propagated especially by the contemporary fascination with psychology and talk that dominated the stage. Reducing humans to mere matter – the present-at-hand – is seemingly the opposite of what Heidegger described as authentic Dasein: resolutely projected possibility. But in his description of the mental state that the Theatre of Cruelty was supposed to combat, his Self is not a scientific object devoid of meaning but rather filled with meaning and in continuity with the world. Rather than being cut off by the uncanny, unhomely nature of the world, theatre can return the self through the flesh. Just as base metals could be converted into precious metals in alchemy, so too does Artaud think that the theatre could have a deep and real effect on its participants. He felt that this effect was inexpressible in rational discourse: for Artaud, the idea of man as a rational animal stinks of separation. The magic of theatre offers the possibility of deeper forces at play in the world to which society must become attuned. In a way, Heidegger too wanted to reawaken the open sense of mystery in the birth of philosophy in the ancient Greeks and a sense of wonder and awe that things are at all. This openness is part of the poetic appreciation of Being.

In short, both thinkers seek to smash the traditional view of subjectivity. For Heidegger this means choosing oneself and one's ownmost possibilities found in Anxiety and Being-towards-death. For Artaud, cruelty released into the theatre like a plague can purge the individual and society of its false being and replace it with force and energy. Each provides a gateway into the question of Being and an attempt to attend to the things themselves. But as we will see in the next chapter, such an approach does not give an adequate account of a solitary individual transcending time and space stranded in the materiality of the body. The theatre also offers an inquiring into Being-with-others as concretely founded in Historicality and Temporality as conceived by Brecht.

Exercises and Topics for Discussion

1. Think about a time when you *didn't* particularly feel like yourself (as we considered at the beginning of the chapter). Try to describe the experience. How did it affect your physical relationship to the world? How did the world 'break down' in its absence? When did you last feel like you were *most* like yourself? What was it like and why?
2. Describe an 'ecstatic' moment in which you experienced a sense of 'flow' – where everything seemed to 'click' and the world seemed to control your actions. It could be when you were playing sport or dancing, or even playing a video game. How does the world appear or disappear in the experience?
3. Try to think about a time when you saw a foreign cultural performance which you didn't understand. What did it make you focus your attention on? Did the materiality of the performance start to come to the fore? What do you think appealed to Artaud when he saw such a performance at the Paris Exposition? Do you think that this is just a form of colonial appropriation of the exotic?
4. Think of a moment when you were overcome by laughter, sadness, shock, or violence. How did it change your relationship to the world and those around you? Did the moment have a lasting effect on you? What was it? Watch a silent film by Charlie Chaplin or The Marx Brothers. What do you think appealed to Artaud in such works? Can you think of a contemporary comedy that has the same effect on you? What other genres or performance forms might bear traces of the Theatre of Cruelty?
5. Can you think of an example of Heidegger's Falling understanding? Are there moments where individuals simply 'take over' others' interpretations of the world? It might be in online forums, glossy magazines, the Oscars, or reality television. How does this change the behaviour of people in society? Conversely, what are some examples of situations that are in some way are about Being-towards-death?
6. Choose a text that you think embodies the Theatre of Cruelty and discuss why. (It could be one of Artaud's works, one that he suggests in his manifestos or an entirely different work.) Perform an excerpt

from it in naturalistic style. Then try the scene focussing on the materiality of the text – its sounds, rhythms, and textures. How might you employ some of the phenomenological concepts in this chapter to your interpretation? How might these elements take on metaphysical significance?

Notes

1 For a discussion of Heidegger's interpretation of Plato in relation to Artaud and consciousness, see Johnston (2004) and Johnston (2008), respectively.
2 For a useful overview of the plague, as well as other Artaudian images, see Singleton (1998).

7

Brecht's Phenomenology of Being-with-others: Authenticity and History

Philosophical Theatre for Political Change

How much money did your parents earn during the year you started school? What sorts of privileges did you have that others did not? How often do you think about how your background has affected your moral choices in life? How does your upbringing affect the way that you move down a hallway, sit on a park bench, get on a train, or hand over your money to a shopkeeper? Rather than think of your choices and actions as inevitable, is it possible that you might behave differently and make alternative choice? If we are making an artistic work, perhaps there is a duty to be honest about who we are and where we have come from. And we can do the same with the characters we present. In this chapter, we turn to an artist who asked such challenging and uncomfortable questions.

'The proof of the pudding is in the eating', director, poet, playwright, lyricist, and theorist, Bertolt Brecht liked to say.[1] For him, theatre is the pudding, the practice of social philosophy is the eating, and political change is the proof. Brecht claims that his theatre is not just about representing the world; it is precisely the place where actors and audiences can face up to possibilities of action in their own lives:

> How can [the theatre] be divorced from spiritual dope traffic and turned from a home of illusions to a home of experiences? How can the unfree,

ignorant man of our century, with his thirst for freedom and his hunger for knowledge; how can the tortured and heroic, abused and ingenious, changeable and world-changing man of this great and ghastly century obtain his own theatre which will help him to master the world and himself? (Brecht, 1964, p. 135)

Consequently, he envisages theatre as a site for staging philosophy and not merely representing the psychological and physical details of life.[2] It is well known that he was fond of quoting Marx who asserted that the point of philosophy is 'not just a matter of interpreting the world but of changing it' (originally from Marx's 'Eleventh Thesis on Feuerbach') (Brecht, 1964, p. 248). In the 1928 programme notes to his production of *In the Jungle of Cities* (*Im Dickicht der Städte*), Brecht declares, '[t]his is a world and a kind of drama where the philosopher can find his way about rather than the psychologist' (Brecht, 1964, p. 24). A year later he writes, '[a]t present it's Germany, the home of philosophy, that is leading in the large-scale development of the theatre and the drama. The theatre's future is philosophical' (Brecht, 1964, p. 24). Clearly, he advocates reuniting theatre and philosophy – those two estranged lovers – and therefore returning philosophy to the world. If Stanislavski is afraid of falling into philosophy, Brecht jumps straight in.

It is perhaps the ultimate heresy to propose any kind of equation between Brecht's practice which enlists the power of popular culture and Heidegger's rejection of the thinking of mass culture and its possession by the They-self (as discussed in Chapter 6).[3] Brecht evidently discussed plans with Walter Benjamin to start an anti-Heidegger reading group and journal despite claiming never to have read any of his philosophical works (Wizisla, 2009, p. 41). In this respect, he saw Heidegger as part of the intelligentsia and establishment against which he railed. But had he engaged with Heidegger's thought, it is possible that he would have been surprised. Neither Heidegger nor Brecht see truth as a static, unchanging entity: for both, it is an event in process. In his own way, Heidegger draws on folk traditions and language as containing an everyday wisdom and insight that can lead to insights into the nature of Being. For Heidegger, true philosophy constitutes a 'moment of vision' (*Augenblick*) – reawakening a sense of wonder at the world. The same is true of Brecht's ideal theatre: to be able to see how the world is and how it might be otherwise. Both theatre and philosophy in this sense should aim to question received notions of human subjectivity. For Brecht, theatre has the ability to disclose historical circumstance, discuss the human self that evolves through time, and attempt to see possibilities for individual and communal existence. These issues are also at the core of Heidegger's phenomenology. Brechtian acting questions traditional conceptions of history and time. Through collaboration with actors and the creative ensemble, Brecht also aims at revealing, questioning and altering social relations. In phenomenological terms, he emphasises Being-with as a fundamental concern of existence. Rather than begin with metaphysical assumptions about the nature of reality and the self, Brecht sees the act of theatre-making as a chance to examine alternative actions and choices. But far from being a detached and purely contemplative activity, he offers the actor an opportunity for applied philosophy capable of transforming society.

In what follows, I consider how various aspects of Heidegger's phenomenology are also separately explored in Brecht's writings on theatre, productions, and work with actors.[4] I will investigate Brecht's theatre theory (epic theatre, *Verfremdungseffekt* and *gestus*) as a call to Authenticity in performance (moving away from a passive self-given from the world towards a self-chosen from the possibilities for action). Through examples from his practice and productions I will explore how Heidegger's themes of Historicality, Temporality, Duration, the Self and Totality are useful for thinking about epic theatre. These topics are taken primarily from *BT*, Division II, Part V, 'Temporality and Historicality' (Heidegger, 1962, p. H372ff). Ultimately, Brecht seeks to create theatre that describes, analyses, and alters the choices we make as a society. I suggest that this is nothing short of a call to authentic Being-with one another.[5]

Authenticity and Rehearsal as Uncovering Truth

Brecht's theatrical revolution was aimed at the dominant set of stage conventions he called 'Aristotelian drama' – illusionistic representation that emphasises the environment's impact on the actions and choices of the individual. For Brecht, Aristotelian drama displays individual choices as inevitable.[6] It administers a theatrical anaesthetic that dulls the senses and seeks to hide the fact of its own construction, reinforced by Richard Wagner's darkened auditorium in 1869 with the aim of submerging the audience into a dream. Half a century later, Brecht wanted to reawaken the audience from this aesthetic slumber and draw attention to the real choices of social existence.

Let's review for a moment. As we have seen, in *BT* Heidegger argues that we have long since forgotten how to ask the question of Being. The only way that we can approach this question phenomenologically is to inquire into the being of that thing which is closest and most mine: Dasein. Dasein is never a thing that can be separated from the world; it is most fundamentally its own *possibilities*. One way to think about this statement is to ask the question, 'who is the real you: your former self at two, twelve, twenty-four, or eighty-six?' There is no completed version of who you are until you have reached your end – at which point you are no longer there. For this reason, Heidegger comes to the conclusion that Dasein is essentially founded in the temporal structure of the world – what is not yet, but might be (Heidegger, 1962, pp. H334–71). At the same time, Dasein is thrown into the world from the past; Dasein's own possibilities are always already handed over beforehand. Dasein is essentially a 'nothing' in its own being apart from Being-in-the-world. Dasein *is* nothing in and of itself, other than the world into which it has been thrown. But this does not lead to a deterministic view of the human subject as we will see. Heidegger suggests by choosing itself from these possibilities with a view that its time will soon come to an end, Dasein takes on an authentic mode of being.

Authenticity (*Eigentlichkeit*) is a problematic term in *BT* since it seemingly indicates a value judgement about Dasein's mode of existing: being authentic versus being inauthentic. On the surface, Heidegger privileges the former over the later (although he denied that this was the case). The term comes from the root *eigen* which means 'to have' or 'to possess' (Inwood, 1999, p. 22). *Eigentlich* can be translated as 'really' or 'actually'. Consequently, Authenticity has the sense of Dasein really being itself or something of its own. Most of the time, we are presumably inauthentic in our everyday attitude of engagement with the world and it is not clear that one could possibly grasp the question of existence and

Being-towards-death at every moment. In other words, we become lost in our preoccupations in the world – as in the work of a carpenter, a doctor, a teacher, or a banker, the profession takes over and the individual fades into the background (Inwood, 1999, p. 24). In this mode, there is nothing that individuates Dasein as itself. We forget the fact that our life will come to an end at some point and that this is what ultimately gives each moment meaning.

But authentic Dasein seizes responsibility for its own actions and finite existence by grasping the meaning of that endpoint at each moment and stands resolute in its actions and choices. Read together with his entanglement with Nazism, Authenticity may also hint at a morally dubious ethics of Being that could be exploited for suspect political ends – the thought that certain types of people are not willing to face their own situation in a truthful way (as Heidegger suggested of Jewish people).[7] Such concerns are apparent when Heidegger describes the 'appropriating event' (*Ereignis*) as the 'destining' of man for *Eigen-tum* of Being and selfhood as the 'ownership' of essence. Heidegger's later writings seem to argue that Authenticity is only necessary for those laying the ground for the question of Being – in other words, for philosophers. But I will argue that the term Authenticity can be helpful in understanding Brecht's theatre as a radical questioning of one's freedom and choices.[8]

In Heideggerian language, Brecht's theatrical process scrutinises Care as a fundamental condition for human existence. Care constitutes the structure of our relation to the world and our dealings with it – the world *matters*. Both Heidegger and Brecht understand the world as the source of our possibilities and potentiality for being and action. Dasein is not simple materiality that can be investigated by the gaze of the physical sciences. It always exists in a specific context, invested in projects, yet with a unique capability of understanding the world. In this sense, Care does not relate to our emotional response to the world and others as human beings (as in 'I care about you'). Care pertains to Dasein's total organism: it constitutes the fact that there is something at stake when we exist and take action in the world. By exploring issues such as the dehumanising effects of war, science, blind faith in economic relations, crime and, ultimately, death, Brecht reveals the conditions of Dasein's Being-with by investigating the outcomes of choice and action for both the individual and society. But Dasein's relationship of Care towards the world is not static. It is thoroughly within time and within history – a thought that is never forgotten in Brecht's theatre.

Having looked back over these key terms from Heidegger, we can see how the consequences of human actions towards one another organise the focus of Brecht's rehearsal process. His method of performance-preparation typically focusses on the choices of characters in their social context that may present no easy solution. In this sense, the process focusses on analysing each character's ethical choices in relation to their story as a whole. The actor's task (in phenomenological terms) is to show when those characters fall into inauthenticity. Do they shy away from taking responsibility for their own circumstances and see them for what they are? Do they grasp that situation and take action accordingly, or turn their back and console themselves with a false consolation and rationalisation? The answers are not without contradiction.

We can see this approach of questioning by examining Brecht's typical way of working on a text with an ensemble or company (Brecht, 1964, pp. 240–46). The general schema for rehearsal might include an initial introduction to the text outlining its central oppositions. During the first reading, the actors interrupt the flow of action when they felt that there was a particular nodal point or change in the scene – readers and listeners are encouraged to shout out 'stop' and interrupt the flow of action. The cast might also perform a naive reading of the play (with no allocation of parts yet, simply changing reader with each new speaker). The company would then discuss the play, its specific circumstances, and its historical, political, social, moral and aesthetic aspects. In anticipation of such an investigation, Brecht also wrote defamiliarising devices into the play text itself through jumping and discontinuous scenes, songs to break up the action, and moments of direct address to the audience. All of these effects are intended to bring the actions and decisions of characters into stark view for the purposes of inciting action for change in the viewer.

Rather than come with a prepared plan, the designer works in parallel with the actors' preparation, letting choices emerge from the process itself rather than be imposed before. From here provisional casting is carried out (in the *Lehrstücke* actors would change rolls even in performance). The actors are encouraged to remember their initial reactions to the play and hold on to the ways they were astounded at the contradictions of the story and actions within it. With this 'super-task' in mind (to borrow Stanislavski's terminology), the actors then work on physical actions, status, and choices of their character (Hurwicz in Witt, 1975, p. 132). Throughout rehearsals, the players are meant to demonstrate their roles and show how the particular actions were never inevitable. The blocking of action or staging arises from this process and deep consideration given to the spatial aspects of the production. Movement is never simply for its own sake, for instance, and each action is always carried out for a purpose. Straight lines are avoided in placing actors on stage, and the spatial blocking tends towards unequal groupings demonstrating social relations. This is meant to emphasise the overall message of the scene together with the significance of character choices at each point.

Full run-throughs would begin at a specified point in rehearsals once the overall shape of the text had been worked out. Each part of the play is meant to relate to the whole as a series of causes and effects. A tempo for the performance is found in these runs with the element of costumes added. Before the performance, speed-runs help to consolidate what each actor is doing when. These are to be carried out with accuracy and clear articulation. Then the results might be recorded and photographed for the *Modellbuch*. Even after opening night, Brecht would give notes and make small changes to both the acting and the text. Importantly, however, the whole process and performance was supposed to be invested with a sense of fun and humour. Of course this process continued to evolve and adapt throughout his career and as Robert Leach points out, many aspects of his process were formalised in the Berliner ensemble model after his death (Brecht, 1964, pp. 240–46 and Leach, 2004, p. 122).

It is not such a stretch to think about Brecht's work with actors in relation to phenomenology given his attention of 'possibilities'. Throughout each stage of preparing for production, the text is never considered holy and unchangeable but always subject to constant revision. Brecht's process nurtures a rejection of the idea that there is ever a final meaning produced either in the world or on stage. This is precisely because of the temporal nature of human existence – and in a way, the work of art shares many characteristics of Dasein's existence – the play becomes a living breathing organism with similarities to our own lives. Brecht considers no individual performance or moment in rehearsal as final, but only ever as *process*. This structure of the 'not-yet' mirrors Heidegger's conception of Dasein which is always essentially incomplete as there is always another moment and choice still to come. Dasein is essential not itself because Being is caught up in what is still yet to come. Brecht would frequently alter lines only to change his mind again the next day – he would facetiously chastise himself in rehearsal asking the actors 'what idiot wrote this?' (Fuegi, 1987, p. 87). Accordingly, he is more concerned with what actually works on stage and is always willing to revise each choice in rehearsal as provisional.

Despite his published criticism and theory, Brecht very rarely mentioned his theoretical writings in rehearsal. Through the collective effort of the theatre ensemble, the Brechtian rehearsal room is transformed into a laboratory in which to work through the possibilities of performance:

> Brecht used his theatre as a laboratory, to experiment with plays and players. Human behaviour, human attitudes, human weaknesses – everything was explored and investigated, to be exposed finally to a public which often enough refused to recognize its image in this very clear, but sometimes perhaps too well-framed, mirror ... For him, the stage was a model of the world – the world we all have to live in. (Weber, 1967, p. 107)

Nevertheless, this is not a laboratory with the reductive scientific gaze of what Heidegger called metaphysics. Brecht doesn't treat people as objects but rather models capable of change (although there may be contradictions in his actual treatment of people in life). Storytelling with a sense of truth is central to this collaboration with the ensemble together with deriving pleasure from the learning process. Truthfulness here is relative to the capacity of the audience to recognise the world as it is through dramatic presentation. Contrary to Brecht's own hope for an atmosphere of fun and playfulness is often the first casualty of war in many classroom productions of his plays. The actor is no mere pawn for the dictatorial director, but rather a fellow philosopher in search of truth in performance. Just as Stanislavski's theatrical truth is not a truth of correspondence to objective reality, so too is Brecht's a truth of discovery through empirical observation. The reality of the actor's own attitudes and social circumstances are never forgotten. I suggest that such a discovery in the theatre-laboratory is the moment of disclosure of Being; but it is a revelation based in collaborative meaning, not an internal source of truth.

In rehearsal Brecht explores a poetic and physical sociology of the stage. This emphasis on social practice parallels Stanislavski's emphasis on action and points towards theatre as a practical and embodied hermeneutic process. However, the concern is not primarily with the psychology or soul of the character. He wants his actors to seek out observed behaviours as they contribute to the overall task of telling the story and thus show their political significance. Whereas he invites the actors to break the mimetic tendency in rehearsal, his own intervening is not so interrupting. His process is less cold artifice than developing a 'feel' for truth:

> During rehearsals Bertolt Brecht sits in the auditorium. His work as a director is unobtrusive. When he intervenes it is almost unnoticeable and always in the 'direction of flow'. He never interrupts, not even with suggestions for improvement. You do not get the impression that he wants to get the actors to 'present some of his ideas'; they are not his instruments.
> Instead he searches, together with the actors, for the story which the play tells, and helps each actor to find his strength. His work with the actors may be compared to the efforts of a child to direct straws with a twig from a puddle into the river itself, so that they may float. (from '*Theaterarbeit*, 1952', in Witt, 1975, p. 126)

This practice requires actors to contemplate the way that the world presents itself to experience by observing their own experiences closely (and the director's task is to open up such a discovery).

But Brecht is wary of the power of performance to manipulate thought and feeling in the audience. He suggests that art cultivating untruth and propaganda functions like a tranquilising drug to the masses (an effect that parallels Heidegger's conception of the Falling understanding of Everydayness). Marx famously claimed that religion is the opiate of the masses but Brecht seems to suggest that such blind and unquestioned religiosity extends to the situation of the theatre spectator. He yearns for a new form of theatre that allows people to see themselves as they are, together with contradictions in their own existence, and take action in their own lives. The Brechtian actor must therefore critically engage with and show these philosophical contradictions on stage by highlighting the choices of the character and showing that things might have been otherwise. This has a corollary in Heidegger's conception of Falling understanding of the world in which Being conceals itself.

The process constantly tests various choices for action by emphasising how identity changes over time. Theatre must also maintain a willingness to adapt and change according to the world. In his exercise 'not ... but', actors would first perform the scene as it didn't happen (prefaced with the statement 'not') and then proceed with the scene as written (saying 'but' before going on and playing it). This effect of showing alternatives was intended to be carried through to performance before an audience (Brecht, 1964, p. 137). This technique is about displaying potentiality – a theatrical investigation of Dasein as 'thrown subject' projecting itself onto its future as a set of possibilities.

In his diaries kept as an assistant director at the Berliner Ensemble, Hans Bunge notes Brecht's approach to rehearsal in his detailed notebook for *The Caucasian Chalk Circle*, an adaptation of a fourteenth-century Chinese play:

> All the inter-relationships were checked out, changed, holes filled, new ideas and changes introduced wherever he had second thoughts. His work as a director is dialectics made visible. (Fuegi, 1987, p. 149)

Brecht is renowned for this attention to detail in rehearsal with actors that Bunge identifies as dialectics. In a sense, dialectics here can be compared to the phenomenological call for returning to the things themselves – here in the process of meaning-making. For example, in the same production, he rehearsed for hours how Grusha, a peasant girl who discovers a child abandoned by the Governor's wife, should pick up a baby, and how to make an entrance onto the stage through a door. In order for actors to understand their parts, he would get them to translate the words into their own dialect. He devised exercises for actors to practice such as folding linen, attitudes of smoking, and singing songs (Brecht, 1964, p. 129). This attention to detail is not for naturalistic depiction, however, but to investigate the social relations between people involved. These details also highlight Everydayness and involved activity as revealing something deeper about the individuals represented than might initially be apparent. The actions reveal something about modes of Being-with.

Rather than emphasise a positivist conception of truth, this type of theatre takes on a perspectival perception of the world replete with vested interests and involvements. In Brecht's famous exercise 'The Street Scene' (1964, pp. 121–29) actors are invited to provide alternative perspectives on the event of an incident on a street corner. Rather than detached observers, each performer's recounting of the scene comments on the actions of those involved, acts some bits out to demonstrate and forms an opinion. In this case, acting is a demonstration of the role rather than becoming a character – as one might act out the events of a tragic accident and step back to comment on them. For this reason, Brecht was quite happy to view the work of untrained actors as epic in their capacity to present observed behaviour – the vividness of a witness's account is exactly the combination of demonstrating and commentary that he was after.[9] Again, the need for observation is key to the performer's success. Like Stanislavski, Brecht indicated that his actors should always be on the lookout for material that might be useful in performance by observing their own lived experience (Brecht, 1961, p. 17).

In addition to weighing up and demonstrating social choices in a context of the real and fictional world as contingent, the actor's role in Brecht's theatre is about bringing the *connectedness* of the world into view. As we have seen, Being-in-the-world hits us all at once and we come to know it through our involved activities, tasks, and projects. In an aesthetic sense, Brecht employs juxtaposed elements of production such as music, movement, gestures, speech, mise en scène to impart a disjointed perspective. In 'The Modern Theatre is the Epic Theatre' he argues contemporary theatre should provoke rational judgements about the fictional situation while at the same time the audience should never lose sight of their own social reality – in this case, the apparatus of the theatre (Brecht, 1950, p. 33ff). Staging, set design, costumes, music, and acting combine as a totality – not because of the essential unity of those elements, but because of the theatre itself draws their Being to attention.

Unlike Wagner's artistic aspirations for the *Gesamtkunstwerk*, where each element is meant to add to the unity of the whole, in epic theatre Brecht forces each element into productive conflict. As I will discuss further later in this chapter, Brecht's famous *Verfremdungseffekt* is intended to bring these elements of the world under scrutiny. By interrupting the illusion of reality, each of the elements of the world becomes significant and available for analysis. So, elements such as acting style (telling the story rather than becoming the character), set design (aimed at interrupting realistic depiction), the half curtain (so that the audience can see the mechanisms of the stage operate), all show up as elements of the world because of their disconnectedness and resistance to absorption on the part of the viewer. A sense of the whole comes into view in Brecht's productions when the audience member forms a judgement about the world only after the elements of that world have been brought to light. The same is true of his approach to acting: rather than show the unity of a character and their mental processes, he wanted actors to show the contradictions, disunities, breaks, and the irrational in their behaviour. Accordingly, the process constitutes stepping out of the natural attitude or involved Care structure of Everydayness (as discussed in the next section).

Brecht is unwavering in asserting that form and content are inseparable in theatre. So if the aim is to emphasise the contradictions of existence, the artistic form must also contain contractions. In a short reflection on theatre, 'Last Stage: Oedipus', Brecht claims that:

> [c]oncern with subject and concern with form are complementary. Seen from inside the theatre it appears that progress in theatrical technique is only progress when it helps to realize the material; and the same with progress in play writing. (Brecht, 1964, p. 24)

Rather than see theatre as radically separated from life, he sees performance as an opportunity for illuminating the world itself: 'By creating this distinction between the world and yourselves/You banish yourselves from the world' (1961, p. 7). The separation between life and art parallels a metaphysical separation between self and world. In contrast, the Brechtian actor is never separated from reality, but always engaged with it:

> As for the world portrayed there [in the theatre], the world from which slices are cut in order to produce these moods and movements of the emotions, its appearance is such, produced from such slight and wretched stuff

as a few pieces of cardboard, a little miming, a bit of text, that one has to admire the theatre folk who, with so feeble a reflection of the real world, can move the feelings of their audience so much more strongly than does the real world itself. (Brecht, 1964, p. 187)

We can compare this view with Heidegger on Authenticity as a truthful engagement with the world as it has been handed over to us, with a restricted set of choices from which we can project our future self:

> But fully comprehending the specificity of that moment would involve placing it in a context wider than the immediate past and future. It would mean seeing it as the point to which one's life has led, and from which the remainder of one's life will acquire a specific orientation. (Mulhall, 2005, p. 155)

Such an interpretation of the term is suggestive of Brecht's own process. Every moment of decision for each character is seen as a point to which their life has led at that moment and which will impact on their life from thereon in. Of course, Brecht wants the actors demonstrating those choices and the audiences watching them to ask the same questions about their own decisions and circumstances. Having painted the broad picture of Brecht as phenomenologist, we now turn to look more closely at some of the technical terms of his dramatic theory in relation to acting that display a phenomenological attitude to the world.

Epic Theatre and Resoluteness

Brecht agrees that individuals and their world are never separate from others there in the world dwelling alongside them. As we saw in the last chapter, in fact, for the most part the Others are an essential part of Desein as it is involved in the world and forgetful of itself, its own being, and its ownmost possibilities (Heidegger, 1962, p. H125). But rather than being dragged along by the interpretation of the They – lacking any will or choice – Brecht thinks that theatre represents a unique opportunity to collectively reconsider our relation to others and call our actions into question. In this type of theatre, Dasein has the possibility of gaining itself back from simply being absorbed in the world, by authentically choosing its ownmost possibilities and becoming what it really *is*. Such a movement is authentic 'resoluteness' as the projection of possibilities:

> Resoluteness, as *authentic Being-one's Self*, does not detach Dasein from its world, nor does it isolate it so that it becomes a free-floating 'I'. And how should it, when resoluteness as authentic disclosedness, is *authentically* nothing else than *Being-in-the-world*? Resoluteness brings the Self right into its current concernful Being-alongside what is ready to hand, and pushes it into solicitous Being with Others. (Heidegger, 1962, p. H298)

In such a grasping of its own possibilities, Dasein finds itself in the world alongside Others there in the world with the same kind of being as itself. Authentic existence is caring about those Others there with us and working together for a common goal rather than in rivalry and mistrust (Heidegger, 1962, p. H122). Authenticity is thus bound up in *how* and *who* Dasein is. This mode of being is where Dasein perceives its own possible futures and takes them over to itself. Resolute Authenticity is an existential way of *seeing*. It is not satisfied with a passive interpretation of 'I' handed over by the world but rather performs a revisionary taking-hold-of-self as possibilities for being – as an authentic Self (Heidegger, 1962, p. H324). Heidegger suggests that resoluteness is not specifically to do with everyday situations and contexts (that he calls 'factical' life). This helps to solve the problem that we should be fully mindful of the gravity of our existential fate at all times. Instead, it is a broader disposition that informs individual actions and choices. One might also say the same of actors: their rehearsal, research, and preparation is not always explicitly at the front of their mind in performance, but rather informs their choices in the moment of performance.

As we have said, the role of the Brechtian actor is to demonstrate and comment upon society while challenging the audience members to change the world:

> The epic theatre is chiefly interested in the attitudes which people adopt towards one another, wherever they are socio-historically significant (typical). It works out scenes where people adopt attitudes of such sort

that the social laws under which they are acting spring into sight. For that we need to find workable definitions: that is to say, such definitions of the relevant processes as can be used in order to intervene in the processes themselves. The concern of the epic theatre is thus eminently practical. Human behaviour is shown as alterable; man himself as dependent on certain political and economic factors and at the same time as capable of altering them. (Brecht, 1964, p. 86)

For Brecht, much dramatic theatre provides a preinterpreted, concealing experience (which he saw as mixed up with capitalist ideology). It is characterised by linear plot development, encourages the spectator to absorb plays passively and provides a view of the human being as a fixed, unalterable entity determined by fate. Epic theatre, on the other hand, emphasises its own constructedness. It is characterised by nonlinear narrative, presents a picture of the world in flux and invites spectators to form judgements about the world (Brecht, 1964, p. 37). In epic theatre, reasoned thought and critical distance are favoured over emotion and immersion. Such a performance style also aims to reject empathy (identification with the characters and emotional involvement on the part of the audience) as the basis of theatre. Brecht challenges Aristotle's unities of time, place, plot, and character and hoped to provide an alternative purpose to his productions as *catharsis* (purging of negative emotions). In short, he hopes to revive theatre by actively engaging audiences, forcing them into an opinion, and challenging them into action in the world by dragging theatre out of the auditorium and into the streets. Although the theory of epic theatre has formal recommendations, Brecht's process of performance is always guided by this practical concern. One of his foremost aims is to gain and communicate an understanding of the historical age in which he was living (Brecht, 1964, p. 190).

The process takes on a philosophical and critical mode of thinking, as Brechtian actors challenge the conditions of their own individual and social construction. It is of note that the term 'epic theatre' was already in use by the time Brecht applied it to his own practice. Contemporaries such as Erwin Piscator (1893–1966) and German agitprop theatre groups had previously evoked the term 'epic'. Traditionally, the epic form deals with larger-than-life heroic characters, singing the praise of their deeds, speech both narrated and in indirect speech, spanning a grand scale of time and locations and somewhat tangential plot lines. Brecht took on some of these characteristics while leaving others behind. The most notable shift in this new employment of the term 'epic' (by Brecht and his contemporaries) was that it did not deal with larger than life heroes, but rather regular people caught up in exceptional circumstances and forced to act from necessity because of the oppressive social structures around them. Illusionistic theatre, according to Brecht, covered up these structures to the point that he felt any theatre that did not revolt against the status quo was an implicit support for it (Brecht, 1964, p. 196). In this sense, Brecht considers himself a proponent of realism in contrast to theatre that constructs an illusory representation of the world on stage. He wants actors to depict believable and contestable social decisions.

By rejecting the so-called Aristotelian understanding of drama, Brecht emphasises *performance* over the text. Aristotle posits that the actual production of a play is the least important element of its essence. In a sense, Brecht's position is a fundamental revolution against the formalist tradition of literary criticism (and also why Brecht has been considered so important for the discipline of performance studies with his emphasis on the performative act itself).[10] So rather than concentrate on theoretical principles he engaged actors and audiences through activity and demonstration. As mentioned, when communicating with actors he rarely used the theoretical terminology for which he has become so famous.[11]

The task of this kind of theatre is to expose social reality in all its ugliness. Instead of being detached from the concerns of everyday life, Brecht hoped that performers would resist fleeing from the world as a They-self towards an unstated, reassuring, illusory reality (in Heidegger's terms). Furthermore, he hoped to expose that reality (what is called 'false consciousness' in Marxist language). Rather than construct a unified picture of the world as a stable subject, Brecht's actors were faced with contradictions, the fragmentary and episodic nature of life as opposed to the smooth narrative offered in the well-made-play. As we have seen, he employs a range of technical means to achieve such an exposure, including the use of a spare stage, minimal lighting, the half curtain, tableaux and an acting style of 'showing'. The goal to all of these effects was to attain the analytical perspective in the audience's consideration of the social problems presented. Brecht is often placed in opposition to both Aristotle and Stanislavski in that he rejects an emphasis on both empathy (in Aristotle) and psychology (in Stanislavski). Nevertheless, especially later in his career, Brecht acknowledged the usefulness of emotion at some points in a production and the importance of a naturalness of acting style.[12] And after all, Brecht was interested in what was useful and successful in the art of acting rather than dogmatically implementing formal devices. In this sense, performance for Brecht is not solely about rationality *per se* but the conditions for the possibility of social existence.

In addition to employing formal techniques, epic theatre is meant to take on new subjects appropriate to the modern age (Brecht 1964, pp. 29, 30; 183ff). In this sense, Brecht seeks a realism not steeped in visual *verisimilitude*, but taking on a new social subject matter characteristic of realism (Brecht, 1964, p. 112). For Brecht, the stale rehashing of past classics was no longer viable. If the theatre is to stage a new meaning relevant to contemporary social concerns, it would have to reach for new forms suited to those concerns. He argues that the rise of market capitalism and growing importance of the scientific method have also brought about a considerable change to the social structure of human societies. Technological innovations, the growing domain of human knowledge, and control over the environment and new developments in the understanding of human culture (namely Marxism) all contributed to significant upheavals in the way that humans relate towards each other (Brecht, 1964, p. 183). Brecht's epic theatre is therefore an attempt to analyse, evaluate and decide upon future action impacting upon how we live together. Mere empathy with the characters on the stage is not enough to stimulate such an attitude to the events presented. For Brecht, character-driven theatre merely supports the playwright's point of view and offers no alternatives for action to the audience. He wants to challenge audiences to think of how things might be different and then take action in their own life based on the experience. But rather than offering the solution to the problems demonstrated, he asks his actors to engage with everyday life where choices are not so clear-cut and at times, and provide answers that pull in different directions.

Brecht later moved away from the term 'epic' and substituted it for 'dialectical theatre'.[13] This emphasised the constantly changing, eternally incomplete nature of the twin artistic and political roles of theatre practice. Later he describes his practice as a philosophical folk-theatre expressing both the philosophical and culturally engaged sides of theatre-making (Brooker in Thomson and Sacks, 1994, p. 191). Rather than settle on a final technique and subject matter, Brecht saw theatre as deeply intertwined with society's needs and requiring development along with society rather than becoming frozen at any point (which Peter Brook [1968, p. 9] later called 'deadly theatre').

The epic actor as philosopher on this account takes a critical stance required by the audience to demonstrate the events and story. In Heidegger's terms, rather than simply being *involved* in the world, the actor and audience member take the attitude of considering the meaning of Being. Moreover, the social, historical and temporal conditions for such a critical examination are also placed under scrutiny. Actors and audience members are supposedly asked to bring their own opinions and judgements under consideration. In the same way, Heidegger realises that to investigate Being, one needs to investigate the entity that is, namely, Dasein. Dasein is for the most part overlooked, taken for granted, misunderstood, or seen as self-evident. Both Heidegger and Brecht bring self-evidence into question, especially in relation to the human subject. This thought will be considered further later in this chapter in considering Brecht's representation of the subjectivity in his productions.

With such intersections between Brecht and Heidegger in mind, it is possible to think about epic acting as the theatrical embodiment of Authenticity with the goal of resolutely winning one's Self back from the world. Rather than succumb to the narcotic illusion of bourgeois theatre (and politics) – parallel to the interpretation of the They handed over by the world – epic theatre practice faces life concretely as thrown possibilities for existence. For the Brechtian actor, Dasein is not simply handed over by the world but has the opportunity to seize itself resolutely in the possibilities that are its very own. But these possibilities are not without paradox. Contradiction is part of the temporal structure of making decisions, facing situations and enacting choices that is always intrinsically incomplete and in process. In his rejection of the tragic inevitability of fate, Brecht firmly presents a model of self and world that is changeable and capable of adopting an attitude in which it can understand itself as such.

Der Verfremdungseffekt and Showing the Things Themselves

And so we come to one of the most commonly misconstrued terms in Brecht's theoretical arsenal. As discussed earlier, epic theatre rejects naturalistic representation and moves towards an attitude of critical observation and engagement in the audience and the actors. This stance is not restricted to acting style. Brecht used the term *Verfremdungseffekt* to describe the result of the overall presentation too. By stepping back from what is obvious and self-evident in an object of analysis, the observer sees the object in a new light and becomes aware of aspects of that thing which are for the most part overlooked in involved activity. This is true of both the phenomenological attitude and the aims of epic acting. Both offer a return to the things themselves.

Brecht employs the term *Verfremdung* as a kind of seeing with the actions, events, and choices portrayed new eyes. The audience is meant to be 'alienated', 'defamiliarised' or 'distanced' from identification, traditional narrative form, and passive mode of understanding.[14] It is important to remember that the sense of alienation here is not in becoming detached from the action so as not to be able to understand it; the opposite is true. As such, the mere employment of techniques does not constitute epic theatre. Not only should we see the world with fresh eyes, but also question why it is the way it is. The goal of the theatre-maker in this sense is to provoke both analysis and social change in the audience rather than be submerged in the illusion.

The term 'alienation' might also cause some confusion in that it differs from both Marx's notion of the alienation of workers from their labour and the Russian formalist 'defamiliarisation' as an aesthetic concept (Brooker in Thomson and Sacks, 1994, pp. 192, 193). Brecht is interested in uncovering social relations and assisting in the ideological struggle against oppression rather than covering it up. Rather than a formalist technique of estrangement (*ostrannenie* in Russian), Brecht wants his actors to make the events look unfamiliar and to incite the response that things don't have to be this way (Brecht, 1964, p. 137). In other words, the *Verfremdungseffekt* is meant to reveal the dialectical progression of social change but one which is inherently unfinished, and requiring action on the part of the audience in order to create change.

Verfremdung refers to a wide range of phenomena in theatre production. Brecht's description of acting style in 'The Street Scene', for instance, is one of demonstration rather than becoming the character – an estrangement from psychology and empathy as conventional approaches to theatre (Brecht, 1964, pp. 121–29). Inspired by Mei Lan-Fang from the Peking Opera, Brecht admired many aspects of what he saw from this foreign style.[15] In his production of *The Mother* (1932), for example, Brecht used a sparse set and projected images onto a canvas. Many distanciation effects are written into Brecht's texts themselves, in the fragmented narrative, particular turns of phrase, the use of songs. Other examples are in the mise en scène: the half-raised curtain, exaggerated costumes, the stylised backdrop painting.[16] The difficulty of pinpointing *Verfremdung* is that it is always culturally and historically relative (Brecht, 1964, p. 201). What one audience sees as strange, another sees as natural. As a result, many of Brecht's techniques have become commonplace today and arguably less effective (Leach, 2004, p. 145). At the core of the technique is the call for social change, revealing current social relations and the fact that the world is still in need of social change.

On the face of it, Brecht's *Verfremdungseffekt* bears a striking resemblance to a description of phenomenological reduction (Husserl's terminology) or the disclosing, clearing space of Dasein (Heidegger's terminology) outside of philosophical discourse. Brecht writes:

> The achievement of the [*Verfremdungseffekt*] constitutes something utterly ordinary, recurrent; it is just a widely practised way of drawing one's own or someone's attention to a thing, and it can be seen in education as also in business conferences of one sort or another. The [*Verfremdungseffekt*] consists in turning the object of which one is to be made aware, to which one's attention is to be drawn from something ordinary, familiar, immediately accessible, into something peculiar, striking and unexpected. What is obvious is in a certain sense made incomprehensible, but this is only in order that it may then be made all the easier to comprehend. Before familiarity can turn into awareness the familiar must be stripped of its inconspicuousness; we must give up assuming that the object in

question needs no explanation. However frequently recurrent, modest, vulgar it may be it will now be labelled as something unusual. (Brecht, 1964, p. 144)

In *BT*, Heidegger describes a corresponding notion of drawing one's attention and awareness to the being of an object is. Ultimately, Heidegger attempts to approach the meaning of Being in general. But in drawing such interest to the being of an entity, that thing becomes strange, unfamiliar or uncanny (*unheimlich*) in Heidegger's terms.

Along the way, the actor is aided by Brecht's writing in that he builds distanciation techniques into the story itself. The interruption of time in epic theatre is demonstrated in *The Caucasian Chalk Circle* (Brecht, 1965a).[17] The play begins with a prologue: two groups of Soviet collective farmers meet to settle a dispute over land ownership in a fertile valley. The main action is a parable told to the disputing farmers and traces the story of Grusha, a servant girl. Grusha takes possession of a baby left behind by the Governor's wife when a town in Georgia is overthrown by revolution. The action jumps back to follow the story of Azdak, the village fool who is appointed judge after the revolution. In the final scene, Azdak settles a dispute when the Governor's wife returns to lay claim to the child that Grusha has come to love. Azdak settles the ownership of the child by placing it in a circle he has drawn on the ground. He says that the real mother will be the one to wrench the child out. Because of her love for the boy, Grusha releases the boy's hand. In the end, the competition is revealed as a test when Azdak declares Grusha's love to be shown and gives her possession of the child.

Temporal *Verfremdung* is evident throughout *The Caucasian Chalk Circle* as actors depict a series of ethical and social dilemmas that the protagonist faces. The framing of the parable told to the Soviet farmers helps to heighten the ability for criticism of the events presented. In a sense, the device is similar to that of a Greek chorus which doubles as both spectator and commentator. Instead of providing an interpretation of the events, however, Brecht leaves it open for the audience to decide and judge the action of the play. Through presenting the events in this way, he is hoping to show that Grusha's tribulations are not just a story, but have real ramifications and relevance to life – both of the Soviet farmers and of the audience. By use of this framed parable, the theatrical time and real time are melted into one. Brecht makes a break from unity in the fiction, allowing the audience to see how Temporality shapes Grusha's actions; the unravelling of events mirror her own turbulent perspective of time.

Distanciation is not only relevant to individual sign systems individually, such as music and gesture; it also operates as a mode of contrast across sign systems. For instance, the actor can only be understood in relation to other elements of the production. We could think about the way that music is a crucial means by which Brecht interrupts the action of the play and the audience's submersion into the time of the story. By taking a step back from everyday absorption in the world and even what he calls Aristotelian dramatic absorption in the story, Brecht hopes to give his audience a critical awareness of the events unfolding. And rather than support the action in a scene, Brecht wanted music to disrupt the audience's illusion:

> [I]n *The Caucasian Chalk Circle* the singer, by using a chilly and unemotional way of singing to describe a servant girl's rescue of the child as it is mimed on stage, makes evident the terror of a period in which motherly instincts can become a suicidal weakness. Thus music can make its point in a number of ways and with full independence, and can react in its own manner to the subjects dealt with; at the same time it can also quite simply help to lend variety to the entertainment. (Brecht, 1964, p. 203)

Verfremdung is encouraged by Brecht's exercise of having actors narrate their character together with the events and behaviours that they are depicting.[18] The audience is meant to take a detached, rational and scientific consideration of those events put forward, yet paradoxically, they are also meant to be invested in the outcome like spectators at a boxing match (Brecht, 1964, pp. 6–9; 44). The self-reflective nature of such a technique also shares the phenomenological concern with the observer. For Heidegger, any understanding of being must take into account the Being conducting the investigation. In Brecht's theatre both the actor and the audience are supposed to be conscious of their own contingent perspective. But *Verfremdung* is not merely supposed to strike the viewer as strange but also startling, creating a sense of astonishment and evoking curiosity and consideration as to how things might be different. The laws of nature are revealed as astounding and more importantly, human behaviour as capable of change (Brecht, 1964, p. 68).

It might be a bold claim to make, but I suggest that the *Verfremdungseffekt* is a theatrical version of the process of phenomenological reduction in Husserl's terminology or a return to the things themselves because it involves an attitude detached from regular involvement in the world. Of course, no observer can ever get back to the thing in itself if by that we mean an objective God's eye view of the world. Human perspective always brings with it a fore-conception through which it interprets the world (Heidegger, 1962, p. H150ff). Brecht's point is not to substitute one view of a stable reality (the ideology of false consciousness) with another – his own revolutionary agenda. The common point is in questioning: a mode of critical examination that is not available in everyday involved activity. For Brecht, illusionistic theatre which relies on the passive reception of ideas in the audience overlooks the possibility of change as does Heidegger's Dasein in Everydayness.

Gestus and Being-with-others

In *BT*, Heidegger emphasises the fact that our world is constituted by a relationship with Others there with us. The world is not made up just of stones, trees, tools and so on, we exist in a way that is always in relation to other people with the same type of being as ourselves – *Mitsein*. The way that we comport ourselves to others is 'Solicitude' (*Fürsorge*) (1962, p. H121). We can take up an authentic or inauthentic understanding of others. The former is to recognise others as having the same type of being as ourselves. The latter is to treat others as mere objects, or faceless numbers (1962, p. H125).

As we will see, *gestus* is a theatrical exploration of Being-with-others in the sense that it encapsulates the essence of a social relationship in gesture, music, or attitude. On the one hand Brecht hopes to make strange the events, decisions, actions and choices depicted in performance. On the other hand, he also wants to present the audience with a multi-layered image of the way that the characters and actors are related to each other in social terms. For Brecht, the world is not inevitably unconquerable. The world is capable of social change. At the core of Brecht's theory of acting is the rejection of inner psychological depiction of characters and its replacement with the depiction of attitudes that are felt between the individuals in the story. Rather than emphasise a fixed, stable identity of the individual Brecht wanted to demonstrate the fragmentary, dislocated behaviours driven by the circumstances of the story, thus understandable, but also changeable. Brecht explains that the term,

> '[g]est' is not supposed to mean gesticulation: it is not a matter of explanatory or emphatic movements of the hands, but of overall attitudes. A language is gestic when it is grounded in a gest and conveys particular attitudes adopted by the speaker towards other men. (Brecht, 1964, p. 104)

So the idea of *gestus* is the representation of the fundamental and relational attitude by means of an image, words or other form of communication, between those figures depicted on stage.[19] According to Willett *gestus* is both 'gist' and 'gesture' (Brecht, 1964, p. 42). It summarises a social relationship through a concrete action. For Brecht, *gestus* is meant to highlight the social relations between characters and invites the audience to question those attitudes in thinking about how things might be different. In this sense, the term is primarily concerned with acting style and provides a method of presentation. At the same time, the *gest* also allows the actor to comment upon the situation having chosen that particular way of presenting things, constituting a political attitude in that choice. The *gest* is not a simple action in itself. The *gest* is always in relation to the artistic presentation as a whole and the surrounding circumstances of that action. Brecht gives the example of a man chasing away a dog. On its own this is not gestic. But a badly dressed man's continual struggle against watchdogs is gestic (Brecht, 1964, p. 104). Brecht comments on (the Elder) Brueghel's paintings and how they depict social relationships in a gestic way. *Gestus* is related to artistic depiction, more than simply in terms of action, gesture and pose, but also bringing a meaning with it in its depiction of attitudes (Brecht, 1964, pp. 157–59). Apart from anything then, the economy of *gestus* lies in its direct impact as an image together with an element of surprise for the audience. *Grundgestus* is the overall social attitude being depicted, perhaps not unlike Stanislavski's super-objective, although with a distinct social emphasis. Brecht was more concerned with behaviours shown through the image than psychological reasoning behind the character. So actions are not supposed to be justified by an internal process but demonstrated, considered and seen as being alterable.

In 'On Gestic Music' Brecht notes that the 'look of pain in the abstract' is not a social gest (Brecht, 1964, p. 104). At this level it does not rise above the animal realm. But on adding the image of a man's degradation to the level of animal, the gest becomes relevant to society. Pain depicted by a man reduced to nothing more than a beast is gestic. Thus, everything hangs on story and what happens *between* those involved. The story is the complete fitting together of gestic elements (Brecht, 1964, p. 200). For Brecht, then, the *gestus* is also central to acting style and more broadly, the rehearsal process. By beginning with the social relations between the characters and developing the overall attitude towards one another, a sense of fragmentation is already achieved.

Brecht's rehearsal practice highlights the inadequacy of language alone to convey the meaning of a performance. He wants meaning to be duplicated in words, action, music, set, physical relations and in short through the entire *mise en scène*. One example is in the medium of the silent film of *Man Equals Man*; Peter Lorre is cited as displaying the character's contradictions.[20] Brecht claimed '[t]his way of acting was perfectly right from the new point of view, exemplary even' (Eddershaw in Thomson and Sacks, 1994, p. 258).

Another example can be found in Brecht's production of *Galileo* in New York, where he worked with Charles Laughton in the lead role.

Having no common language, the two worked together in rehearsal and used physical actions to convey the meaning:

> This system of performance-and-repetition had one immense advantage in that psychological discussions were almost entirely avoided. Even the most fundamental gests, such as Galileo's way of observing, or his craze for pleasure, were established in three dimensions by actual performance ... We were forced to do what better equipped translators should do too: to translate gests. For language is theatrical in so far as it primarily expresses the mutual attitude of the speakers. (Brecht, 1964, p. 165)

So by uncovering a physical depiction of our Being-with-one-another Brecht is inviting open reflection upon the type of solicitude we take towards our Being-with others (*Mitsein*). But rather than suggest a simple solution to caring for others (Solicitude) the world presents conflicting and competing demands and interests.

A third example of the *gestus*, or more precisely the mode of acting that Brecht was hoping for, can be found in his last note to the Berliner Ensemble before their production of *Mother Courage and Her Children* in London (1956):

> For our London season, we need to bear two things in mind. First: we shall be offering most of the audience a pure pantomime, a kind of silent film on stage for they know no German ... Second: there is in England a long-standing fear that German art (literature, painting, music) must be terribly heavy, slow, laborious, and pedestrian ... The audience has to see that here are a number of artists working together as a collective (ensemble) in order to convey stories, ideas, virtuoso feats to the spectator by a common effort. (Brecht, 1964, p. 283)

Brecht's gestic approach to acting leads performers to concentrate on the socially situated depiction of the story (and the social context of the performance itself) rather than the internal, psychological workings of the individual. To achieve this end, he suggests that the actors rehearse in their own accents rather than take on the characters'; actors should convert the present tense of their scenes into the past tense; narrate what their characters are doing, saying 'he said' and 'she said'; should switch roles to avoid identifying too closely with one or the other. Brecht also took on untrained actors whom he felt were better at displaying the attitudes necessary rather than the psychologically trained actors from actor-training institutions of the time. In short, *gestic* action consciously redeploys everyday behaviour and portrays characters as strangers or as if recounted from memory. Through such demonstration the actors can show the contradictory emotions, motives and actions rather than try to smooth these over through an illusionistic narrative. Different parts of the story are challenged by the different perspectives portrayed as bystanders to an accident, for instance. Rather than act out what happened, the participants show what it was like and adopt an attitude to the scene. As such, the audience is invited to make a judgement and see possible un-adopted alternatives to the action. In this way, it is hardly possible merely to consider these methods theoretically. The *gestus* is necessarily a physical embodiment on stage of different possibilities and perspectives.

The gestic mode removes the actor from submersion in the character, refuses to take for granted that their social relationships must be as they are, and puts Being-with up for question. In other words, Brecht wanted both actors and audiences to question everyday Being-with-one another (which is for the most part inauthentic) and investigate possible alternatives (Heidegger, 1962, p. H124). To a certain degree, Brecht seeks a philosophical and intellectual naivety, leaving it up to the audience to learn, critique, enjoy and be incited to action. But this naivety is not meant in terms of a superficial or erroneous understanding of events depicted but rather as a fresh look avoiding the habitual received understanding of those events. The emphasis on social action reflects on human beings not as mere things, but rather as people who care about one another. We live in a world that is never exhausted by description of material objects: 'Brecht sought in this context particularly, so it seems, to combine theory and practice in a shared and undemonstrative working philosophy' (Brooker in Thomson and Sacks, 1994, p. 198). Having looked as some of Brecht's key theoretical concepts in action, we now turn to his broader conception of how human individuals find themselves in the world – again, with a little help from Heidegger.

Historicality, Temporality, and Selfhood

One of the defining features of *BT* – with implications for historiography – is its rejection of the view that history is simply a collection of facts about the past (Heidegger, 1962, p. H380). Heidegger refuses to acknowledge that the study of history functions in the same way as the physical sciences (1962, p. H375). He maintains that our understanding of the past is always constructed through a worldview specific to the present. Historicality is therefore a necessary condition for Being in any age. History is a fundamental part of the uniquely human way that we experience the world and forms a condition for the human subject. All experience is always from within history. As such, Historicality is a necessary part of Being-in-the-world that we have as humans.

Heidegger also argues convincingly that Temporality is a twin necessary condition for Being, together with Historicality. All human experience is not only situated within a world but also experienced within time. As with Historicality, time is not something we can put under the microscope and discover independently of human experience. Time is not a thing at all – time isn't like a rock or a hammer. Heidegger thinks that there has been a long history of misunderstanding surrounding the concept of time in terms of a spatial analogy. Time is not 'a series of nows', like boxes passing on a conveyor belt, filled up one by one (1962, p. H422ff). Instead, we need to think of Temporality as one of the necessary conditions for existence and experience at all. As we have discovered, the world becomes visible only through our relation to objects in our environment and others that exist there with us in the world (1962, p. H416ff). The stuff of our world becomes significant only in the context of our daily concerns and practical tasks that we undertake. Similarly, Temporality is revealed only through the interaction with the world around us. Time is neither simply something objectively there in the world (the position of realism), nor simply in our minds (idealism). In the jargon, Temporality is 'equiprimordial' with Historicality as a basis for our Being-in-the-world (1962, p. H377).

Consequently, there is nothing in our regular experience that suggests that time is something present-at-hand. On the contrary, experience comes first as an undifferentiated whole unfolding in a temporal context – what

Henri Bergson calls *durée* (duration). Bergson claims that the conscious perception is in constant 'flow' – the continuous progress of the past that gnaws into the future (Bergson, 2001). Generally, we do not see the passing of discrete moments, but rather see time as continuous and uninterrupted. It is only after this human experience of connectedness within time that we can start to think of discrete, separable moments rather than vice-versa. Durational time is not the passing by of seconds, or the turning of the sun, but rather how long it takes for the kettle to boil or when the day has cooled off enough so that it is comfortable to water the garden.

The two-fold conditions of Temporality and Historicality also have a bearing on what we understand as a Self. Dasein does not experience itself as a series of selves that pass from one moment to another. Quite the opposite is true for the most part. Dasein experiences itself in flow with the world (in fact, the self is mostly not even apparent when Dasein goes about its daily business). The same might be said of groups and communities of individuals. We can also think about the notions of 'within-history' and 'within-time-ness' of society as a whole (1962, p. H382). The argument is that Being unfolds historically to people of the age and has a general tendency to conceal and hide itself (1962, pp. H19–26). Most of the time, we don't even notice time, history, and self, but in the theatre each of these elements can be brought into critical view – and this is exactly what Brecht intended.

With this perspective in mind, I suggest that we can build upon theatre scholar Meg Mumford's list of what she calls 'H-effects' (historicising effects) in Brecht:

- distancing (contemporary phenomena) by placing them in the past;
- presenting events as the product of historically specific conditions and choices;
- showing difference between the past and the present and evidencing change;
- showing similarities between the past and present and urging change;
- revealing received versions of history as the views of the ruling class;
- giving air to suppressed and interventionist histories;
- presenting all versions of history as serving vested interests (Mumford, 2009, p. 72).

Since theatre is so deeply imbued with time and history, it lends itself as an obvious vehicle for conscious investigation of these phenomenological aspects of existence.[21] But Brecht moves against the type of theatre that suppresses awareness of its own conditions of creation – what he sees as a sedating illusory effect inherent in Aristotle (Brecht, 1964, p. 33ff). The notion of epic theatre thus seeks to increase the critical distance of the performer and spectator from the story and characters. So by having a half-curtain, by having projections and captions, by singing songs in a style out of joint with the subject matter of the action, by having oversized stilts for the performers and half-masks, and so on, the audience has its attention drawn to the uncanniness of those elements. In the same way as Brecht argues that traditional forms of theatre covered up their own constructedness, Heidegger's phenomenology notes that we tend to overlook the temporal and historical structures of Being-in-the-world in everyday lives.

The concept of Historicality is crucial to epic theatre and acting in that Brecht rewrote and adapted plays from the past with a view to making them relevant to contemporary audiences and debates (Brecht, 1964, p. 190). He writes extensively on the need to make theatre relevant to modern audiences in 'A Short Organum for Theatre' (Brecht, 1964, pp. 179–205). In this essay, Brecht expresses his wish to view historical events in light of a contemporary understanding of the world through his historical adaptations on stage. He hopes to highlight the historically contingent values of the past and likewise show the equally conditional values of the present-day. Living through the rise of the National Socialist Party in Germany, Brecht felt that he was living in an especially significant age that would be of crucial importance to world-history. He wants to communicate the importance of contemporary events to his audiences by looking to lessons from the past. Walter Benjamin recalls a conversation with Brecht on this very matter in which Brecht reportedly said:

> We must neglect nothing in our struggle against that lot. What they're planning is nothing small, make no mistake about it. They're planning for thirty thousand years ahead. Colossal things. Colossal crimes. They stop at nothing. They're out to destroy everything. Every living cell contracts under its blows. That is why we too must think of everything. They

cripple the baby in the mother's womb. We must on no account leave out the children. (Benjamin, 1983, p. 120)

If only Heidegger had heeded such a warning. The challenge for the Brechtian actor is to depict actions as historically situated – a task that is aided in the subject matter of Brecht's plays. Historicality is central to his production of *The Life of Galileo* (1947), for instance (Brecht, 1980). Dealing with Galileo's discoveries in astronomy, Brecht highlights the power struggles in determining truth in the objective sciences while showing human aspects of daily existence in presenting this historical character on stage. The Vatican resists Galileo's assertion that the earth is not the centre of the universe. At the same time, the great scientist needs to find a way to earn money for survival in daily life. Brecht highlights Galileo's financial strain to pay the milkman, the necessities of tutoring in order to survive, and the opportunism that drives economic needs. Galileo's daughter pleads for him to recant his discoveries when his life is severely threatened. Despite the watchful eye of the Inquisition the near blind scientist completes the *Discoursi* in secret. At the end of one version of the play they are smuggled out of Italy by Galileo's long-time pupil, Andrea.

In addition to these grand power struggles, *The Life of Galileo* draws attention to the development of history not as a series of facts, but rather as founded in the daily concerns and social responsibilities that drive life. The values, actions and beliefs of the characters are always formed from a historical worldview and a specific social perspective. (Consider the Pope's inability to accept the scientific discoveries that Galileo presents because of the ramifications they will have on the power of the Church.) Objective facts are by no means self-evident in this story, but are always seen from the perspective of individual actions and interests. In practice, Brecht was loose with historical facts in his adaptation of the historical character. He hoped to draw out these human, social elements of his plays. Well aware of the way in which a historical age determines our understanding of Being, he tried to show the connection between the manipulation of science for the sake of political power in Galileo's time and the contemporary development of the nuclear bomb. *Galileo* opened in New York shortly after the bombing of Hiroshima and Nagasaki in 1945. Perhaps this was one reason the play was poorly received in America (Fuegi, 1987, p. 91).

In the rehearsal and collaboration between Brecht and Laughton, both men closely negotiated history and the lived experience of the present. Working in Laughton's house, the two would meet in the garden and run barefoot over the damp grass, discussing gardening: 'The gaiety and the beautiful proportions of the world of flowers overlapped in a most pleasant way in our work' (Brecht, 1964, 166). Drawing from all manner of sources, from Leonardo da Vinci's drawings to Hokusai's graphics and Brueghel's paintings, Laughton was not turned into a bookworm, but rather sought out behaviour to aid in his performance. In the actual production itself, maps, historical documents, and works of art were projected onto the stage, highlighting the notion of history being played out (Brecht, 1964, p. 203). In this way, *Galileo* itself and the process by which it was produced showed the connection and contradictions between the everyday experience of life and the historical movement of power. Ultimately, the everyday always has its place within history.

Brecht used many historically defamiliarising techniques to performance preparation. For instance, actors were encouraged to narrate their character's words and actions in the past tense (with 'he said' or 'she said' before each line). In the 'not ... but' exercise (Brecht, 1964, p. 137), actors would describe what the character does not do before describing what they do (he doesn't say, 'I will forgive you', but rather 'you'll pay for that'). In fact, this exercise in particular highlights the nature of the human subject as *possibility*.

Obviously, theatre is an art form that also takes place within time – a specific duration (in the period that the audience watches the performance, for instance). Brecht understood that the conception of time was particularly important in allowing a critical engagement with events in the drama. He played with the discrepancy of dramatic and real time as it passed in the performance. His theory of epic theatre recommends the fragmentation of narrative, jumping montage of scenes and a general lack of adherence to the Aristotelian unities of time, action and place draw attention to the constructedness of the drama. By interrupting the realistic depiction of events, Brechtian acting was meant to bring the theme of Temporality explicitly to the fore. Benjamin notes in his essay, 'What is Epic Theatre' (second version), 'Epic theatre and tragic theatre have a very different kind of alliance with the passing of time. Because the suspense concerns less the ending than the separate events, epic theatre can span very extensive periods of time' (Benjamin, 1973, p. 17). In dramatic theatre the audience is concerned with the outcome of events as they unfold in the fictional time. In epic theatre, the audience should not be concerned with the outcome of the action, but rather be freed up for rational analysis of the events that take place. In this way, the audience stands outside of time in order to judge (whereas, of course they are always within real time of the performance). The goal-oriented actions of the characters within time become available for rational criticism by the audience because they have a detached, temporal relation to the events.

At the same time, the social reality of the audience and contemporary historical time is also foregrounded in epic theatre. As mentioned earlier, Brecht saw parallels between Galileo's story and the development of the nuclear bomb. Similarly, *Mother Courage and Her Children* was intended as a warning for Switzerland (where Brecht was residing when he wrote the play) against acquiescence and making profit from the war. And it hardly seems necessary to say that Mother Courage's own story is an investigation of the way that small practical decisions of life can lead to a horrific picture of 'life as a whole' with the background of war. Such a single-minded pursuit of profit overlooks the human life of her family. In microscopic detail such a quest for profit is understandable, but in the overall temporality of her life, she fails to evaluate the value of her relationships. In the same way, audiences were meant to question their own historical situation and the ultimate ends of contemporary social and political decisions.

A deliberate drawing-attention-to-time is evident throughout *The Caucasian Chalk Circle*, for instance. Brecht famously employs a framing prologue in which Soviet farmers dispute the ownership of a plot of land. The device invites the audience (as well as the farmers) to contemplate the meaning of the fable of Grusha, the peasant-girl's journey to save the abandoned child of an aristocrat. In a sense, the device is similar to that of a Greek chorus which doubles as both spectator and commentator – collapsing 'fictional' and 'real' time. Instead of providing an interpretation of the events, however, Brecht leaves it open for the audience to decide and judge the action of the play. The prologue is intended to show that Grusha's tribulations are not just a story, but have real ramifications and relevance to life – both of the Soviet farmers and of the audience. Brecht makes a break from unity in the fiction, allowing the audience to see how Temporality shapes Grusha's actions; the unravelling of events mirrors her own turbulent perspective of time as the play jumps from scene to scene: discontinuous time and contradiction rather than scientifically objective and linear time.

Tempo and an increased pace of performance were important for Brecht in his notes to the production. So his attention to time is not simply in terms of the fictional reality of the play, but in the lived experience of the production in the auditorium. This pace reinforces the effect of Grusha's own frenetic journey: 'A stepping up of the tempo serves not only to shorten but even more to enliven the performance. The majority of scenes and figure *gain* by higher speeds' (Brecht, 1967, p. 99).

By rejecting a view of history as the inevitable development of self-consciousness (as put forward in his idol G.W.F. Hegel's teleological view of the progress of world history), Brecht demonstrates a uniquely human experience of time and action within the world. As mentioned, in *The Life of Galileo*, the eponymous great scientist is portrayed in terms of everyday human existence, needing money to pay the milkman, taking up tutoring in order to make ends meet and other small day-to-day worries. Rather than taking the 'big H' historical view of scientific discoveries, a uniquely *human* time is emphasised in these small actions of the man. Brecht recognises that acting is an art form suited to engaging with the human experience of time and its relation to the transitory subject. Time is also the central concept in Heidegger's revisionary formulation of both the human subject and the concept of Being.

One of Brecht's earliest plays, *Man Equals Man*, takes subjectivity (what it means to be a human subject) as its main concern: 'tonight you will see a man reassembled like a car/Leaving all his individual components just as they are' (Brecht, 1979, p. 1). In this play, the actors are staging an argument about subjectivity. Set in British India the story looks at Galy Gay, an Irish dock worker who is transformed into a ruthless soldier through the events of the play. Three soldiers blackmail and trick Galy Gay into believing that he is someone else – their missing companion:

> Across the stage strode giant soldiers, holding onto a rope so as not to fall from the stilts concealed in their trousers. They were hung about with rifles and wore tunics smeared with lime, blood and excrement. According to the story they were soldiers of a British detachment in India, murderous machines and marauders preparing for a frontier attack, an attack called 'defensive war' in the play. And side by side with these three giants, shaped not only by the crust of their uniforms but also by the logic of bourgeois laws, statutes and regulations, there dangled the soft-hearted and friendly petty bourgeois Galy Gay, 'a man who cannot say no'. (Tretyakov in Witt, 1975, p. 72)

Galy Gay's story brings into question the idea of the human subject as a linear progression within time. Heidegger also asserts that it is a mistake to think of time merely as a series of nows (what he would call a Cartesian understanding of spatiality). He also proposes a radical rethinking of the concept of the human subject (1962, pp. H317–32). According to Heidegger, Western philosophy has understood the human subject as something that remains constant throughout time, separated from the body. This thing, 'the subject', has been theorised variously as the 'soul' (Plato's eternal Forms) through to a 'transcendental subject' (Descartes' thinking thing). Heidegger follows his teacher, Husserl, in his demand for a return to the things themselves, a radical empiricism of objects available to consciousness (Husserl, 2001). Heidegger questions whether we really do experience the world as a disjointed series of phenomena brought together in consciousness and whether we really do gather disparate moments into a unified subject (Heidegger, 1962, p. H373).

In *Man Equals Man*, Brecht comments on the mutable nature of character and identity, the contingent circumstances of human existence, and upon the social environment of every human being. The play purports to demonstrate that subjectivity is not a stable constant, but rather performed in relation to desires and the survival of the individual. Brecht questions the concept of personhood and whether identity papers and pay slips can verify *who* anybody is. The title itself, 'Man Equals Man', highlights the ease with which society can substitute one person for another. This is remarkably similar to Heidegger's concept of *das Man* – the anonymity of social interpretation from the outside. The They-self is an inauthentic understanding of subjectivity in so far as it lacks individuality (Heidegger, 1962, p. H126). Numerical values of characters are projected onto the stage: '4 − 1 = 3' (when three soldiers lose their fourth member), '3 + 1 = 4' (when Galy Gay takes his place) and '1 = 1' (in scene 8 when it is demonstrated that man equals man).

Brecht's production critiques the idea of a core self that persists throughout a 'series of nows' in much the same way as Heidegger sets out philosophically. Human experience is based on a continuity of duration, not a fragmented integration of discrete events. Galy Gay is swept along by the actions of those around him while the one thing that remains constant is his desire to profit from his situation. Despite the farcical elements of such a scenario (i.e. Galy Gay gives a eulogy at his own funeral and sells an elephant which is really several men holding a hose pipe), Brecht is commenting seriously upon the changeability of human nature. Subjectivity is not something constant throughout a series of moments, but rather contingent upon circumstances. In a direct address to the audience in the interlude, Brecht highlights this point that Galy Gay

> has some kind friends by whom he is pressured
> Entirely in his own interest
> To conform with his world and its twists and turns
> And give up pursuing his own fishy concerns. (Brecht, 1979, p. 38)

Brecht's critique of subjectivity parallels Heidegger's argument that the Self is not something separate from the world that remains constant throughout time. On the contrary, the Self is fashioned by the environment, and experiences a flow in the duration of events rather than measurably discrete moments. For Brecht, however, the self is capable of making choice and taking action; it is never wholly decided by the world.

Any theory of the subject as a series of moments unified into a whole presents the major problem of explaining exactly what that whole is. Heidegger thinks that if only the 'now' is actual (the current segment in the series) then it is impossible to apprehend the past and future as constitutive of the human subject (since they are not available in the same way as the current segment). Heidegger's thinking in *BT* is very much influenced by Bergson and Husserl on this point. The now is the only available aspect of the subject that we can truly have before our eyes, yet it seems to lack the wholeness of who we would say a person really is. With such a difficulty of getting the whole of human existence into view, Heidegger proposes a revision of the metaphysics of subjectivity. As we have seen, metaphysics, for Heidegger, is any philosophical system that proposes an explanation of Being based in the false presumption that Dasein is a *thing* like other things in the world. Heidegger's phenomenology begins with the things themselves, the way phenomena present themselves to experience. Experience is primary. In order to find out what a self is, we need to begin with the human experience of a self rather than assuming it as a thing, available for scientific (physical and material) analysis.

As a lived experience, the whole of the Self consists of the past, the present sensory environment and future possibilities. The present already contains the past and the future in memories and anticipations. This way of thinking proposed by Heidegger denies that the subject is something *present-at-hand* (a mere thing to be observed under the microscope). Rather than model the human subject on a spatial analogy (as a physical thing), we should begin from the totality of our human experience which already includes the past and the future. In other words, the whole is constituted by the given circumstances of our environment, the projects that we wish to achieve and the possibilities that lie in that situation.

Brechtian actors, too, are concerned with making sense of life as a whole. *Mother Courage and Her Children* (1939) follows the life tragedies of a woman who runs a canteen wagon during the Thirty Years' War (Brecht, 1966). She loses two sons to the army, and has a third killed by the enemy during an armistice. Her only remaining child, the dumb daughter, Kattrin, is killed trying to warn the village of an oncoming attack from the opposing soldiers. Throughout all of this, Mother Courage maintains a determination to survive and profit from the war – even amidst such personal loss. The whole of her life is brought into view in this unifying feature of survival at any cost.

By stitching a series of scenes together, epic acting brings the whole of life into view with stark reality. Brecht's theatre is precisely a reflection on that whole. He hoped to engage audiences to think about other possible outcomes for his plays. If Mother Courage had acted differently, would the outcome have been the same? By encouraging such counterfactual thinking, Brecht shows that *possibilities* are as much a part of subjectivity as actuality. He points towards the meaning of 'the whole' not as something that can be understood *ontically* (as a scientific, physical thing) but rather *existentially* (already invested with meaning and possibilities).

In Brecht's 1951 production of *Mother Courage* there is an unmistakable image of the *gestus* – Helene Weigel's 'silent scream' depicts a clear moment of vision of life as a whole:

> As she hears the salvo that signals the execution of her son Swiss Cheese, Weigel's Courage is seated on a low stool with her hands in her lap. She clenches her rough skirt, leaning forward with a straight, tense back against her shoulders; her mouth tears open until it seems that her jaw will break, but no sound comes forth. For a moment, her whole physicality has the impossible, angular contortion of one of Picasso's screaming horses in *Guernica*. Then she snaps her mouth shut, brings her torso and head back into alignment, and collapses the tension in her torso, slumping in on herself. (Rouse, 1984, p. 34)

This paradigmatic example of *gestus* reveals a conception of time not merely as a scientific measure, but as a fully human conception of lived experience. It is as though the whole story of the play were encapsulated in this one moment. Yet even Courage continues on and it is up to the spectator to suffer outrage at her actions. This sense is repeated in the final scene when Mother Courage herself is epitomised in Weigel's actions at the end of the production:

> Courage's daughter has been shot trying to alert the city of Halle to an impending enemy attack. Courage is now alone She must drag her wagon herself back into the war, back into the train of the army that feeds her. She cannot afford to wait to bury Kattrin herself, so she pays a peasant family to bury her daughter for her. She fishes a handful of coins from the leather purse at her waist, starts to hand them to the peasants, looks at the coins, hesitates, slowly puts one coin back in her purse, then gives the rest over in payment. Even as she displays her character's total collapse, Weigel demonstrates once again the basic contradiction between businesswoman and mother that has led to that collapse. (Rouse, 1984, p. 37)

This moment brings the meaning of life into stark contrast against Mother Courage's choices. Death which is so near to Dasein in this instance is met with an inauthentic response of self-interest. Or is it necessary survival? It is up to the audience to realise that authentic Being-with-others care and love for those close is the basis for authentic existence.

A Theatre of P-Effects

In addition to Mumford's list of H-effects quoted earlier, I suggest that Brecht's theatre also employs 'P-effects' (phenomenological effects), although he did not formulate them in these terms:

- challenging a view of history as a collection of objective facts;
- recognising the being of any social agent is always within history;
- investigating lived human experience of time rather than scientific/objectively-measurable time;
- uncovering time not as a series of 'nows' privileging the present, but a 'self' that is thrown from the past and with projects set out for the future;
- revealing human action as 'possibility' and not 'actuality'; and
- showing the essence of Dasein's being as thrown possibility.

If we can interpret this type of performance as a call to authentic understanding of the possibilities of social action, Brecht's approach to acting highlights some important aspects of Being examined by Heidegger in *BT*. But this is not a concept of truth that can be detached from the lived human experience – unproblematic, unchanging and unalterable. Brecht's practice can be understood through the complex interaction between Being-in-the-world and the social, temporal and historical world itself. It makes no sense to conceive of the human subject outside of time and history and this is precisely why theatre is such a powerful vehicle for showing these elements. Acting is essentially both historical and temporal. By choosing the theatre as a medium for philosophical communication, Brecht emphasised a uniquely human relation to the world not as simply scientific and physical, but rather as an engagement already invested with meaning that constitutes human Being-there.

A Brechtian rewriting of Heidegger would have Heidegger disclose his own position of writing, disclose the social and political underpinnings of his perspective, and demonstrate how his Authenticity contradicts any ideology founded in National Socialism. Being authentic necessarily involves seeing Others there with us in the world as a fundamental part of our own existence. So to treat others in such a way as to overlook their Dasein is to fall prey to a different kind of falling understanding. In many ways, this is similar to Levinas' critique of Heidegger and emphasis on ethics as fundamental to phenomenology.

On the other hand, we need to find new ways of thinking about Brecht. Since his death, his plays have been staged widely, his writings read in schools, and his theories transformed into a mindlessly repeated catechism. It is unfortunate that his works are often approached as museum pieces thereby overlooking Brecht the revisionist and experimenter. In fact, he continually stresses the need for making theatre relevant to the times – both form and content. Heiner Müller notes, 'to make use of Brecht without being critical of him is to betray him' (cited in Leach, 2004, p. 142).

The Brechtian actor has the challenge of drawing attention to the temporal and historical structures that are key to this human understanding of the world. Through the influence of dialectics Brecht stresses process both in a fictional context (drawing attention to the social and environmental formation of actions performed by his characters) and in his practical engagement with theatre (denying any form of finality in his rehearsals and writing, always being open to criticism and revision). He maintains that the analysis of social relations in the fictional reality should be equally applicable to the real world. In this way, he overcame the metaphysical tendency to understand the human subject merely as another thing alongside other things in the world. Epic theatre's emphasis on social relations as fundamental to our historical and daily existence extends beyond a spatio-physical conception of humanity towards an understanding of human life as a unique site of Being. Finally, by inciting the possibility of social change in the audience, Brechtian acting highlights the world not as fixed and unalterable, but what Heidegger describes as inter-meshed with our own Being-in-the-world, a radical continuity between the human subject and its environment that unfolds throughout time.

This phenomenological interpretation sees Brecht as demonstrating Being through the historico-temporal structures of the world. He wished that both actors and spectators would seize an authentic understanding of their own existence and resolutely take action as grasping their ownmost possibilities. That is the *theory*, anyway. In practice, his theatre was also very entertaining. Brecht himself emphasised humour, entertainment and a sense of fun that he felt was essential to successful acting:

> If the critics could only look at my theatre as the audience does, without starting out by stressing my theories, then they might well see theatre – a theatre, I hope imbued with imagination, humour and meaning – and only when they began to analyse its effects would they be struck by certain innovations, which they could then find explained in my theoretical writings. (Brecht, 1964, p. 248)

Rather than simply frame his work in the construction of meaning, I suggest that his work is deeply phenomenological in its search for 'truth' of the lived subject:

> On Brecht's stage everything must be 'true'; but he prefers a particular sort of truth, the truth which comes as a discovery. During the presentation he will point beamingly with an outstretched hand at an actor who has just shown something special or something important in human nature or human circumstance. (Witt, 1974, p. 127)

Such a discovery of truth in rehearsal is not so much uncovering a pre-existent or eternal meaning or truth. The beaming outstretched hand is a moment of unearthing or 'disclosure' of Being in rehearsal; it is a revelation based in shared meaning and understanding. For Brecht, theatre is an iterative practical and embodied process. Indeed, as a place for the discovery of truth, rehearsal coincides with Heidegger's description of truth as *aletheia* in the work of art, as I will consider in the next and final chapter.

Exercises and Topics for Discussion

1. Choose a power relationship to represent. It could be something like the relationship between a lecturer and student, a mayor and local resident, a waiter and customer. Create a series of three tableaux to demonstrate the relationship. Now shift the power situation to different people. Provide a detached commentary on your representation as you enact it. How do the participants react to a situation of powerlessness?
2. Play out 'Little Red Riding Hood' (or other fairy-tale) from different points of view. For instance, imagine that the wolf is the last of his species and his wood is being cut down for a new development. Now imagine that the story is from the perspective of an orphaned girl and there is a lack of state resources to take care of the child. Now a woodcutter, whose skills are no longer needed in a technologically advanced society. Now from the perspective of a grandmother who has no access to aged care facilities and needs to rely on her granddaughter in order to cope.
3. Create a video campaign for social media on a political topic that interests you. How can you interrupt the flow of the story to get the audience to focus on the construction of the medium? How could you get the audience to think about alternatives to action here? How can you be honest about your own position in relation to the judgements you make in the clip?
4. Take an everyday interaction such as shaking hands with the master of ceremonies at a graduation event. Map out the Care structure of this occasion. Emphasise the power relationship by doubling it. Now double it again. Find a heightened physicality for the relationship. Now play with different temporalities. Play the action out over two minutes. Play it backwards. Put the action in a different historical period. Play the scene with a view to the fact that life will one day come to an end and this puts a perspective on the action. What changes?
5. Look at a piece of political propaganda such as Leni Riefenstahl's *Triumph of the Will*. Think about the ways in which 'tradition' is drawn upon to naturalise the power of the leader. Now look at a speech by a dictator such as Hitler. How does he construct a physical *gestus* of a

leader? How is the leader positioned in relationship to others there and to the natural world?
6. Think about an event or choice that caused you to rethink your life. How would you describe your attitude in terms of 'authentic resoluteness'? How did it change your actions from that point onwards? Was the change long lasting or did you fall back into old habits? Do you think Authenticity is possible at every moment in one's life? How does your social, financial, political, religious, and gendered context affect and create your sense of Authenticity?

Notes

1 See Fuegi (1987, p. 87), Eddershaw in Thomson and Sacks (1994, p. 254) and Brecht (1964, p. 248).
2 See *The Messingkauf Dialogues* for a theatrical treatment (albeit unfinished) by Brecht (1965b).
3 Brecht's friend Sergei Tretyakov claims to have 'seen foam appear on the lips of dignified German professors as they screamed that Brecht has no resemblance to a poet, that he had smuggled himself into literature like a fox: a man who rhymed "sein" with "Dasein" could not call himself a poet' (Witt, 1974, p. 79). It seems likely that Tretyakov is referring to Heidegger as one of these professors. See Collins and Selina (1999, p. 68), who place Heidegger and Brecht in opposition with respect to popular culture.
4 In *Bodied Spaces*, Stanton Garner (1994) also provides some analysis of Brecht in terms of phenomenology. He specifically focusses on the subversion of presence, the body in pain and the objectification of the body in the *Verfremdungseffekt*.
5 See Doug Rosson's 'Re-Examining Heidegger to Uncover Creativity in the Iteratively Bound Performer' in McCutcheon and Sellers-Young (2013, pp. 179–94) for a discussion of artistic agency in the creative act as opposed to social constructivism.
6 See Leach (2004, p. 111) for a brief discussion of Socialist realism, formalism, naturalism and realism.
7 See Ott (1993) and Young (1997).
8 These themes are central to Sartre's philosophy. It would be equally appropriate to present an existentialist interpretation of Brecht. But it is useful here to find tensions between Heidegger and Brecht to see how the latter can speak back to the former.

9   See 'Two Essays on Unprofessional Acting' (Brecht, 1964, pp. 148–53).
10 See for instance *The Drama Review* Autumn, 1967, *12*(1) devoted to Brecht in which Richard Schechner's appropriates his agenda of social revolution. Schechner was greatly influenced by Brecht's theories in his own call for a return of 'efficacy' in performance (see 'From Ritual to Theatre and Back' in Schechner, 1976).
11 See Eddershaw, 'Actors on Brecht' in Thomson and Sacks (1994) and McDowell, 'Actors on Brecht: The Munich Years' in Martin and Bial (2000).
12 See 'Some Things that can be Learnt from Stanislavsky' (Brecht, 1964, p. 36) and Hurwicz in Witt (1974).
13 See Willett's editorial note in Brecht (1964, pp. 281, 282).
14 See Leach (2004, pp. 118, 119) and Willett (1959, pp. 177–81) for a discussion of translations of *Verfremdungseffekt*.
15 See 'On Chinese Acting' in Martin and Bial (2000).
16 See Casper Neher's 1954 design for *The Caucasian Chalk Circle*, for instance (Fuegi, 1987).
17 For an extensive discussion of the production of *The Caucasian Chalk Circle* see Fuegi (1987).
18 See 'A Dialogue about Acting', 'Alienation Effects in Chinese Acting', 'New Technique of Acting', and 'From a Letter to an Actor' in Brecht (1964).
19 According to Brooker in Thomson and Sacks (1994) and Willett in Brecht (1964), the term was used by Lessing in 1767 and Kurt Weil on the gestic nature of music. It appeared in Brecht's own writings with his notes to the 'Rise and Fall of the City of Mahogany' and 'On Gestic Music' (Brecht, 1964).
20 See 'The Question of Criteria for Judging Acting', Notes from *Mann ist Mann* in Brecht (1964).
21 For a discussion of space and time in Brecht's theatre, see Bryant-Bertail (2000).

8

Conclusion: Lights Up on Manual Philosophy

KING LEAR: O, ho, are you there with me? No eyes in your head, nor no money in your purse? Your eyes are in a heavy case, your purse in a light; yet you see how this world goes.

GLOUCESTER: I see it feelingly.

(Shakespeare, *King Lear*, 4.6.128–30)

The World Disclosed: Your Fingerprints Were All Over It

During a recent postperformance discussion in which students reflected on their final practical performance assessment, a young actress claimed that she could tell that one of her classmates had collaborated on another group's work. 'Your fingerprints were all over it', she said. The metaphor immediately reminded me of Lucian of Samosata's suggestion that actors are 'manual philosophers' mentioned earlier in Chapter 2 and the idea of working with one's hands. The student's remark also draws attention to the materially intersubjective practice of theatre-making and the tactile nature of performing. We can think about the haptic work of rehearsal as akin to sculpting with the hands or (as Michelangelo wrote about the art of the sculptor) revealing the hidden form inside a block of marble.[1] Theatre scholar Margaret Eddershaw uses a similar metaphor writing about Brecht, whose 'directorial method was based on investigation and varied experimentation that could extend the smallest gesture – eyes, fingers ... Brecht worked like a sculptor on and with the actor' (Eddershaw in Thomson and Sacks, 1994, p. 257). While rehearsing a performance, an imprint of the theatre-maker's self (completely unique to their own being) is left on collaborators and audience in the moment of performance.

The word 'manual' comes from the Latin '*manus*' (hand) and by extension, one's manipulation of the environment through instruments and tools. Given Heidegger's exposition of the ready-to-hand (*Zuhandenheit*) in *BT* as a mode of encountering objects when we look around in the world, the phrase is handy. In the art of acting, however, it is not just the hands, but the whole body – and I argue the whole being of Dasein – that is both the user and the tool. Or rather, it is not merely an operator and equipment but artist and artwork. Actors work on *themselves* as the material and emotional support for the work of art in the moment of performance. 'Manual' can also mean doing something by hand as opposed to electronically or automatically (an association equally pertinent here). As I understand it, driving a manual rather than automatic car gives a greater responsiveness to the road, driving conditions, and control over the car. Theatre-practitioners who work on automatic will not open up a world in the same way as those who pay attention to the specificity of their Historicality, Temporality, and Being-with others. We might even take a step further and suggest that the art of acting can foster an existential sense of touch – a feeling for the possibilities of Being.[2]

The sense of touch is also particularly relevant to Dasein's Being-in-the-world. In *BT* section 42, Heidegger argues that we are not 'in' the world merely as an object is in space (Heidegger, 1962, pp. H55, H56).[3] When we say that the chair touches the wall, technically the statement isn't accurate because, as Heidegger argues, the space between the two objects will never equal zero. The primary meaning of 'touch' here is that which is encounterable in the world. The wall can't encounter the chair in the same way that Dasein can. By extension, we can only be 'touched' by things in that they make an impression in the encounter precisely because

Dasein has a world. We can be touched by theatre in such an encounter as it discloses a world. It makes an impression on the audience when successful. So when Gloucester says that he can see the world 'feelingly' in the epigraph at the start of this chapter, it has the double meaning of feeling with his hands (compensating for his blindness) and also seeing the world with his feelings (having been through the trials and tribulations of recent events).

Basic Problems in Theatre Phenomenology

The comparative approach adopted in this book advances the thought that theatre can press back on philosophy. So for instance, aspects of Heidegger's thinking might be inflected by Brecht's emphasis on social relationships together with the economic and historical context for individual choice. Stanislavski's fear of falling into philosophy speaks back with an unwillingness to reduce human existence to a specific technique, approach, or definition of Being-in-the-world. Unrestrained by a rigid philosophical system, he is able to open up the question of Being through fostering the conditions for the slippery state of creative inspiration. Artaud's struggle for self-expression in words enacts a rejection of formal literary criticism as a measure for value in artistic creativity and calls for a return to the body as a site of Being. His writings point out the irreducible and inexpressible essence of individual existence together with the failure of rationality and representation in articulating complete existence.

When I began thinking about theatre and philosophy many years ago, I thought that the appropriate philosophical question to ask in theatre studies is 'what is theatre?' in a manner similar to the key question in aesthetics, 'what is art?' Such an approach would distil the necessary and sufficient conditions of theatre – a mode of inquiry that I am now convinced isn't particularly helpful. The problem may be similar to Wittgenstein's (2001) example of the difficulty of stipulating exactly what a 'game' is in any single rigid definition. But although there might not be one unifying definition that accounts for everything that is a game (and discounts everything that is not), we have no problem in using the word game correctly. Games may have a family resemblance in a series of overlapping but non-essential qualities. Marvin Carlson (1996, p. 1) notes that 'performance', too, is an essentially contested concept and although no single definition of the term will eventuate, the dialogue of disagreement about it is productive. Likewise, if you are still hoping for a simple definition of theatre phenomenology:

> It should now be obvious that phenomenology is not a homogeneous and dogmatic philosophy but a way of reopening the basic philosophical issues that deal with the foundational questions of all human endeavours. (Stewart and Mickunas, 1990, p. 140)

Phenomenology is also essentially contested because questioning is at the heart of its approach together with the question of what questioning is in the first place. Nevertheless, we can say that there is a basic set of problems in phenomenology with respect to theatre: the nature of freedom and choice; embodiment; intersubjectivity; the meaning of existence; the transcendent dimensions of experience; meaning in language; movement; space; and time. Theatre phenomenology takes itself into question and asks what questioning is in the first place. This could be investigated in the theatrical process itself and even in the resulting work. A phenomenological interpretation of theatre may not necessarily show anything new, but it will help to reformulate age-old questions by making the blindingly obvious apparent. Another overarching task of phenomenology is to give an account of the unity of human consciousness by illuminating the basic understandings implicit in all human behaviours. And finally, phenomenological analysis must also acknowledge its own limits by coming to terms with what it cannot achieve through its method. The danger of such a broad definition is to include all description as phenomenological, but this would be an error. The key move of the theatre phenomenologist is to challenge the fundamental principles behind received notions of theatre – presence, rationality, naturalness, dualism, positivism, aesthetic properties, and so on. Without doubt, such an unsettling of foundations has already happened in the last half-century or so of academic scholarship in theatre and performance studies. This challenge to foundational concepts is an attempt to avoid naturalistic assumptions about the ontological status about the world. They are not meant to plunge us into solipsism or get bogged down in our subjective reactions to the world. Instead, the task is to open up the phenomena of everyday experiences so that they become accessible to philosophy.

Theatre phenomenology of the Heideggerian flavour I have served here looks into what type of Being can create and encounter theatre in the first place. What kind of entity is Being-in-the-world, Being-with-others, has phenomenological moods, is thrown into the world towards death? What kind of being cares about the world and its dealings with it, always from within time and history? I have tried to demonstrate how theatre contains processes for 'clearing' or 'lighting' (*Lichtung*) and revealing Being in the Event (*Ereignis*) of performance. When the lights of the theatre come up at the end of the show, hopefully we see the world differently (at least for a while, if the performance did its job). Unlike Nietzsche, who interprets ancient Greek tragedy (*Oedipus at Colonus* and *Prometheus Bound*) according to story and myth, here I have attempted to focus on the process of theatre-making.[4] In 'The Ode on Man in Sophocles' *Antigone*', Heidegger also interprets Sophocles' poetry without really thinking about the performance process that brings it to life (Heidegger, 2000, pp. 156–76). Actors and theatre-makers have the ability to foster the same sense of wonder that the pre-Socratic philosophers felt when they observed the world around them – the stars, the sky, natural disasters, and mathematical harmony in nature. Heidegger suggests that this attitude underpins phenomenology. For the theatre phenomenologist such wonder allows the rich description of theatrical phenomena, and perhaps even for creating performances.

In Chapter 3, I suggested that we might begin to explore the meaning of phenomenology in the exercise of communicating to an alien what it means to tie a shoelace. As Heidegger's grandfather was a shoemaker, it seems to be an appropriate example. Throughout his childhood artisanal tools of manual labour surrounded him. I suggested that a good way to proceed is to tack between observing a particular experience or phenomenon and the world or context that makes it possible. Such a hermeneutic method is an attempt to approach and describe 'the thing itself' without amputating it from its context. The method finds a parallel in the processes of actor training, rehearsal, and performance. One remembers that there is no tying a shoelace 'in general' but only ever in specific given circumstances. The meaning of a shoe will depend on who you are and what you are doing. When Estragon takes off his boot in *Waiting For Godot* it is in a world different from *Miss Julie* where the mistress tightens her boot before having it kissed by the servant Jean. Yet another world is gleaned in Launce's shoes in *The Two Gentlemen of Verona* when he uses them to represent his father and mother. Who would have thought that the world could be revealed in a shoe?

A Theatre of Truth: *Aletheia*

I noted in Chapter 1 that people often talk of truth in rehearsal rooms around the world. What does it mean to be 'in the truth of the moment', to give an 'authentic performance', to 'really believe' in the character? What does it mean to 'give an honest and sincere performance'? Is theatrical truth different from philosophical truth? Throughout this book, I have alluded to Heidegger's appropriation of the ancient Greek term αλαθεία (*aletheia*) and asked you to keep the word at the back of your mind. For Heidegger, works of art have the ability to disclose the world and in many ways share in the being of Dasein. The type of truth uncovered in theatrical performance, then, is not universal or to be apprehended in purely scientific terms. Truth in theatre is firmly grounded in the historical world, at a specific time, within time, and by a particular group of people.

Heidegger contrasts his own exegesis of truth with what he calls the traditional conception. In section 44 of *BT*, 'Dasein, Disclosedness, and Truth' (1962, pp. H212–30), he rejects the idea of truth as the correspondence or agreement of a judgement with its object. Truth is not a relation between knowledge and the Real (1962, p. H216). In other words, we don't represent things to ourselves as pictures in our heads and then check the reality against that picture. Instead, he suggests that truth is the *uncovering* of an entity towards which an assertion is made (1962,

p. H218). When I say 'that is true', the 'is true' refers to 'the thing itself'. Being true is a Being-uncovering. Heidegger appropriates Aristotle's term *aletheia* to encapsulate this conception of truth. The most primordial phenomenon of truth for him is in this ancient Greek sense of 'uncovering'. And according to Heidegger, this uncovering is precisely the task of phenomenology – to show things as they are in themselves in the way that they show themselves. Truth shows not only *what* is uncovered but also *how* it is uncovered. Such a conception therefore originates in the being of Dasein: 'Dasein as constituted by disclosedness, is essentially in the truth. Disclosedness is a kind of Being which is essential to Dasein' (Heidegger, 1962, p. H226).

In 'The Origin of the Work of Art' (first delivered in 1935 as a public lecture at Freiburg), Heidegger dwells on this truth-revealing function of art (Heidegger, 1977).[5] An investigation of theatrical acting through Heidegger's later writings might well be the topic of another book entirely in itself. But it is worth considering briefly how in this essay, he comes to the conclusion that art 'is a becoming and a happening of truth' (1977, p. 196). He begins by reflecting upon art (in general) as the precondition for particular art works, and artists as the creators of those works. But art is that which makes an artist, so the origin of art and the artist is reciprocal. To break into the infinite regress of this relationship between art, the artwork, and the artist, Heidegger begins again with the 'thingly' aspect of a work of art, and then the relation of things to equipment, moves forward to consider the concept of truth as *aletheia*, and finally the way in which (great) art both reveals and creates the world. Ultimately, he argues that all art has its essence in poetry:

> Art lets truth originate. Art, founding preserving is the spring that leaps to the truth of beings in the work. To originate something by a leap, to bring something into being from out of its essential source in a founding leap – this is what the word origin (*Ursprung* – primal leap) means. (1977, p. 202)

There are a number of concerns that might be offered to this conception of art. Firstly, by starting with the 'thingly' nature of a work, Heidegger seems to privilege the fine arts over performance. The two examples he uses in the lecture to show how the world is revealed by the work of art are van Gogh's *Peasant Shoes* as revealing the work world of the peasant and a Greek temple as a historical object which no longer has its world in the same way as when it was in use – the gods have now fled the temple. Acting does not begin with a material object, but with a whole self. And more often than not performance leaves no stable support through which it survives in history. The moment of performance disappears at its own birth (though it may well leave traces in the physical world and ripples in Being-with-others). Secondly, by placing poetry as the essence of all art Heidegger places emphasis on language, perhaps privileging the medium in which he himself worked, although *poiesis* refers more broadly to creating or making (Heidegger, 1977, p. 197). By considering acting as manual philosophy here, I have tried to move away from understanding Being in terms of language towards the whole of Dasein and its world and this may entail expression beyond written poetry. Thirdly, Heidegger may be misguided in his romanticised view of ancient Greek culture as a kind of pre-Fall state of philosophical plenitude. Coupled with his fetish for German folk culture as the inheritor of this tradition, something of his ill-considered political orientation may lurk below the surface. Fourthly, unlike Heidegger, we might not look to great works of art, but to theatre-making on a local level not concerned with 'world historical' people but to an intimate communion between actors and audience. Young (2001, pp. 64–68) points out that when Heidegger began to write about art, he took on Hegel's thesis that the age of great art was over and in doing so alienated himself from the art of his own age that he very much admired. A world ruled by reason and aesthetics (the formal appreciation of works of art in relation to beauty and the aesthetic experience) supplanted or rather killed off the 'Greek paradigm' of art with the advent of the modernity. Heidegger goes on to suggest that art is no longer essential to Being in the modern world. But unlike Hegel, Heidegger thought that there was a possibility of the return of great art (Young, 2001, pp. 1, 2). Perhaps this is similar to Richard Schechner's call for a return of efficacy to theatre (Schechner, 2003).

But need we raise art to such lofty heights? It might also be argued that we no longer live in a historical age where there is a single cultural expression that can 'found' or 'gather' a people in the way Heidegger suggests. In a contemporary era of cultural fragmentation there may well be no one 'great art' that can bring the world together. Even as individuals we live across many worlds. But this is precisely the capacity for theatre to harvest a sense of the local, the intimate, the small-scale, and the specific. In some cases, the immediacy of theatre can be a threat.

Here we can recall the persistent feeling of 'ontological queasiness' supposedly provoked by theatre and acting that stems from a concern that they present a false and degenerate representation of the world that threatens to destabilise our sense of what is real and what is not (Barish, 1981). Instead of the actor making their own representations correspond with a preexisting external truth, the rehearsal process is a matter of uncovering truth. Performance can be a moment of truth-revealing. It is an imaginative leap. The truth of acting is not a representation of the world, a correspondence between the stage and reality, but rather an uncovering and disclosure of Dasein in itself: of 'Being There'. For Constantin Stanislavski, this was the truth of artistic creativity, for Antonin Artaud it was the truth of unmediated experience, and for Bertolt Brecht it was the truth of social relationships played out on stage. From this perspective, acting is not about representing, but rather unconcealing Being by letting it show itself from itself.

Binocular Vision or Seeing Double: Semiotics and Phenomenology

In this book I have attempted to look into the possibilities of theatre phenomenology. As suggested, the project might continue by bringing the works of phenomenologists other than Heidegger into dialogue with theatre. Various other creative activities might also become the focus.

One issue that remains is the relationship between phenomenology and semiotics in theatre studies. Bert States (1985) first proposed that these two methodologies are complementary in that they respectively bring the processes of signification and the materiality of the stage into view. He suggests that they constitute a 'binocular vision', using the metaphor of sight and, by extension, the way in which our two eyes combine visual data into a single image and allow the perception of depth. Mark Fortier's (1997) *Theory/Theatre* also suggests that phenomenology and semiotics are complementary approaches. For him, phenomenology reveals the embodied nature of theatre and the way in which it gives itself to consciousness:

> Phenomenology's primary concern is with the engagement in lived experience between the individual consciousness and the real which manifests itself not as a series of linguistic signs but as sensory and mental phenomena – the 'world' as encountered in perception and reflection rather than the 'earth' as things in themselves. In way, the emphasis is on the presence or unconcealing of the world for consciousness rather than its absence through language, and therefore with the interplay with the real rather than its inevitable deferral. Phenomenology is concerned with truth, no matter how mediated, provisional and revisable. (Fortier, 1997, p. 29)

Similarly, *The Routledge Companion to Theatre and Performance* contrasts phenomenology with semiotics in its usefulness for approaching the experience of the spectator and performer by emphasising the role of the senses, feelings, and descriptive modes of analysis (Allain and Harvey, 2006, pp. 186, 187).

While contrasting semiotics and phenomenology might be useful for introductory purposes by comparing a focus on embodied perception and the signifying function of theatre, I suggest that such a binary relationship is reductive. I was recently talking to an ophthalmologist friend about the topic of binocular vision and he mentioned that rather than simply take the data that we receive through each eye and combine it together, in fact we use a number of different cues that we use to perceive depth and distance. Some of these can be achieved with the use of just one eye. A more sophisticated analysis would recognise that interpreting the world as a series of signs is only one way in which we apprehend it. And it is not easily separated from other ways of experiencing the world. But it is by no means the only way that we consciously encounter life. The point is not dissimilar to the way Heidegger's phenomenology challenges the thought that 'knowing' is the fundamental way in which we experience the world. Interpreting theatre as a sign system does not exhaust the content of the experience. Semiotics, therefore, emphasises a specific mode of accessing phenomena (as a set of signs) and might be thought of in the context of a broader phenomenological inquiry. The world hits us all at once and the meaning of a sign is not separate from the experience. Anyone who has witnessed a performance that defies putting into words knows how inadequate language is to describe what they felt at the time. Similarly, the meaningfulness of the world feeds back in to the way that we see and interpret it in the first place. In this respect, the phenomenal world is contingent upon the meaningful totality of our past experiences and present activities.

Theatre scholar Patrice Pavis (1997, p. 214) suggests that we 'remain on the side of the signifier' – the materiality of the object of perception – for as long as possible in the process of performance analysis though the tendency will be to formulate that meaning into a set of statements. This advice is helpful not only in describing but also making performance. If theatre scholar Anne Ubersfeld is right in claiming that theatre practitioners are 'semiologues sauvage' (intuitive semioticians) perhaps we can extend the comparison in thinking of actors as phenomenologists in the wild.[6] Some might argue that domesticating such naturally occurring intuition would change it inherently. I wonder whether introducing a phenomenological method to a set of actors would simply be confusing or stimulating and illuminating. What might such a hybrid actor-philosopher sound like?

Part of the challenge is sustaining a dialogue between theatre and philosophy. The creative work of theatre needs to be allowed to speak in order to bring about such a conversation. And arguably, such an interpretation changes the very nature of the work itself. But an interpretive approach that also has a sense of 'openness' to the world and work will be able to return to the things themselves too. Of course, Jean-Paul Sartre, Albert Camus, Gabriel Marcel, and Alain Badiou have written plays in which they express philosophical ideas by creative means. The challenge is to widen our study beyond playwrights to other practitioners in the creative process. To a certain degree, theatre-makers already work with phenomenological concepts though they might not explicitly use phenomenological language. For Merleau-Ponty, the description of savage being (the unwieldy beast that constitutes our lived experience of the world) can never be exhausted but leads further into a boundless matrix of meaning. The task is to follow Ariadne's golden string through the maze.

What's Your Next Gig? From Phenomenology to Creativity

Actors often find it frustrating that just when they have secured employment and arrive to start work on a show or film, the first question they get is 'what's your next gig?' It's enough to plunge a successful artist back to reality and into a spiral of despair. Fortunately, I have a suggestion for theatre phenomenology's next job. My hope is that future theatre makers themselves might contribute to philosophy. By embarking upon a phenomenological pathway to performance, for instance, the production itself might offer a philosophical thought however provisional and elusive. Such a task is to make philosophy a rich and fertile source in the process of theatre-making.

In many ways philosophical processes are 'naturally' occurring in the creative act. James Thomas (2009, p. 218), for instance, suggests that, in the task of interpreting a dramatic script, actors, directors, and designers should attempt to formulate the 'main idea' of a play by distilling the essence of the play into a single statement. The procedure of reducing the work to its essence performs the eidetic reduction in the creative process (without the jargon). And rather than arrive at a simplistic and fixed interpretation of the play, it provides a creative locus for the production process that can change over the course of rehearsal. Likewise, the analysis of other elements of the given circumstances in the text constitutes an exploration of Being-in-the-world (minus the philosophical language) for the character in context. I wonder whether phenomenological questions to the surface could aid in the creative process.

I often recall the maxim of an acting teacher at a major acting conservatoire who proclaimed 'the playwright is god' – implying that the meaning of the play is to be found by forensic attention to the text and interpreting it only as it is given on the page. Other directors at the school were much looser in their interpretation of a play text, paying more attention to their own creative intentions in a project. Regardless of emphasis in the creative process, a phenomenological approach requires attending to the work and listening to the call of Being. This means focussing on the text in its relation to the world and tacks between the two (combining the approaches of these two acting teachers). The creative act begins by enlisting the dramatic text as a pretext for artistic exploration. If there is no text, as in a devised or improvised performance, then the actor has no choice but to start with Dasein while integrating other creative sources. The process should involve *letting* things show themselves *from* themselves in *the way* that they show themselves. Otherwise, the result will be 'out of touch'.

And so we finally return to Lucian's discussion of pantomime. Timocrates, the teacher of Lesbonax of Mytilene, is reported to have said after accidentally seeing a performance:

> How much have I lost by my scrupulous devotion to philosophy! I know not what truth there may be in Plato's analysis of the soul into the three elements of spirit, appetite, and reason: but each of the three is admirably illustrated by the pantomime; he shows us the angry man, he shows us the lover, and he shows us every passion under the control of reason; this last – like touch among the senses – is all-pervading. (1905, pp. 257, 258)

Notes

1   See Michelangelo's Sonnet 15, quoted in Anthony Blunt's (1962, p. 168) *Artistic Theory in Italy, 1450–1600*.
2   Laura Marks (2000) uses the phrase 'haptic visuality' in the context of critical film theory, adapting the concept from Gilles Deleuze. In contrast to 'optical visuality', which entails the separation of the viewing subject and object, haptic visuality emphasises material presence and embodiment.
3   Of course, Merleau-Ponty (1962) is the primary phenomenologist to deal with touch in his analysis of perception. But the type of 'touch' I am implying here is an existential sense of touch.
4   See Nietzsche (1999) in which these tragedies as paradigms of the Apollonian and Dionysian drives competing in drama.

5 For a discussion of this essay in relation to a specific rehearsal process, see Johnston (2011b).
6 Gay McAuley, one of the founders of Performance Studies at the University of Sydney, noted down the phrase 'semiologues sauvage' from a public lecture that Ubersfeld gave. I first heard it from my colleague, Paul Dwyer, who adapted the phrase from McAuley. The term has an embodied oral history of its own.

Bibliography

Allain, P. and Harvey, J. (eds) (2006) *The Routledge Companion to Theatre and Performance* (Abingdon and New York: Routledge).
Appadurai, A. (1990) 'Topographies of the Self' in C. A. Lutz and L. Abu-Lughod (eds), *Language and the Politics of Emotion* (Cambridge: Cambridge University Press).
Aristotle (1996) *Poetics*, trans. M. Heath (London and New York: Penguin Books).
— (2000) *Nicomachean Ethics*, trans. R. Crisp (Cambridge: Cambridge University Press).
Artaud, A. (1958) *The Theater and Its Double*, trans. M. C. Richards (New York: Grove Press).
— (1968) *Collected Works*, Vol. 1, trans. V. Corti (London: Calder and Boyars).
— (1970) *The Theatre and Its Double*, trans. V. Corti (London: John Calder).
— (1971) *Collected Works*, Vol. 2, trans. V. Corti (London: Calder and Boyars).
— (1972) *Collected Works*, Vol. 3, trans. V. Corti (London: Calder and Boyars).
— (1974) *Collected Works*, Vol. 4, trans. V. Corti (London: Calder and Boyars).
— (1988) *Selected Writings*, S. Sontag (ed), trans. H. Weaver (Los Angeles and Berkley: University of California Press).
Auslander, P. (1995) '"Just be Yourself": Logocentrism and Difference in Performance Theory' in *Acting (Re)Considered* (London: Routledge).
— (ed) (2003) *Performance: Critical Concepts in Literary and Cultural Studies* (London: Routledge).
Austin, J. L. (1962) *How To Do Things With Words*, J. O. Urmson (ed) (London: Clarendon Press).
Bachelard, G. (1994) *The Poetics of Space*, trans. M. Jolas (Beacon Press: Boston).
Badiou, A. (2013) *Rhapsody for the Theatre*, trans. Bruno Bosteels (London: Verso).
Bakewell, S. (2016) *At the Existentialist Café* (London: Penguin).
Bakhtin, M. (1984) *Rabelais and His World*, trans. H. Iswolsky (Bloomington: Indiana University Press).

Barish, J. (1981) *The Antitheatrical Prejudice* (Berkley and Los Angeles: University of California Press).
Beistegui, M. de, and Sparks, S. (eds) (2000) *Philosophy and Tragedy* (London: Routledge).
Benedetti, J. (2004) *Stanislavski: An Introduction* (New York: Routledge).
— (1990) 'A History of Stanislavski in Translation', *New Theatre Quarterly*, 6(23), 266–78.
— (1998) *Stanislavski and the Actor* (London: Methuen).
— (2005) *The Art of the Actor: The Essential History of Acting, From Classical Times to the Present Day* (London: Methuen).
Benjamin, W. (1983) *Understanding Brecht*, trans. A. Bostock (London: Verso).
Bergson, H. (2001) *Time and Free Will: An Essay on the Immediate Data of Consciousness*, trans. F.L. Pogson (Mineola, NY: Dover Publications).
Binswanger, L. (1963) *Being-in-the-world: Selected Papers of Ludwig Binswanger*, trans. Jacob Needleman (New York: Basic Books).
Blackburn, S. (2000) 'Enquivering', *The New Republic*, 223(18), 43–47.
Bleeker, M., Sherman, J. F. and Nedelkopoulou, E. (2015) *Performance and Phenomenology* (New York: Routledge).
Blunt, A. (1962) *Artistic Theory in Italy: 1450-1600* (Oxford: Clarendon Press).
Bourdieu, P. (1977) *Outline of a Theory of Practice*, trans. R. Nice (Cambridge: Cambridge University Press).
Brecht, B. (1960) *Plays/Bertolt Brecht* (London: Methuen).
— (1961) *Poems on Theatre*, trans. J. Berger and A. Bostock (Frankfurt am Main: Scorpion Press).
— (1964) *Brecht on Theatre: The Development of an Aesthetic*, J. Willett (ed) (London: Methuen).
— (1965a) *The Caucasian Chalk Circle*, trans. E. Bentley (New York: Grove Press).
— (1965b) *The Messingkauf Dialogues*, trans. J. Willett (London: Methuen).
— (1966) *Mother Courage and Her Children: A Chronicle of the Thirty Years' War*, trans. E. Bentley (New York: Grove Press).
— (1967) 'On "The Caucasian Chalk Circle"', *The Drama Review*, 12(1), 88–100.
— (1976) *Poems 1913–1956* (London and New York: Eyre Methuen).
— (1979) *Man Equals Man and The Elephant Calf* (London: Eyre Methuen).
— (1980) *The Life of Galileo* (London: Eyre Methuen).
Brentano, F. (1977) *Psychology from an Empirical Standpoint*, trans. R. George (London: University of California Press).

Brook, P. (1968) *The Empty Space* (London: MacGibbon and Kee).
— (1988) *The Shifting Point* (London: Methuen).
Bruns, G. (1989) *Heidegger's Estrangements: Language, Truth, and Poetry in the Later Writings* (New Haven, CT: Yale University Press).
Bryant-Bertail, S. (2000) *Space and Time in Epic Theater: The Brechtian Legacy* (Rochester, NY: Camden House).
Butler, J. (1990) *Gender Trouble: Feminism and the Subversion of Identity* (London: Routledge).
Camp, P. (2004) 'The Trouble with Phenomenology' *Journal of Dramatic Theory and Criticism*, *19*(1) Fall, 79–97.
Carlson, M. A. (1993) *Theories of the Theatre: A Historical and Critical Survey from the Greeks to the Present* (Ithaca, NY: Cornell University Press).
— (1996) *Performance: A Critical Introduction* (London and New York: Routledge).
Carnicke, S. M. (1998) *Stanislavsky in Focus* (Amsterdam: Harwood Academic Publishers).
Cartledge, P. (1997) 'Deep Plays: Theatre as Process in Greek Civic Life' in P. E. Easterling (ed), *The Cambridge Companion to Greek Tragedy* (Cambridge: Cambridge University Press).
Casey, E. S. (1991) 'Imagining and Remembering' in *Spirit and Soul, Essays in Philosophical Psychology* (Dallas, TX: Spring Publications), 136–54.
— (2002) 'Between Geography and Philosophy: What does it mean to be in the place-world?' *Annals of the Association of American Geographers*, *91*(4), 683–93.
Chekhov, A. (2009) *4 Plays & 3 Jokes*, trans. S. M. Carnicke (Indianapolis, IN: Hackett).
Cole, T. and Chinoy, H. K. (eds) (1970) *Actors on Acting: The Theories, Techniques, and Practices of the World's Great Actors, Told in their Own Words* (New York: Crown Publishers).
Collins, J. (2000) *Heidegger and the Nazis* (Cambridge and New York: Icon Books).
Collins, J. and Selina, H. (1999) *Introducing Heidegger* (Cambridge: Icon Books).
Counsell, C. (1996) *Signs of Performance: An Introduction to Twentieth-Century Theatre* (London: Routledge).
Cresswell, T. (2004) *Place: A Short Introduction* (Malden, MA: Wiley Blackwell).
Cull, L. K. (2012) 'Performance as Philosophy: Responding to the Problem of "Application"', *Theatre Research International*, *37*(1), 20–27.
Cull, L. K. and Lagaay, A. (2014) *Encounters in Performance Philosophy* (London and New York: Palgrave Macmillan).
Curran, K. and Kearney, J. (2012) 'Introduction', *Criticism*, *54*(3), 353–64.

Derrida, J. (1978) *Writing and Difference*, trans. A. Bass (London: Routledge).
— (1989) *Of Spirit: Heidegger and the Question*, trans. G. Bennington and R. Bowlby (Chicago: University of Chicago Press).
— (1994) 'Maddening the Subjectile', *Yale French Studies, 84*, 154–71.
Derrida, J. and Thévenin, P. (1998) *The Secret Art of Antonin Artaud*, trans. M. A. Caws (Cambridge, MA: MIT Press).
Diderot, D. (1957) *The Paradox of Acting*, trans. W. H. Pollock (New York: Hill and Wang).
Dreyfus, H. L. (1991) *Being-in-the-world: A Commentary on Heidegger's Being and Time, Division I* (Cambridge, MA: MIT Press).
Dreyfus, H. and Spinosa, C. (2002) 'Highway Bridges and Feasts: Heidegger and Borgmann on How to Affirm Technology' in H. Dreyfus and M. Wrathall (eds) *Heidegger Reexamined: Art, Poetry, and Technology* (New York: Routledge), 175–93.
Dreyfus, H. and Wrathall, M. (2005) 'Martin Heidegger: An Introduction to His Thought, Work, and Life' in *A Companion to Heidegger*, H. Dreyfus and M. Wrathall (eds) (Oxford: Blackwell).
Dufrenne, M. (1973) *Phenomenology of the Aesthetic Experience*, trans. E. Casey (Evanston IL: Northwest University Press).
Esslin, M. (1961) *The Theatre of the Absurd* (Garden City, NY: Anchor Books).
Ewen, F. (1970) *Bertolt Brecht: His Life, His Art and His Times* (London: Calder and Boyars).
Farias, V. (1989) *Heidegger and Nazism*, trans. J. Margolis and T. Rockmore (Philadelphia: Temple University Press).
Fortier, M. (1997) *Theory/Theatre: An Introduction* (New York: Routledge).
Foucault, M. (1984) *The Foucault Reader*, P. Rabinow (ed) (New York: Pantheon Books).
— (1988) *Madness and Civilization: A History of Insanity in the Age of Reason*, trans. R. Howard (New York: Vintage Books).
— (2002) *The Order of Things: An Archeology of the Human Sciences* (London and New York: Routledge).
Fraleigh, S. H. (1987) *Dance and the Lived Body: A Descriptive Aesthetics* (Pittsburgh: University of Pittsburgh Press).
Fuegi, J. (1987) *Bertolt Brecht: Chaos According to Plan* (Cambridge: Cambridge University Press).
— (1995) *The Life and Lies of Bertolt Brecht* (London: Flamingo).
Gadamer, H.-G. (1979) *Truth and Method* (2nd edn) (London: Sheed and Ward).

Garner, S. B. (1994) *Bodied Spaces: Phenomenology and Performance in Contemporary Drama* (Ithaca, NY: Cornell University Press).
— (2001) 'Theater and Phenomenology', *Degrés: Revue de synthèse à orientation sémiologiques*, 107–08 (Autumn–Winter), B1–17.
Geertz, C. (1973) *The Interpretation of Cultures: Selected Essays* (New York: Basic Books).
— (1983) *Local Knowledge: Further Essays in Interpretative Anthropology* (New York: Basic Books).
Gerassi (1989) *Jean-Paul Sartre: Hated Conscience of His Century. Vol. 1, Protestant or Protester?* (Chicago: University of Chicago Press).
Glendinning, S. (2007) *In the Name of Phenomenology* (Abingdon and New York: Routledge).
Goffman, E. (1956) *The Presentation of Self in Everyday Life* (Edinburgh: University of Edinburgh Social Sciences Research Centre).
Goodall, J. R. (1994) *Artaud and the Gnostic Drama* (Oxford and Melbourne: Clarendon Press).
Grant, S. (2005) 'Practical Intersubjectivity', *Janus Head*, 8(2), 560–80.
— (2006) *Gathering to Witness*. Unpublished PhD Thesis, University of Sydney, Sydney.
— (2012) 'Genealogies and methodologies of phenomenology in theatre and performance studies', *Nordic Theatre Studies: Yearbook for Theatre Research in Scandinavia*, 24, 8–20.
Grayling, A. C. (1998) *An Introduction to Philosophical Logic* (Oxford: Blackwell).
Green, N. (1970) *Antonin Artaud: Poet Without Words* (New York: Simon and Schuster).
Grotowski, J. (1969) *Towards a Poor Theatre*, trans. E. Barba (London: Methuen).
Guignon, C. (2005) 'The History of Being' in *A Companion to Heidegger*, H. Dreyfus and M. Wrathall (eds) (Oxford: Blackwell).
Hegel, G. W. F. (1977) *The Phenomenology of Spirit*, trans. A. V. Miller (Oxford: Oxford University Press).
— (2001) *Hegel on the Arts: Selections from G.W.F. Hegel's Aesthetics, or the Philosophy of Fine Art*, trans. H. Paolucci (Smyrna, DE: Griffon House).
Heidegger, M. (1962) *Being and Time*, trans. J. Macquarrie and E. Robinson (London: Blackwell).
— (1975) *Poetry, Language, Thought*, trans. A. Hofstadter (New York and Sydney: Harper and Row).
— (1977) *Basic Writings: from Being and Time (1927) to The Task of Thinking (1964)*, trans. D. F. Krell (London: Routledge).

— (1982) *The Basic Problems of Phenomenology*, trans. A. Hofstadter (Bloomington, IN: Indiana University Press).
— (1996) *Hölderlin's Hymn, 'The Ister'*, trans. W. McNeil and J. Davis (Bloomington: Indiana University Press).
— (1998) *Pathmarks*, W. McNeill (ed) (Cambridge: Cambridge University Press).
— (1999) *Contributions to Philosophy: From Enowning*, trans. P. Emad and K. Maly (Bloomington, IN: Indiana University Press).
— (2000) *Introduction to Metaphysics*, trans. G. Fried and R. Polt (New Haven, CT: Yale University Press).
Houser, N. (2010) 'Peirce, Phenomenology and Semiotics' in P. Cobley (ed), *The Routledge Companion to Semiotics* (London and New York: Routledge), 89–100.
Husserl, E. (2001) *Logical Investigations (Two Vols.)*, trans. J. N. Findlay (London and New York: Routledge).
Ihde, D. (2003) *Postphenomenology: Essays in the Postmodern Context* (Evanston, IL: Northwestern University Press).
Inwood, M. J. (1999) *A Heidegger Dictionary* (Malden, MA: Blackwell Publishers).
Jackson, M. (ed) (1996) *Things As They Are: New Directions in Phenomenological Anthropology* (Bloomington, IN: Indiana University Press).
Jannarone, K. (2010) *Artaud and His Doubles* (Ann Arbor, MI: University of Michigan Press).
Johnston, D. (2004) 'Active Metaphysics', *Philament*, 4 (August) http://www.arts.usyd.edu.au/publications/philament/issue4_Commentary_Johnston.html
— (2008) 'Overcoming the Metaphysics of Consciousness: Being/Artaud' in *Being-there: After, Proceedings of the 2006 Conference of the Australasian Association for Drama, Theatre and Performance Studies, Sydney: University of Sydney.* http://ses.library.usyd.edu.au/handle/2123/2527
— (2010) 'Phenomenology, Time and Performance', conference proceedings from *time.transcendence.performance*, Melbourne: Monash University.
— (2011a) 'Theatre-making as *Aletheia*: Rehearsal and the Production of Truth', *Theatre Research International*, *36*(3), 213–27.
— (2011b) 'Stanislavskian Acting as Phenomenology in Practice', *Journal of Dramatic Theory and Criticism*, Fall *26*(1), 65–84.
Jones, M. T. (1998) 'Heidegger the Fox: Hannah Arendt's Hidden Dialogue', *New German Critique*, *73*, 164–97.
Kant, I. (1952) *Critique of Judgment*, trans. J. C. Meredith (Oxford: Clarendon Press).

Kaufmann, W. (1992) *Tragedy and Philosophy* (Princeton, NJ: Princeton University Press).
Kohansky, M. (1984) *The Disreputable Profession: The Actor in Society* (Westport, CT: Greenwood).
Krasner, D. and Saltz, D. (eds) (2006) *Staging Philosophy: Intersections of Performance, Theater and Philosophy* (Ann Arbor: University of Michigan Press).
Legrand, S. (2008) '"As Close as Possible to the Unlivable": Michel Foucault and Phenomenology', *Sophia*, 47(3), 281–91.
Leach, R. (2004) *The Makers of Modern Theatre: An Introduction* (London and New York: Routledge).
Leder, D. (1990) *The Absent Body* (Chicago: University of Chicago Press).
Lehmann, H. T. (2006) *Postdramatic Theatre*, trans. K. Jürs-Munby (London and New York: Routledge).
Levinas, E. (1991) *Totality and Infinity: An Essay on Exteriority*, trans. A. Lingus (Dordrecht: Kluwer Academic Publishers).
Lewis, J. L. (2013) *The Anthropology of Cultural Performance* (New York: Palgrave Macmillan).
Ley, G. (1999) *From Mimesis to Interculturalism: Readings of Theatrical Theory Before and After 'Modernism'* (Exeter: University of Exeter Press).
Lucian (1905) *The Works of Lucian of Samosata, Vol. 3*, trans. H. W. Fowler and F. G. Fowler (Oxford: Clarendon).
McCutcheon, J. and Sellers-Young, B. (2013) *Embodied Consciousness: Performance Technologies* (Houndsmills and New York: Palgrave Macmillan).
Machiavelli (1991) *The Prince*, trans. G. Bull (Hammondsworth: Penguin).
Marks, L. (2000) *The Skin of the Film: Intercultural Cinema, Embodiment, and the Senses* (Durham, NC: Duke University Press).
Martin, C. and Bial, H. (eds) (2000) *Brecht Sourcebook* (London: Routledge).
Maude, U. and Feldman, M. (eds) (2009) *Beckett and Phenomenology* (London and New York: Continuum).
May, S. (2016) *A Philosophy of Comedy on Stage and Screen* (London and New York: Bloomsbury).
McKenzie, J. (2001) *Perform or Else: From Discipline to Performance* (New York: Routledge).
Merleau-Ponty, M. (1962) *The Phenomenology of Perception*, trans. C. Smith (London: Routledge).
Merlin, B. (2003) *Konstantin Stanislavsky* (New York: Routledge).
Meyer-Dinkgräfe, D. (1996) *Consciousness and the Actor: A Reassessment of Western and Indian Approaches to the Actor's Emotional Involvement from the Perspective of Vedic Psychology* (Frankfurt am Main: Peter Lang).

Meyrick, J. (2003) 'The Limits of Theory: Academic versus Professional Understanding of Theatre Problems' *New Theatre Quarterly*, 19(3), 230–42.

Milling, J. and Ley, G. (2001) *Modern Theories of Performance: From Stanislavski to Boal* (New York: Palgrave).

Moran, D. (2000) *Introduction to Phenomenology* (London and New York: Routledge).

Moran, D. and Mooney, T. (eds) (2002) *The Phenomenology Reader* (New York: Routledge).

Mulhall, S. (2005) *Heidegger and Being and Time* (2nd edn) (London and New York: Routledge).

Mumford, M. (2009) *Bertolt Brecht* (London and New York: Routledge).

Nagler, A. M. (ed) (1952) *A Sourcebook in Theatrical History: Twenty-five Centuries of Stage History in More than 300 Basic Documents and other Primary Material* (Mineola, NY: Dover).

Natanson, M. (1973) *Phenomenology and the Social Sciences* (Evanston, IL: Northwestern University Press).

Nietzsche, F. (1968) *Nietzsche Contra Wagner*, trans. W. Kaufmann (New York: Viking Press).

— (1999) *The Birth of Tragedy and Other Writings*, trans. R. Speirs (Cambridge: Cambridge University Press).

— (2007) *The Genealogy of Morality*, trans. C. Diethe (New York: Cambridge University Press).

Nussbaum, M. C. (1990) *Love's Knowledge: Essays on Philosophy and Literature* (New York: Oxford University Press).

Ott, H. (1993) *Martin Heidegger: A Political Life*, trans. A. Blunden (London: Harper Collins).

Parry, J. (ed) (2011) *Art and Phenomenology* (Abingdon and New York: Routledge).

Patke, R. S. (2013) *Modernist Literature and Postcolonial Studies* (Edinburgh, Edinburgh University Press).

Pavis, P. (1997) 'The State of Current Theatre Research', *Applied Semiotics/ Sémiotique Appliquée*, 1(3), 203–30.

Pitches, J. (2006) *Science and the Stanislavsky Tradition of Acting* (London and New York: Routledge).

Plato (1980) *The Laws of Plato*, trans. T. L. Pangle (New York: Basic Books).

— (1987) *Early Socratic Dialogues* (Hammondsworth and New York: Penguin).

— (1992) *Republic*, trans. G. M. A. Grube and C. D. C. Reeve (Indianapolis: Hackett).

Pinkard, T. (2002) *German Philosophy 1760–1860: The Legacy of Idealism* (New York: Cambridge University Press).
Power, C. (2008) *Presence in Play: A Critique of Theories of Presence in the Theatre* (Amsterdam and New York: Rodopi).
Puchner, M. (2002) *Stage Fright: Modernism, Anti-theatricality, and Drama* (Baltimore: Johns Hopkins University Press).
— (2010) *The Drama of Ideas: Platonic Provocations in Theater and Philosophy* (Oxford and New York: Oxford University Press).
— (2013) 'Please Mind the Gap between Theater and Philosophy,' *Modern Drama*, 56(4) (Winter), 540–53.
Rayner, A. (1994) *To Act, To Do, To Perform: Drama and the Phenomenology of Action* (Ann Arbor, MI: University of Michigan Press).
Read, R. and Jerry, G. (eds) (2005) *Film as Philosophy Essays in Philosophy after Wittgenstein and Cavell* (New York: Palgrave Macmillan).
Reinelt, J. G. and Roach, J. R. (eds) (1992) *Critical Theory and Performance* (Ann Arbor: University of Michigan Press).
Roach, J. R. (1985) *The Player's Passion: Studies in the Science of Acting* (Newark and London: University of Delaware Press).
Rossiter, A. P. (1961) 'Ambivalence: The Dialect of the Histories' in *Angel with Horns* (London: Longmans).
Rouse, J. (1984) 'Brecht and the Contradictory Actor', *Theatre Journal*, 36(1), 25–42.
Rozik, E. (2002) 'Acting: The Quintessence of Theatricality', *SubStance*, 31(2), 110–24.
Sartre, J.-P. (1967) *Essays in Existentialism* (New York: Citadel Press).
— (1976) *Sartre on Theater*, trans. F. Jellinek (New York: Pantheon).
— (1992) *Being and Nothingness*, trans. H. Barnes (New York: Washington Square Press).
Sauter, W. (1997) 'Approaching the Theatrical Event: The Influence of Semiotics and Hermeneutics on European Theatre Studies', *Theatre Research International*, 22(1) (supplement), 4–13.
Schechner, R. (1976) *Ritual, Play and Performance* (New York: Seabury Press).
— (2003) *Performance Theory* (London and New York: Routledge).
— (2006) *Performance Studies: An Introduction* (New York: Routledge).
Schechner, R. and Appel, W. (eds) (1990) *By Means of Performance: Intercultural Studies of Theatre and Ritual* (Cambridge and New York: Cambridge University Press).
Schechner, R. and Turner, V. (eds) (1985) *Between Theater and Anthropology* (Philadelphia: University of Pennsylvania Press).

Scheer, E. (ed) (2000) *100 Years of Cruelty: Essays on Artaud* (Sydney: Power Publications).
— (2004) *Antonin Artaud, A Critical Reader* (London and New York: Routledge).
Schiller, F. (1967) *On the Aesthetic Education of Man, in a Series of Letters*, trans. E. M. Wilkinson and L. A. Willoughby (Oxford: Clarendon).
Schrift, A. (1990) *Nietzsche and the Question of Interpretation: Between Hermeneutics and Deconstruction* (New York and London: Routledge).
Schütz, A. (1967) *The Phenomenology of the Social World*, G. Walsh and F. Lehnert (eds) (Evanston, IL: Northwestern University Press).
Sheehan, T. (ed) (1981) *Heidegger: The Man and the Thinker* (Chicago: Precedent).
— (2001) 'A Paradigm Shift in Heidegger Research', *Continental Philosophy Review*, 32(2), 1–20.
Sheets, M. (1966) *The Phenomenology of Dance* (Madison: University of Wisconsin Press).
Sherratt, Y. (2013) *Hitler's Philosophers* (New Haven, CT and London: Yale University Press).
Shepherd, S. and Wallis, M. (2004) *Drama/Theatre/Performance* (London and New York: Routledge).
Smith, B. (2000) 'Premodern Sexualities', *Publications of the Modern Languages Association*, 115(3), 318–29.
— (2010) *Phenomenal Shakespeare* (Chichester and Malden, MA: Wiley-Blackwell).
Singleton, B. (1998) *Le Théâtre et son double* (Valencia: Grant and Cutler).
Spiegelberg, H. (1971) *The Phenomenological Movement: A Historical Introduction* (2nd edn) (The Hague: M. Nijhoff).
Stanislavski, C. (1979) *Building a Character*, trans. E. R. Hapgood (London: Methuen).
— (1980a) *An Actor Prepares*, trans. E. R. Hapgood (New York: Methuen).
— (1980b) *My Life in Art*, trans. J. J. Robbins (London: Methuen).
— (1981) *Stanislavski's Legacy: A Collection of Comments on a Variety of Aspects of an Actor's Art and Life*, trans. E. R. Hapgood (London: Eyre Methuen).
— (1983) *Creating a Role*, trans. E. R. Hapgood (London: Eyre Methuen).
— (2008) *An Actor's Work: A Student's Diary*, trans. J. Benedetti (London and New York: Routledge).
States, B. O. (1983) 'The Actor's Presence: Three Phenomenal Modes', *Theatre Journal*, 35(3), 359–75.
— (1985) *Great Reckonings in Little Rooms: On the Phenomenology of Theater* (Berkeley: University of California Press).
— (1996) 'Performance as Metaphor', *Theatre Journal*, 48(1), 1–26.

Stern, T. (2013) *Philosophy and Theatre: An Introduction* (Abingdon and New York: Routledge).
Stewart, D. and Mickunas, A. (1990) *Exploring Phenomenology: A Guide to the Field and its Literature* (2nd edn) (Athens: Ohio University Press).
Tassi, A. (1995) 'Philosophy and Theatre: An Essay on Catharsis and Contemplation', *International Philosophical Quarterly*, 35(4), 469–81.
— (1998) 'Philosophy and Theatre', *International Philosophical Quarterly*, XXXVIII No. 1(149), 43–54.
— (2000) 'The Metaphysics Of Performance: The "Theatre Of The World"', *Paideia, Metaphysics*, http://www.bu.edu/wcp/Papers/Aest/AestTass.htm.
Thamer, H. U. (1996) 'The Orchestration of the National Community: The Nuremberg Rallies of the NSDAP', trans. A. Taylor, in G. Berghaus (ed), *Fascism and Theatre: Comparative Studies on the Aesthetics of Performance in Europe, 1925–1945* (Providence, RI, and Oxford: Berghan Books).
Thomas, J. (2009) *Script Analysis for Actors, Directors and Designers* (Oxford: Focal Press).
Thomson, P. and Sacks, G. (eds) (1994) *The Cambridge Companion to Brecht* (Cambridge: Cambridge University Press).
Turner, V. (1990) 'Are There Universals of Performance in Myths, Ritual and Drama?' in W. Appel and R. Schechner (eds), *By Means of Performance* (Cambridge: Cambridge University Press).
— (1982) *From Ritual to Theatre: The Seriousness of Human Play* (New York: Performing Arts Journal Publications).
Vork, R. (2013) 'Things That No One Can Say: The Unspeakable Act in Artaud's Les Cenci', *Modern Drama*, 56(3), 306–26.
Walton, K. (1990) *Mimesis as Make-Believe: On the Foundations of the Representational Arts* (Cambridge, MA: Harvard University Press).
Weber, C. (1967) 'Brecht as Director', *The Drama Review*, 12(1), 101–07.
Whyman, R. (2008) *The Stanislavsky System of Acting: Legacy and Influence in Modern Performance* (Cambridge and New York: Cambridge University Press).
— (2011) *Anton Chekhov* (New York: Routledge).
Wikander, M. (2002) *Fangs of Malice: Hypocrisy, Sincerity, & Acting* (Iowa City: University of Iowa Press).
Willett, J. (1959) *The Theatre of Bertolt Brecht* (London: Eyre Methuen).
Williams, B. (1996) 'Contemporary Philosophy: A Second Look' in N. Bunnin and E. P. Tsui-James (eds), *Blackwell Companion to Philosophy* (Oxford: Blackwell), 23–34.
— (2002) *Truth and Truthfulness: An Essay in Genealogy* (Princeton, NJ and Woodstock, UK: Princeton University Press).

Wilshire, B. (1982) *Role Playing and Identity: The Limits of Theatre as Metaphor* (Bloomington, IN: Indiana University Press).
— (1982) 'Theatre as Phenomenology: The Disclosure of Historical Life', in R. Buzina and B. Wilshire (eds), *Phenomenology: Dialogues and Bridges* (Albany: State University of New York Press).
Witt, H. (1974) *Brecht As They Knew Him*, trans. J. Peet (New York: International Publishers).
Wittgenstein, L. (2001) *Philosophical Investigations*, trans. G.E.M. Anscombe (Oxford: Blackwell).
Wizisla, E. (2009) *Walter Benjamin and Bertolt Brecht: The Story of a Friendship* (New Haven, CT: Yale University Press).
Young, J. (1997) *Heidegger, Philosophy, Nazism* (Cambridge, New York, and Melbourne: Cambridge University Press).
— (2001) *Heidegger's Philosophy of Art* (Cambridge and New York: Cambridge University Press).
Zarrilli, P. (ed) (1995) *Acting (re)Considered: Theories and Practices* (London: Routledge).
— (2001) 'Negotiating Performance Epistemologies: Knowledges About, For, and In', *Studies in Theatre and Performance*, *21*(1), 31–46.
— (2002) 'The Metaphysical Studio', *The Drama Review*, *46*(2), 157–70.
— (2004) 'Towards a Phenomenological Model of the Actor's Embodied Modes of Experience', *Theatre Journal*, *56*, 653–66.
Zarrilli, P., McConachie, B., Williams, G. J., Sorgenfrei, C. F. (eds) (2006) *Theatre Histories: An Introduction* (London and New York: Routledge).

Index

A

Absolute, the   37
action   3, 7, 20, 22, 28, 58, 68, 76, 77, 83–104, 116, 129, 131, 133, 135–37, 139–41, 143–45, 147, 149–52, 154–57, 160–64, 166, 169–73
Adorno, Theodor   49
aesthetics / aesthetic   14, 31, 47, 60, 64, 66, 69, 87, 113–14, 125, 126, 134, 136, 141, 149, 177, 178, 182
Ahmed, Sarah   71
aletheia   22, 46, 171, 180–81
An Actor's Work: A Student's Diary   83–105, 104 n.1, 105 n.8
anthropology   9, 45, 58, 65
Antigone   179
Anxiety (*Angst*)   36, 41, 105 n.7, 110–11, 121–26, 128
Appadurai, Arjun   18
Arendt, Hannah   39, fn 52, 55
Aristotle   12, 23, 38, 40–42, 114, 117, 133, 145, 146–47, 152, 160, 181
  Metaphysics   40, 42
  Nicomachean Ethics   42
  Physics   40, 42
  Poetics   23
art   10 n.1, 11, 13–14, 24, 47, 51, 56–57, 61, 71–73, 76–77, 79 n.6, 87, 92–93, 97, 112–13, 115–18, 120, 123, 126, 131, 137, 139, 141–42, 156, 162, 171, 176–77, 180–83
Artaud, Antonin   8–10, 13, 23, 107–30, 177, 183
  The Theatre and its Double   111, 115, 118, 123
Auslander, Philip   73–75, 88
Austin, J.L.   24 n.1
Authenticity / authentic   8, 34, 40, 49, 90, 93, 110–11, 114, 116, 124, 128, 131, 133–36, 143–44, 148, 153, 170–71, 173
Averageness   120
Ayer, A.J.   49

B

Bachelard, Gaston   60
bad faith   34
Badiou, Alan   25 n.12, 185
Bahktin, Mikhail   114
Barish, Jonas   22, 183
Baudrillard, Jean   6
Beckett, Samuel   66, 68, 71, 79 n.4
  Waiting for Godot   180
behaviour   7, 34–35, 44, 57, 58–59, 85, 96, 104, 113, 116, 127, 129, 138–42, 145, 152–55, 157, 162, 178

behaviourism 57, 87
Being 3, 7, 9–10, 20, 23, 25 n.7,
    31, 34–36, 38–45, 47–48, 50,
    55, 72–73, 75–77, 84–85, 88,
    90–91, 104, 108–14, 118–19,
    121–24, 127–28, 132, 134–35,
    138, 140–41, 143–44, 148,
    151–52, 158–59, 161, 164,
    167, 169–71, 176–77, 179,
    181–83, 187
  the history of 40, 72 –73
  the meaning of 31, 43, 44, 45, 47,
    55, 72, 84, 116, 148, 151
  the question of 7, 10, 20, 38–40,
    88, 113–14, 128, 134–35, 177,
Being-in-the-world 8, 35, 50, 84,
    92–93, 101, 111, 122, 134,
    141, 144, 158, 160, 169, 171,
    176, 177, 179, 186
  (*être-au-monde*) 35
Being-towards-death 36, 107, 111,
    121, 124–25, 128, 129, 135
Being-with-others / Being-with
    25 n.7, 36, 58, 99–101, 118–
    121, 128, 133, 135, 141, 144,
    153–157, 169, 176, 179, 182
Benjamin, Walter 132, 160–62
Bergson, Henri 42, 159, 167
binocular vision 67, 183–84
Binswanger, Ludwig 57–58
biology 45, 124
bits (beats) 89, 96
Bourdieu, Pierre 6, 59–60
  body hexis 59
  doxa 60
  habitus 59
Brecht, Bertolt 8–10, 13, 23, 67,
    74–75, 128, 131–74, 176–77,
    183

The Caucasian Chalk Circle 140,
    151–52, 163
In the Jungle of Cities 132
The Life of Galileo 155–56,
    161–62, 164
Man Equals Man 155, 164–66
The Mother 150
*Mother Courage and Her
    Children* 156, 163, 167–69
Brentano, Franz 30, 32–33, 38–39,
    42, 57
Broadhurst, Susan 71
Brook, Peter 9, 148
Brueghel the Elder, Pieter 155,
    162
Butler, Judith 6, 62, 70

C

Camp, Pannill 70
Camus, Albert 185
capitalism 17, 35, 147
Care 25 n.7, 36, 42, 54, 91–93,
    119, 124–25, 135–36, 142,
    172
Carlson, Marvin 178
Casey, Ed 60
catharsis 114, 145
Chaplin, Charlie 129
Chekhov, Anton 17–18, 25 n.5,
    68, 87, 97
The Cherry Orchard 17
Circumspection (*Umsicht*) 42
communion 99–101, 105 n.8, 182
comparative literature 78 n.1
Concern (*Besorgnis*) 42, 44, 93,
    122, 124, 144
consciousness 4, 10 n.2, 19, 23,
    28–36, 39, 48, 49, 52 n.4,
    54–55, 57, 60, 66, 76–77,

84–85, 88–89, 95, 102–103, 108, 130 n.1, 165, 178, 184
Corneille, Pierre   25 n.12
creativity   75, 83–84, 86, 89, 94, 126, 177, 183, 186
cruelty   111, 113–14, 114, 117, 128
Cull, Laura   5–6, 16

D

da Vinci, Leonardo   162
dance   71, 77, 79 n.4, 94, 108
danger   118
Darwin, Charles   87
Dasein   41, 44–45, 47, 49, 51 n.1, 58, 84, 92–3, 109, 111, 113, 116–20, 122–24, 128, 134–38, 140, 144, 148, 150, 153, 159, 167, 169–70, 173 n.3, 176–77, 181–82, 187
Daseinsanalysis   58
de Beauvoir, Simone   62
de Certeau, Michel   60
de Saussure, Ferdinand   61, 64
death   31, 42, 45, 123–26, 135, 169
deconstruction   21, 41, 62, 65, 74
Deleuze, Gilles   109, 187 n.2
Derrida, Jacques   40–41, 49, 61–62, 70, 77, 109, 115, 121, 126
Descartes, René   28, 31–32, 103, 114, 117, 165, 103
Destruktion   8, 45, 72–74, 109–13
dialectical materialism   87
dialectical theatre   147
dialectics / dialectic   34, 74, 140, 149, 170
Diderot, Denis   14, 77, 79 n.9, 87

différance   49, 61, 74
Dilthey, Wilhelm   42
Diprose, Rosalyn   71
disability   71
discourse   15, 23, 46, 48, 57, 60–62, 78 n.7, 114, 116, 122
Distantiality   119
Dostoevsky, Fyodor   97
drama-theatre-performance (distinction)   21
dualism / dualist   28–29, 35, 39, 42–43, 52 n.7, 78, 79 n.8, 88, 108, 178
Dufrenne, Mikel   66
Duns Scotus   38
duration   133, 159, 166
Dwyer, Paul   188 n.6
dysfunction   107, 127

E

Eckhart, Meister   52 n.9
eidetic reduction   33, 186
embodiment / embodied experience   4, 18–19, 28, 31, 34, 51, 60, 63, 66–67, 70–71, 84, 89, 94, 103, 121, 126, 139, 148, 157, 171, 178, 184, 187 n.2
emotion   3, 10, 18, 24, 54, 63, 79 n.9, 85–87, 97–98, 100, 102, 114, 121, 135, 142, 145, 147, 152, 157, 176
emotion memory   89, 98, 100
empiricism   29–30, 87, 164
Engels, Friedrich   87
environment   27, 34–36, 42–43, 54, 57–60, 88, 92–97, 99–102, 104, 119, 122, 133, 147, 158, 165–67, 170, 176

epic theatre 9–10, 133, 141, 143–149, 151, 160, 162–63, 170
épistemé 87, 89, 105 n.4
epistemology 14, 18–19, 28
epoché 33, 51, 56
essence 29, 32–34, 55, 62–63, 78, 115, 181
ethics / ethical 14–15, 18–19, 31–32, 34, 37, 51, 55, 64, 68, 135–36, 151, 170
ethnography 58–59
eurocentrism 10 n.2
Event (*Ereignis*) 22, 47, 135, 179
Everydayness 116, 121, 127, 139, 140, 142, 153
existentialism 52 n.5, 66, 173 n.8
exteriority 37
externalism 30–31

F

facticity / factical experience 41–43, 48
falling 42, 52 n.9, 91, 111, 113–18, 122, 126–27, 129, 139–40, 170
Fichte, Johann 87
film philosophy 16, 25 n.4
flow 129, 159
Fortier, Mark 88, 184
Foucault, Michel 18, 25 n.6, 41, 62–63, 87, 105 n.4, 109
Frankfurt School, the 49

G

Gadamer, Hans-Georg 39, 60–61
Garner, Stanton 7, 52 n.6, 67–68, 76, 79 n.4, 173 n.4
Geertz, Clifford 58–59, 65

gender 21, 62, 68, 71, 173
Gesamtkunstwerk 141
Gestalt psychology 35
gestus 10, 133, 153–157, 168, 172
given circumstances 87, 89, 92–93, 95, 98, 102, 180, 186
givenness 29, 33, 95
Gnosticism / Gnostic 111, 117, 126
Goffman, Erving 66, 76
Goldman, William, *The Princess Bride* 4
Gogol, Nikolai 87
Grant, Stuart 69–70
Grosz, Elisabeth 71
Grotowski, Jerzy 74–75
grundgestus 155

H

Habermans, Jürgen 49
Hartmann, Karl von 87
Hegel, G.W.F. 15, 32, 44, 87, 164, 182
Heidegger, Martin 6–8, 20, 22–23, 25 n.3; n.7, 30–31, 34–49, 52 n.3; n.4; n.8, n.9, 53, 55, 58, 72–74, 79 n.4; n.5; n.6, 83–84, 88, 90–94, 99, 101, 105 n.7, 109–24, 128–29, 132–36, 138–40, 143–44, 146, 148, 150–53, 157–58, 161, 164–67, 169–71, 173 n.3, 176–77, 179–84
Being and Time (BT) 8, 25 n.7, 31, 39, 41–47, 52 n.3, 83–84, 123, 133–34, 139, 151, 153, 158, 166, 169, 176, 180
'The Origin of the Work of Art' 181–83

hermeneutics   15, 38, 40, 60–61,
    65, 67, 179
Historicality   8, 25 n.1, 36, 61, 66,
    128, 133, 158–61, 176
historicism   31
historiography   62
history   23, 29, 36, 47, 62, 60,
    72–73, 79 n.5, 85, 109, 133,
    136, 158–62, 164, 169
Homer   12
Horkheimer, Max   49
humanism   47
Hume, David   36
Husserl, Edmund   30–36, 38–39,
    41–42, 44–46, 48–50, 57–60,
    66, 90, 150, 153, 165, 167
  Cartesian Meditations   36
  Logical Investigations   32, 38

I

Ibsen, Henrik   16, 87
idealism   30, 87, 158
Idhe, Don   50
inauthenticity / inauthentic   90–91,
    110, 116, 136, 118, 134, 136,
    153, 157, 166
Ingarden, Roman   66
inspiration   10, 23, 83–86, 88, 90,
    93, 99, 177
intential fallacy   56
intentionality   29, 31–32, 39 , 68
interdisciplinarity   16, 65, 78 n.1
interintersubjective /
    intersubjectivity   56–57, 66,
    100, 175, 178
involvement   53–54, 90–92,
    95–97, 99, 101–102, 104, 119,
    121, 141, 153

J

Jackson, Michael   60
James, William   87
Jaspers, Karl   41
Jones, Amelia   71

K

Kant, Immanuel   32, 36, 44
Kierkegaard, Soren   16, 42, 52 n.9
knowledge   14–15, 19, 27, 30–31,
    37, 41, 57, 62–64, 89
  embodied   27, 89
  practical   19, 24, 42
  propositional 19, 24
Kuppers, Petra   71

L

Lan-Fang, Mei   150
language   8, 15, 35–37, 48–50,
    57, 61–63, 65–66, 68, 72,
    74–75, 84, 108, 111, 115–16,
    116, 126, 132, 155, 178, 182,
    184–85
Laughton, Charles   155, 162
Leach, Robert   88, 137
Lebensphilosophie   41
Leder, Drew   69, 107
Lehrstücke   136
Les Cenci   126–27
Lessing, Gotthold   174 n.19
Levelling / levelled down   120
Levinas, Emmanuel   32, 34, 36–37,
    51, 55, 170
  Totality and Infinity   36
liminal / liminoid   20–21, 25 n. 8
logic (philosophical)   12, 14, 22,
    35, 63
logocentrism   62, 73–75, 88
logos   46, 62

Lorre, Peter 155
Lucian of Samosata 11–13, 20, 175, 187
   On Pantomime 11–13, 187
Luther, Martin 42
Lyotard, Jean–François 71

M

Machiavelli, Niccolo 14
magic 'if' 89, 92
manual philosophy 4, 8, 11, 13, 103, 175, 176–77, 182
Marcel, Gabriel 55, 185
Marcuse, Herbert 39
Marx Brothers 114, 129
Marx, Karl 13, 87, 132, 139, 149
Marxism 35, 47, 49, 74, 146, 147
McAuley, Gay 188 n.6
McCutcheon, Jade 19
McKenzie, Jon 71
Merleau-Ponty, Maurice 31–32, 34, 35–37, 39, 49, 51, 52 n.6, 55, 60, 69, 185, 187 n.3
   le corps phénoménal 36
   le corps propre 36
   material body (*Körper*) 52 n.7
   Phenomenology of Perception 35
metaphyiscs (philosophy) 14, 30, 40–42, 44–45, 49–50, 62, 64, 72–73, 84, 88, 90–91, 101, 108–10, 112, 120, 127, 130, 138, 167
method of physical actions 9
Method, the 97
Michelangelo 175–76
mineness 91, 101
Miss Julie 180
Modellbuch 137

moment of vision (*Augenblick*) 42, 72, 132
mood 85, 97–100, 102, 104, 105 n.7, 111, 121–126, 179
Müller, Heiner 170
Mumford, Meg 159, 169

N

Natanson, Maurice 29, 56
natural attitude 33, 54, 56, 58, 85, 101
naturalism (philosophy) 31
Nazism / Nazi / National Socialism 37, 39, 47, 49, 52 n.10, 135, 160, 170
New Criticism 55
Nietzsche, Friedrich 15, 109, 179, 187 n.4

O

objectivism 29
Oedipus at Colonus 179
ontological difference, the 25 n.7
ontological queasiness 22, 183
ontology 14, 22, 28, 40, 47, 52, 108, 110, 112–13
ostrannenie 149
Other, the 18, 32, 37, 51, 55, 118, 124, 99, 101, 102, 104, 118–20, 124, 143

P

paradox of acting 77, 87
Pavis, Patrice 185
Pavlov, Ivan 87
Peirce, Charles Sanders 63–64
   firstness / secondness / thirdness 63–64
   icon / index / symbol 64

perception   3, 22–23, 29, 33, 35–36, 41–42, 46, 51, 54–55, 70–71, 86, 159, 184–85
performance analysis   65, 67, 69, 185
performance philosophy   6, 16
performance studies   15–16, 20–21, 35, 37, 65, 69–70, 78 n.1, 146, 179, 188 n.6
performativity   68, 70 –71
phenomena / phenomenon   28–30, 34, 45, 54–55, 59, 70, 76, 165, 167, 179, 184–85
phenomenology   4–10, 15, 20, 23, 27–35, 40, 42, 44–45, 47–50, 53, 55–61, 63–72, 75–76, 84, 88–90, 102, 110, 137, 160, 167, 170, 177–79, 181, 183–84
  applied   53
  comparative   56, 76, 177
  creative   76
  definitions of   4, 6, 27–50, 177–86
  descriptive   23, 43, 69, 76, 78
  phenomenological interpretation   5, 71, 90, 101, 171, 178
  phenomenological method   33, 41, 53, 64, 112, 185
  phenomenological reduction   33, 95, 101, 150, 153
philosophy   4–9, 12–23, 28–31, 33, 37, 39–40, 44, 47–50, 56, 65–66, 72, 75, 84, 89, 111, 116, 127–28, 132–33, 165, 177–79, 186–87
  analytic   15–16, 22, 49, 69
  'applying'   5–8, 13, 133
  continental   15–16
  the history of   18, 29, 31, 44, 56

Picasso, Pablo   168
Piscator, Erwin   145
plague   110, 112–14, 125, 128, 130 n.2
Plato   12, 14, 117, 130 n.1, 165, 187
  Ion   14
  The Republic   14
poetry   14, 23, 47–48, 50, 110–12, 114–15, 118, 128, 179, 181–82
poiesis   182
positivism   49, 57, 141, 178
possibility / actuality   31, 43, 92, 102, 124, 134, 162, 168–69
postdramatic theatre   66
postmodernism   50, 62, 66
postphenomenology   50
post-structuralism   15, 18, 41, 48, 50, 63, 70, 79 n.7
Power, Cormac   70
pragmatism   64
prana   88
praxis   43
presence   43, 49, 66, 70, 73, 173 n.4, 178, 184
present-at-hand (*vorhandenheit*)   51, 94, 116, 119, 124, 128, 158, 167
Prometheus Bound   179
psychology   9, 45, 57, 87, 122, 128, 139, 147, 150
Publicness   119–20

R

Racine, Jean   39 n.12
rationality / rational   28, 32, 40, 44, 62, 109, 114, 128, 147, 177–78

Rayner, Alice   68, 76
ready-to-hand (*zuhandenheit*)   93, 119, 176
Rabelais and His World   114
relativism   22, 31
religion   9, 42, 61, 114, 139
resoluteness   42, 144, 173
'restored behavior'   20
Ribot, Théodule   88
Ricoeur, Paul   60–61
Roach, Joseph   18, 24, 67
Romanticism   112
Rousseau, Jean-Jacques   14
Russell, Bertrand   49
Ryle, Gilbert   58

S

Sartre, Jean-Paul   14, 32, 34–35, 51, 55, 173 n.8, 185
  Being and Nothingness   34
  en-soi   34–35
  pour-soi   34–35
Saxe-Meiningen Company, the Duke of   87
Schechner, Richard   20–21, 182
Scheler, Max   42, 66
Schelling, Friedrich   87
Schlegel, Friedrich   20
Schleiermacher, Friedrich   38
Schopenhauer, Arthur   16
Schütz, Alfred   58
self / Self   8, 15, 18, 20, 35–36, 49, 57–58, 60, 65–66, 74–78, 85–86, 88–93, 98–102, 107–108, 110, 115–17, 120–21, 126, 128–29, 133–35, 142–44, 148, 158–59, 166–67, 169
Sellers-Young, Barbara   19

semiosis   63
semiotics   63–64, 67, 69, 75, 183–5
Seneca   15
Shakespeare, William   15, 63, 67–68, 71, 79 n.1, 175
  Hamlet   3, 68–69
  King Lear   175
  Macbeth   68
  Othello   90
  Two Gentlemen of Verona   180
Shchepkin, Mikhail   87
signifier / signified   61, 64, 185
Smith, Bruce   63
sociology   9, 45, 58
solicitude   124, 153, 156
sophistry   13
Sophocles   179
space / place (distinction)   60, 68, 79 n.2, 94
spatiality   60, 93, 165
St. Paul   42
stand-up comedy   71, 77, 79 n.4
Stanislavski, Constantin   8, 9, 10, 23, 74–75, 77, 83–105, 132, 137, 138, 141, 147, 177, 183
state of mind   97–99, 104, 121
States, Bert   7, 67, 76, 183
subjectivism   29
subjectivity   18, 41, 68, 128, 133, 164–68
Sulerzhitsky, Leopold   88
supertask   97, 137
symphilosophy   20

T

tasks   89, 95–96, 102
Tassi, Aldo   22

technology 14, 19, 70–71, 147
Temporality / temporal 25 n.7, 31, 34, 41, 45, 61–62, 66, 68, 72, 88, 92, 98, 123–25, 127–28, 133, 152, 158–59, 162–64, 171, 176, 134, 151
theatre history 7, 10 n.2, 20, 24
Theatre of the Absurd 66
Theatre of Cruelty 9, 109, 111, 116–18, 120, 123, 125–29
theatre phenomenology 20, 67, 76, 177–79
theatre studies 5, 8, 15, 21, 65–71, 76, 177, 183
theoria 44
They, the (*das Man*) 110, 119–22, 128, 132, 143, 148, 165–66
thick description 59
things themselves / the thing itself 29–30, 32, 39, 42, 47–48, 50, 55, 69, 85, 90, 103, 109, 128, 140, 149, 153, 165, 167, 180–81, 185
Thomas, James 186
throw / thrownness 116, 140
time 20–21, 31, 38–40, 42, 45–46, 49, 54, 68, 101, 124–26, 128, 133, 136, 151–52, 158–60, 162–66, 168–69, 171, 178–80
Tolstoy, Leo 87, 97
Totality 37
tradition / traditional thought 5, 30, 37, 43–44, 72, 110–13, 114, 116, 125–27, 172, 182
tragedy 15, 66, 179
transcendence 9, 34, 37, 40
transcendental ego 49–50

transcendental reduction 33
Tretyakov, Sergei 165, 173 n.3
truth 13–15, 20–22, 24, 30, 32, 39, 46–47, 62, 64, 72–75, 84–86, 88, 90, 100, 103, 132–33, 138–39, 141, 169, 171, 180–81, 183–84, 187
  correspondence theory of 22, 39, 46, 138, 180
  representationalist theory of 39
Tuan, Yifu 60
Turn, the (*Kehre*) 47
Turner, Victor 20–21

U
Ubersfeld, Anne 185, 188 n.6
uncanny 51, 95, 102, 105 n.7, 122, 128, 151

V
van Gogh, Vincent 182
Vedic science 10 n.2
Verfremdungseffekt 133, 142, 149–53, 173 n.4, 174 n.14
via negativa 74–75
Vienna Circle, the 49
Voltaire 15

W
Wagner, Richard 16, 134, 141
Weigel, Helene 168
Weil, Kurt 174 n.19
Whyman, Rose 87–88
Williams, Bernard 16
Wilshire, Bruce 7, 20, 66, 76
Wittgenstein, Ludwig 177

world (*Welt*) / worldhood   3–4,
7, 9–10, 13, 14, 17–20,
23–24, 27–31, 33, 35–44,
46–48, 50–51, 53–61, 65,
67–69, 71–73, 75–77, 83–86,
88–104, 107–9, 111–29,
131–46, 148–50, 152–54,
156–60, 164–67, 169–71,
175–77, 179–85, 187

Y

yoga   88

Z

Zarrilli, Phillip   10 n.2, 18, 69, 76

Printed by Printforce, the Netherlands